The Powers of
Prophecy

Practica. Das künfftig ist
vnd geschehen sol/das hat gepracticiert vnd
gemacht Jacob pflawm von Vlm. Im jar.1500. Vnd der
anfang diser Practica hat angeheßt Im jar.1520.
Vnd wirt noch etliche jar weren.

Getruckt im.M.D.xxvij. Jar.

Title page of the second edition of pseudo-Pflaum's *Practica* [Nürnberg?], 1527, courtesy of the British Library. The perennial vision of a glorious eschatological crusade is here portrayed in sixteenth-century, Germano-imperial terms.

The Powers of Prophecy

THE CEDAR OF LEBANON VISION

FROM

THE MONGOL ONSLAUGHT TO THE

DAWN OF THE ENLIGHTENMENT

Robert E. Lerner

CORNELL UNIVERSITY PRESS
Ithaca and London

Hardcover edition originally published by the University of California Press, 1983.

First printing, Cornell Paperbacks, 2009.

Printed in the United States of America.

A bibliographic record of the hardcover edition is available from the Library of Congress.

Cornell University Press strives to use environmentally responsible suppliers and materials to the fullest extent possible in the publishing of its books. For further information, visit our website at www.cornellpress.cornell.edu.

Uxori carissime

CONTENTS

ACKNOWLEDGMENTS

Sometime in the future, if the world endures, the research for a book like this will be done, alas, mostly by pushing buttons. My expression of dismay is not meant to suggest that the research product will be poorer; on the contrary, whenever the contents of all surviving medieval manuscripts are exhaustively catalogued and computerized, the research product will be as rich as can be, assuming that human art in interpretation remains constant. But research will be infinitely less fun. In hunting for copies of the "Cedar of Lebanon" vision I have travelled across Alps and fields of lavender, worked in libraries from Baroque to Bauhaus, and engaged in correspondence that has left my faculty letter box customarily resplendent with varicolored foreign commemorative stamps. Hence were I to thank here all the librarians and scholars who offered me aid and information directly or by mail, the list would be far too long. Instead I offer blanket thanks to all librarians who have sent me photocopies from manuscripts (my index of manuscripts will indicate the sources) and acknowledge more specific kinds of help as scrupulously as possible in my footnotes.

A handful of acknowledgments remain that most clearly belong up front. The National Endowment for the Humanities, the American Council of Learned Societies, and Northwestern University provided generous and indispensable financial support. Northwestern's Marjorie Carpenter, the best interlibrary loan librarian this side of the Fortunate Isles, performed cheerful ongoing service and a few magic tricks. Vita Maniscalco combed the entire typescript, and then again the galleys, with her customary alertness, looking for (and finding) infelicities and worse. William Paden sacrificed many hours helping me with Old French and Catalan. Two nearby colleagues and superb medievalists, Richard Kieckhefer and Charles Radding, talked shop with me regularly and helped provide the stimulation that makes scholarship vigorous. Charles Radding and Walter Wakefield read through my entire typescript and offered numerous valuable suggestions for improvement. The footnotes amply show that I received the greatest aid in technical matters from Alexander Patschovsky, but I wish to thank him again for his unfailing generosity and also to express my admiration for his *Können*. My masters in the general field of eschatology and prophecy are Herbert Grundmann, Bernhard Töpfer, and Marjorie Reeves.

ABBREVIATIONS

AfK	*Archiv für Kulturgeschichte*
Bignami-Odier, *Rupescissa*	Jeanne Bignami-Odier, *Études sur Jean de Roquetaillade (Johannes de Rupescissa)* (Paris, 1952)
BL	British Library (formerly Library of the British Museum)
BN	Bibliothèque nationale
Bodl.	Oxford, Bodleian Library
Cgm	Codex germanicus monacensis (Bayerische Staatsbibliothek, Munich)
Clm	Codex latinus monacensis (Bayerische Staatsbibliothek, Munich)
Donckel, "Visio"	Emil Donckel, "Visio seu prophetia fratris Johannis. Eine süditalienische Prophezeiung aus dem Anfang des 14. Jahrhunderts," *Römische Quartalschrift*, 40 (1932), 361–379
Essays... Wilkinson	*Essays in Medieval History Presented to Bertie Wilkinson* (Toronto, 1969)
Expositio... Joachim	*Expositio magni prophete Joachim in librum beati Cirilli de magnis tribulationibus* (Venice, 1516)
Grauert	Hermann Grauert, "Meister Johann von Toledo," SbM, 1901, no. 2, 111–325

Holder-Egger, 15, 30, 33	Oswald Holder-Egger, "Italienische Prophetien des 13. Jahrhunderts," NA, 15 (1890), 143–178; 30 (1905), 323–386; 33 (1908), 96–187
Hugo de Novocastro	Hugo de Novocastro, *Tractatus de victoria Christi contra Antichristum* (Nürnberg, 1471)
JWCI	*Journal of the Warburg and Courtauld Institutes*
Lerner, "Refreshment of the Saints"	Robert E. Lerner, "Refreshment of the Saints: The Time After Antichrist as a Station for Earthly Progress in Medieval Thought," *Traditio*, 32 (1976), 97–144
Maier	Anneliese Maier, "Handschriftliches zu Arnaldus de Villanova und Petrus Johannis Olivi," *Analecta sacra Tarraconensia*, 21 (1948), 53–74
MGH	*Monumenta Germaniae Historica*
NA	*Neues Archiv der Gesellschaft für ältere deutsche Geschichtskunde*
Pelster	Franz Pelster, "Die Quaestio Heinrichs von Harclay über die zweite Ankunft Christi und die Erwartung des baldigen Weltendes zu Anfang des XIV Jahrhunderts," *Archivio Italiano per la Storia della Pietà*, 1 (1951), 25–82
PL	*Patrologiae cursus completus . . . series latina*, ed. J. P. Migne (Paris, 1844–1864)
Pou y Marti	José Maria Pou y Marti, *Visionarios, Beguinos y Fraticelos Catalanes (Siglos XIII–XV)* (Vich, 1930)
Reeves, *Influence of Prophecy*	Marjorie Reeves, *The Influence of Prophecy in the Later Middle Ages: A Study in Joachimism* (Oxford, 1969)

RS   Rolls Series (*Rerum Britannicarum medii aevi Scriptores*) (London, 1858–1891)

SbM   *Sitzungsberichte der königlichen bayerischen Akademie der Wissenschaften, philosophisch-philologische und historische Classe* (Munich)

STC   *Short Title Catalogue*

Thorndike   Lynn Thorndike, *A History of Magic and Experimental Science*, 8 vols. (New York, 1923–1958)

Töpfer   Bernhard Töpfer, *Das kommende Reich des Friedens. Zur Entwicklung chiliastischer Zukunftshoffnungen im Hochmittelalter* (Berlin, 1964)

UB   Universitätsbibliothek

Vat.   Biblioteca Apostolica Vaticana

Ward   H. L. D. Ward, *Catalogue of Romances in the British Museum*, 3 vols. (London, 1883–1910)

INTRODUCTION

"Among all forms of mistake," George Eliot once observed, "prophecy is the most gratuitous." Although this dictum is pure common sense, the hazards of prophesying have not hindered men and women throughout the ages from trying to divine the future in various ways. No doubt people will continue to do so (a prophecy) as long as humanity exists. Because the quest for clairvoyance seems to be a basic human drive, the history of the writing and reception of prophecy should comprise an important part of the emerging study of past mentalities. The following is offered in that conviction as an investigation into the subject of medieval prophecies and eschatological expectations.[1]

Medieval Christians knew for certain that time would have a stop, for Scripture revealed that Antichrist would some day come and that afterwards the world would end in fiery judgment. Since the last chapter of human history had already been published, historians such as Otto of Freising and Vincent of Beauvais could close their world chronicles with confident treatments of last things. But, in the face of trials and instability, it was natural for many to wonder about the nature and duration of the intervening events, and many accordingly issued predictions that attempted to link up the present to the last pages of the history book.

The prophecies of a few outstanding eschatological thinkers, such as Joachim of Fiore or Saint Bonaventure, have attracted some

1. Throughout this book the word *prophecy* is used in its everyday meaning of a prediction about the future and *prophet* as the issuer of such a prediction.

modern historians who have treated their ideas primarily from the intellectual-historical or theological point of view.[2] Another modern approach has been to look for extremist "radical" predictions in the hope of finding in them either harbingers of revolutionary ideology or catalysts for popular uprisings.[3] But there has hitherto been almost no attempt to look for the typical, to study commonplace prophetic ideas as expressions of collective and recurring concerns.[4]

Historians have come late to the quotidian and have come latest to it in inquiring about mentalities. Prophecy in particular has been regarded as either unfruitful or treacherous terrain: only recently was the warning issued that "prophecy confronts the historian with difficult questions for which few historians would be so foolhardy as to propose easy answers," that "surely most would admit that in its total scope prophecy is beyond the grasp of current methodology and

2. For works concerning "Joachim and Millenarianism" that have appeared in the last two decades, see Carl T. Berkhout and J. B. Russell, *Medieval Heresies: A Bibliography 1960–1979* (Toronto, 1981), 69–76. A useful review of a variety of research on medieval prophecy is Bernard McGinn, "Apocalypticism in the Middle Ages: An Historiographical Sketch," *Mediaeval Studies*, 37 (1975), 252–286.

3. The basic study that looks for harbingers of revolutionary ideology in high-medieval prophetic thought is Töpfer. See also Tilman Struve, "Utopie und gesellschaftliche Wirklichkeit: Zur Bedeutung des Friedenskaisers im späten Mittelalter," *Historische Zeitschrift*, 225 (1977), 65–95. On prophecies as supposed catalysts for uprisings, see Norman Cohn, *The Pursuit of the Millennium*, 3d ed. (New York, 1970). In partial criticism of Cohn, see Conclusions, pp. 183–197.

4. Bernard McGinn, *Visions of the End: Apocalyptic Traditions in the Middle Ages* (New York, 1979), is an extremely valuable anthology which presents much material that will help in the pursuit of this goal; nonetheless, McGinn concentrates on reviewing the appearance and evolution of eschatological themes in idea-historical fashion rather than on searching for everyday eschatological assumptions. I do not pretend that my own study is about "popular religion" if "popular" is taken to mean unlearned. Occasional scraps of information in chronicles and inquisitorial protocols are the only sources I know of that might cast scattered light on what completely uneducated people thought about the future, but these are probably insufficient to allow for generalizations. My evidence directly pertains only to the literate, but it was spontaneous and informal, rather than school-bred, and was generally the property of monks and priests of no exceptional distinction who had ongoing, everyday contacts with the nonclerical world.

evidence."[5] While conceding some truth to these caveats, I do not accept their counsel of despair, for "current methodology" can always be improved and the evidence for the study of medieval prophecy is not sparse but abundant.

Apart from formal treatises on last things and numerous biblical commentaries that broached eschatological questions, a plethora of short prophecies circulated throughout Western Europe in the high and later Middle Ages. Because almost all were pseudonymous, they have seldom been treated in monographs on individual thinkers, and hitherto very few scholars have thought them sufficiently dignified to be worth studying for themselves. But for the student of mentalities they are a fascinating and extremely valuable source. In what follows, I have attempted to write the history of one of them, the "Cedar of Lebanon" vision, which circulated from the thirteenth century to the seventeenth in numerous different forms.

It may seem surprising that a history of a short prophecy should be as long as a book, but there are good reasons for this. Most of the handful of scholarly articles that have been written on short prophecies are galleries of gaffes. Usually a scholar who decided to "write one up" did so because he had discovered one or a few new copies which he thought were all that survived: since the text was short, it could be described or edited quickly and another brick for medieval scholarship laid into place.[6] But anyone who studies the genre will

---

5. T. A. Sandquist, "The Holy Oil of St. Thomas of Canterbury," *Essays . . . Wilkinson*, 330.

6. A striking example of numerous scholarly false starts is the case of treatments and editions of a prophecy beginning *In vigilia namque ascensionis*, or in German *Am auffart abent*. The German version was first studied and edited, respectively, by Carl Koehne, "Die Weissagung auf das Jahr 1401," *Deutsche Zeitschrift für Geschichtswissenschaft*, n. F., 1 (1897), 352–362, and Friedrich Lauchert, "Materialien zur Geschichte der Kaiserprophetie im Mittelalter," *Historisches Jahrbuch*, 19 (1898), 844–872 (at 852–867), both of whom realized that there was a Latin original but thought that it was lost, and neither of whom realized that the Latin text was about a century older than the German translation. Then Alexander Reifferscheid, *Neun Texte zur Geschichte der religiösen Aufklärung in Deutschland während des 14. und 15. Jahrhunderts*, Festschrift der Universität Greifswald (Greifswald, 1905), 43–46, presented another edition of the German version without knowledge of Lauchert's superior work. Later,

soon learn that short prophecies can seldom be dealt with so expeditiously. Most of them circulated for centuries in scores of copies and numerous mutations. Thus what might at first seem a unique copy can turn out to be a late variant. In some cases seemingly independent prophecies prove to have been no more than parts or pastiches of others. Enough short prophecies have made fools of their editors to show that the student of any one of them must be prepared to engage in much patient sleuthing and cumulative research.[7]

Even the patient and careful student of a short prophecy, however, does not necessarily have to write a book about it. Once he feels sure he knows the earliest form of his text, he might edit it and be finished. But that is the approach of the textual scholar. The historian of mentalities, on the contrary, will find the later copies to be just as interesting as the earliest ones and the history of the appearances of and reactions to such copies more illuminating than narrow analysis of the text alone. An attempt to identify and appraise dominant attitudes must therefore cast wide nets over long periods of time. Only a full-length study could pursue the Cedar of Lebanon prophecy in numerous countries and contexts over hundreds of years.

My approach is not entirely new but bears some kinship to a work that has never received its due recognition, a remarkable monograph on the "Toledo Letter" published in 1901 by Hermann Grau-

---

one copy of the Latin text was discovered and edited by Donckel, "Visio," but he was ignorant of the existence of at least six other Latin copies, several of which would have helped him to avoid numerous errors. Recently Thomas Hohmann, "Deutsche Texte unter dem Namen 'Heinrich von Langenstein,'" *Würzburger Prosastudien II: Kurt Ruh zum 60. Geburtstag*, ed. Peter Kesting (Munich, 1975), 232–233, has attempted to give a complete list of the German copies but has overlooked at least half as many as he lists and reverts to a pre-Donckel state of scholarship by revealing ignorance of the Latin original.

7. As Herbert Grundmann wrote to Emil Donckel in a letter of 25 June 1933 informing him of some of the oversights and mistakes made in his treatment of *In vigilia namque ascensionis* (see preceding note): "Ich habe es deshalb immer vorgezogen, keine einzelnen Stücke zu publizieren, ehe ich mir nicht einen Ueberblick über möglichst viele Prophetien und ihre Zusammenhänge verschaffen habe. Was ein einzelner gelegentlich auffindet, ist immer ganz zufällig, und der Oeffentlichkeit ist, wie mir scheint, mit der Vorführung solcher gelegentlicher Funde wenig gedient." (A copy of this letter is in the Grundmann papers in Munich, access to which was kindly granted to me by Frau A. Grundmann.)

ert.[8] Grauert was the first to demonstrate that medieval prophecies had their own life histories insofar as they were continually rewritten and promulgated over the course of centuries with altered details and often with new dates. (He was able to show that the Toledo Letter first appeared in Christian Europe in the later twelfth century and reappeared with impressive regularity until the end of the fifteenth.) Beyond merely tracing the reappearances of a text, Grauert was also interested in collective psychology (there were Abels and Enochs even before the Flood) and used his evidence to demonstrate medieval preoccupation with astrology and recurrent fears about the end of the world.

Grauert's study is outstanding, but I hope to go beyond it in both method and conclusions. The central methodological weakness of his work is that he adduced far too little unpublished manuscript evidence. Most of the copies of the Toledo Letter he treated came from chronicles, but these, whether he knew it or not, represented only a small percentage of the surviving total. In fact the letter was copied so often in different manuscripts of all sorts that a fresh treatment could multiply Grauert's evidence at least fourfold and consequently result in new conclusions about all the different phases of its life.[9] Ignorant of the bulk of occurrences of his text, Grauert was insufficiently informed about how it circulated, who read it, and all the uses to which it was put. And insufficiently informed about medieval prophecy in general, Grauert was unable to demonstrate how his particular prophecy related to other texts and to the broad outlines of basic medieval prophetic and eschatological expectations.

8. Grauert (see list of abbreviations). M. Gaster, "The Letter of Toledo," *Folk-Lore*, 13 (1902), 115–133, is an English summary of Grauert's findings. F. Baer, "Eine jüdische Messiasprophetie auf das Jahr 1186 und der dritte Kreuzzug," *Monatsschrift für Geschichte und Wissenschaft des Judentums*, 70 (1926), 113–122, 155–165, argues for Jewish origins, but these would be at most very distant ones.

9. For example, a very early copy in MS Admont 381, fos. 107^r–109^v, kindly called to my attention by Dr. A. Patschovsky, would help to illuminate Western Christian origins, and a very late copy in MS UB Augsburg, Oettingen-Wallerstein'sche Bibliothek (formerly housed in Maihingen and Schloss Harburg), II, 1, 2°, 85, f. 30^v, would show that the prophecy circulated even later than Grauert thought. The file I have been keeping on previously unknown occurrences of the Toledo Letter is available for consultation.

That Grauert elected to avoid a hunt for unpublished manuscripts is not surprising. Manuscript searches are always laborious, and,
when their object is unpublished copies of prophecies, they are bound
to be frustratingly incomplete. Short prophecies were copied any-
where. One can try to search for them methodically in chronicles and
prophetic anthologies, but that by no means exhausts the possibilities
because they were also added to blank spaces in other kinds of manuscript books and at random on flyleaves. Notice of them does not always appear in published manuscript catalogues because until recently
cataloguers felt no obligation to report every text in every manuscript, and short prophecies were just the sort of seeming trivia they
ignored. Thus only the best described collections can be crossed off
the searcher's list, while the many large ones that have been inade-
quately catalogued would need to be swept by seven maids with
seven mops, so to speak, because unless every page of every high- and
late-medieval volume were turned, one could not be certain that a
sought-for prophecy was not missed.

Two examples from my own experience best illustrate the fact
that no prophecy-hunter's search will be complete until the last
known scrap of medieval writing has been catalogued and indexed.
While I was working in the Bayerische Staatsbibliothek in Munich,
a prophecy on an unbound single sheet fell out of an unrelated manuscript onto my lap: clearly it had been stuck there at random in the
fifteenth century and never noticed since.[10] At least I could take
credit for that "discovery" myself, but I only learned of a thirteenth-
century prophecy of one Peter of Little Hornmead when a colleague
in administrative history told me that it lay in the London Public
Record Office filed among "Chancery Miscellanies": some thirteenth-
century clerk had refrained from throwing it into what passed for his

---

10. This is a prophecy for the years from 1470 to 1478 with the incipit *Anno
lxx⁰ erunt tempora frigida*, placed in Cgm 754, a fifteenth-century German MS
consisting of a German translation of the Dialogues of Gregory the Great. The
prophecy, assigned the folio number 201 after I found it, was copied on a loose
paper sheet by a hand different from that of the main text. Related versions are
in MSS Clm 3586, f. 260^{r-v}, and Clm 18770, f. 189^r; another was apparently in
MS Innsbruck, Servitenkloster I b 28, fos. 176^v–177^v, but this MS (main text,
Reformatio Sigismundi) has disappeared from the Servitenkloster without a
trace.

waste basket.[11] These experiences make me certain that shortly after this book appears I will learn of several important missing copies of the Cedar of Lebanon text that had just been waiting for the print to dry to come out of hiding.

Nonetheless, if I have certainly not found every surviving copy of my prophecy, I have found a great many—sometimes with the generous aid of librarians or other scholars, sometimes by scent, and sometimes by fortuity's recompense for drudgery. My evidence, then, is more extensive than Grauert's and I hope to be able to tell a more complete story. I have selected the Cedar of Lebanon prophecy because it had numerous avatars and was in sum extremely popular and long-lived. Drawing on a comparative wealth of evidence, I hope to be able to show in what circumstances the prophecy emerged, how and why it was constantly rewritten, and what functions the original text and its numerous descendants fulfilled for its readers over the centuries.

In emphasizing the wealth of evidence, I do not mean to suggest that all my findings are indisputable, for I am thoroughly aware that this is not the case. Parts of what follows are frankly, perhaps shamefully, speculative for two major reasons. One is that the evidence, however extensive, has survived at random. This is of course true of any evidence found in medieval manuscript books: the survival rate of manuscripts over the passage of many centuries is notoriously indeterminate owing to the depredations of rats and rain, dissolutions of monasteries, pillagings, and wars. But prophecies clearly were lost far more often than most other texts because they were copied more spontaneously. Prophecies that were copied on single sheets were bound to have disappeared more quickly than books, and prophecies copied on flyleaves were easily lost either in rebinding or when a front leaf was snipped off for the purpose of destroying a prior ownership mark. Thus even were it possible to locate every surviving copy of the Cedar of Lebanon vision, it would still be impossible to know about all those that once existed. Since I could only draw conclusions from the evidence at hand, I have had to do some hypothesizing about places of origin, paths of transmission, and states of texts.

11. The thirteenth-century parchment is numbered C47/34/12/20. Professor Franklin J. Pegues kindly conveyed this information to me.

Were I to find new copies of the text, they might easily disprove some of these hypotheses.

The other grounds for uncertainty are that medieval prophecies are rife with obscure allusions. The meaning of some of these may have been clearer to contemporaries than to us, but there is good reason to believe that many prophets invented fully incomprehensible obscurities because they thought them appropriate: had a prophet been forced to say what he meant by a certain line, he would have had to answer that he could not tell. This makes matters extremely difficult for the modern commentator who not only can easily be mistaken in interpreting what was once intelligible, but also has no touchstone for distinguishing the originally intelligible from the eternally unintelligible. Hypotheses in such areas are unavoidable; I only hope that I have not too frequently tried to make sense out of nonsense with the schoolmasterly self-assurance of Humpty-Dumpty glossing the Jabberwock.

Whatever my inevitable mistakes, I trust that they will not vitiate my main argument that a study of the Cedar of Lebanon text in its manifold appearances reveals the persistence of certain deeply imprinted mental patterns. That leads me to state, in conclusion, that the outcome of this book proved to be very different from my original conception. When I started this project, I had in mind the idea of writing a "biography" of a prophecy: I intended to describe the life cycle of a text from birth, through adolescence and "identity-crisis," to maturity, senescence, and death. That notion was based on the assumption that the words of the prophecy not only changed greatly, but that such change reflected changing attitudes caused by the passage of four centuries. Study, however, showed that while the text certainly did change, in the most basic ways it stayed the same. Thus if I have written a biography, it has been of a textual Peter Pan. While I regret that this result deprives me of some biological metaphors, I do think it helps to establish an important conclusion; namely, that human mentalities have their persistencies just as much as demographic patterns, field systems, and trade routes do. The Cedar of Lebanon prophecy appears today as gratuitous error, but it spoke truth to its readers for ages.

Chapter I

THE MONGOLS ARE
COMING

Batu Khan, grandson of Genghis, knew well how to inspire fear. Advancing from the Asian steppes toward Europe in 1237 and slaughtering so many in his path that "no eye remained open to weep for the dead," he sent an imperious demand for submission to Bela IV, king of Hungary. Bela might be rich and strong, Batu wrote, but not strong enough to defend himself against the "messenger of the king of heaven to whom is given power on earth to exalt the submissive and oppress his enemies." The Mongol warned the "kinglet of the Hungarians" that it would be best to surrender immediately, especially since Bela had already been foolish enough to enrage Batu by sheltering a contingent of fleeing Cumans, Batu's "servants." "It is easier," Batu declared, "for the Cumans to flee than for you, since they are without houses and wander with their tents.... But you who dwell in homes, having castles and cities, how can you escape from my hands?"[1]

1. A critical edition of the letter, found in the report of Brother Julian discussed immediately below, is in Heinrich Dörrie, *Drei Texte zur Geschichte der Ungarn und Mongolen* (*Nachrichten der Akademie der Wissenschaften in Göttingen*, philosophisch-historische Klasse, 1956, no. 6; Göttingen, 1956), 179. Dörrie prefers the reading of "King" to "kinglet" without knowing that "kinglet" is found in the oldest MS text (see n. 4 below). The authenticity (which is not in

This dreadful missive was brought to Hungary at the end of 1237 by a Hungarian Dominican, Brother Julian, who also brought back more bad news.[2] In 1235 Julian had made a missionary trip to the Volga regions, where he had found pagan Hungarians whom he thought were ready for conversion to the Roman Christian faith. Inspired by Julian's discovery, four other Hungarian Dominicans went east in 1236 to follow up on his work: when they did not return, the intrepid Julian, who had already heard rumors of the Mongol advance, set out to look for them. By this time he was unable to advance farther than the grand duchy of Suzdal (Vladimir) in Russia. There he learned that the Mongols had conquered all the regions to the east, and—worse—that they were still advancing. Indeed, Iuri, the grand duke of Suzdal, bade Julian report to the king of Hungary that the Mongols were plotting night and day how they could first conquer Hungary and then advance "to Rome and beyond."[3]

At Iuri's court, Julian obtained the copy of Batu's frightening demand for submission. The Great Khan had dispatched this by means of his own emissaries, who had been intercepted and imprisoned by Iuri, so Julian took the letter back himself. Although it was written in Mongolian with Arabic characters, he found a pagan on his return trip who could translate it. Having located two of the missionaries for whom he was searching, Julian left Suzdal in the autumn of 1237, shortly before the grand duchy was overrun by the Mongols.

Back in Hungary around the beginning of 1238, Julian addressed a report of his findings to the papal legate at the Hungarian court. Herein he included a description of Mongol military tactics, as well

doubt) and authorship of the letter are treated by Dörrie. The best brief account of the Mongol advance toward Europe is J. J. Saunders, *The History of the Mongol Conquests* (London, 1971), 73–89. Saunders, 221, n. 30, explains that the source of the quotation "no eye remained open" has not yet been identified.

2. Best on Julian's travels is Dörrie, 127–131, who refutes the argument of Denis Sinor, "Un Voyageur du 13e siècle: le Dominicain Julien de Hongrie," *Bulletin of the School of Oriental and African Studies*, 14 (1952), 589–602, that Julian made only one instead of two trips. Dörrie is followed by Jean Richard, *La Papauté et les missions d'orient au moyen âge (XIIIe–XVe siècles)* (Rome, 1977), 26–30, which offers a convenient summary of the events. See also Gian Andri Bezzola, *Die Mongolen in abendländischer Sicht (1220–1270)* (Bern, 1974), 40–53, now the standard treatment of Western attitudes toward the Mongols.

3. Julian's report, Dörrie, 162–182.

as Iuri of Suzdal's warnings about the Mongols' ambitions and a copy
of Batu's letter. Understandably, Julian's report caused great conster-
nation. King Bela obtained a copy for himself and sent a copy to his
uncle, the patriarch of Aquileia on the Adriatic. The latter, in turn,
sent copies to the bishop of Brixen and the count of Tirol, urging
both to transmit the news farther. Clearly one purpose behind this
southerly transmission of Julian's report was to seal the Alpine passes
against possible Mongol attack.

From the Tirol, Julian's report was sent north again to Germany.
The earliest surviving copy was transcribed in the Swabian Benedictine monastery of Ottobeuren around July of 1241, after many of
Batu's threats had already become reality. True to his word, the Khan
had in fact advanced on Hungary, where he effortlessly succeeded in
destroying Bela's defending army on 11 April 1241. All the West lay
exposed to the Mongol terror. Had events on the borders of China
not dictated the withdrawal of Batu's armies from Europe the following year, the Alpine passes might well have been put to the test.

The exploits of Batu are not of as much interest here, however,
as the manuscript from Ottobeuren, hitherto thought lost but in fact
preserved in the University Library of Innsbruck.[4] Written at the

---

4. MS UB Innsbruck 187. The MS was found in Innsbruck in the first half of
the nineteenth century by J. F. Böhmer, who utilized its documentary material
for his *Regesta imperii* (see next note). Learning of the existence of the MS
from Böhmer, J. F. Hormayr used it for an edition of Julian's letter in his
Goldenen Chronik von Hohenschwangau (Munich, 1842), II, 66–69. Because
Hormayr did not indicate the location of the MS, subsequent students of Julian's
letter, including Sinor and Dörrie, remained ignorant of it, an ignorance that
has hampered attempts to provide a critical edition. Twentieth-century editors,
first Laszlo Bendefy, "Fontes authentici itinera fr. Iuliani (1235–1238) illustran-
tes," *Archivum Europae Centro-Orientalis*, 3 (1937), 1–52, and then Dörrie,
simply fell back on the Hormayr copy in lieu of the MS itself, and Dörrie mistakenly inferred that the MS was less valuable for providing a critical text than
one copied later in the thirteenth century. The MS came to Innsbruck from the
monastery of Stams (founded in 1273) but was certainly written in Ottobeuren,
which had close medieval contact with Stams. Brief descriptions of it, which
recognize its origins at Ottobeuren but say nothing of its copy of Julian's letter or of any prophetic material, are Paul Lehmann, "Mitteilungen aus Handschriften, I," SbM, 1929, no. 1, 14–15, and Hansmartin Schwarzmaier, "Mit-
telalterliche Handschriften des Klosters Ottobeuren," *Studien und Mitteilungen
zur Geschichte des Benediktiner-ordens und seiner Zweige*, 73, no. 2/4 (1962),
7–23 (at 22).

height of the Mongol threat, the manuscript contains Julian's report, a collection of other documents and texts, mostly concerning the Mongols, and the earliest known copy of a short Latin prophecy of dire events soon to come.[5] That prophecy was to circulate throughout Europe in various forms for centuries, long after Batu and Bela were forgotten. It is the subject of this book.

The short prophecy precedes the copy of Julian's report in the Ottobeuren manuscript and is written in the same hand. But there is no reason to believe that Julian's report and the prophecy came from the same source because the other texts about the Mongols in the manuscript are of disparate provenance. Most likely a monk of Ottobeuren with Mongols on his mind copied together a number of related texts that came to the monastery from different directions. Still, Julian's report provides essential background for determining the origins and comprehending the meaning of the prophecy.

There are seven known copies of the prophecy, but five are of no help in determining its origin. Four are English, but the prophecy certainly was not written in England, and the English copyists did not say where the text came from, probably because they themselves

---

5. There is unfortunately no published catalogue of the important UB Innsbruck MS collection; I have been aided somewhat by the old handwritten *Zettelkatalog*. MS 187 falls into two parts, written by two coeval hands, the second of which ends with a colophon indicating completion in Ottobeuren in 1241. The first scribe must have worked in Ottobeuren in that year too because the letters in the first part, with the exception of Julian's earlier report, all date from 1241 (none later than June) and because most were sent to addressees in Swabia. All of the documents in the first part of the MS are calendared in J. F. Böhmer, *Regesta imperii, V: Regesten des Kaiserreichs*, ed. J. Ficker and E. Winkelmann (Innsbruck, 1881-1901) (=BFW). In order of their appearance in the MS they are BFW 11357, 11309 (Julian's report), 11328, 3210, 11341, 11349, 3209, 11338, 11337, 11325. BFW 3210 is also edited from the Innsbruck MS in MGH, *Leges*, *sect. IV: Constitutiones II*, 322-325. The nondocumentary texts in the first part of the MS have characteristically been ignored; they are: Latin hexameters on the divine essence (f. 1r); the short prophecy to be treated here (f. 2r); and a short dialogue between "Alexander and Aristotle" about future trials to be brought by the Mongols, incipit: "Alexander Macedo quesivit ab Aristotile magistro suo, dicens: 'Dic michi quod erit in futuro tempore'" (f. 8r-v). To my knowledge the copy of the short dialogue is unique and unstudied: there is no mention of it in Bezzola or in George Cary, *The Medieval Alexander* (Cambridge, 1956). (I am extremely grateful to Herr Dr. Neuhauser of the University Library for numerous kindnesses during my stay in Innsbruck.)

did not know.[6] A fifth copy appears without word of provenance in a prophetic anthology written in Italy in the late thirteenth century.[7]

The provenance sleuth is therefore forced to rely on the two remaining copies, and even the one from Ottobeuren provides a false lead: a statement that the prophecy was a message revealed miraculously to a monk in the Cistercian cloister of "Snusnyacum." That name might have told us where in Europe to look for origins had there ever been such a place. But no cloister or town of "Snusnyacum" is known to have existed, nor was there ever a Sunsnyacum, a Sinisnyacum, a Smisnyacum, or a Simsnyacum, other paleographical, but not real geographical, possibilities. The monastic locale was thus almost certainly invented to lend an alleged miracle an aura of specificity.

The Ottobeuren manuscript is of real aid in showing that an early reader thought the prophecy alluded to the advent of the Mongols, an interpretation well borne out by the contents of the text. The subject matter, in turn, helps point to a place of origin. Since the one Latin-Christian country best informed and most concerned about the Mongols before the middle of 1241 was Hungary, that country was probably the locale of the composition. Further support for this hypothesis comes from the seventh copy, one included in the chronicle of Alberic of Trois-Fontaines, a Cistercian of Champagne. Alberic did not refer to the prophecy's origins, but scholars have long noted that he was particularly well informed about events in Hungary and that much material in his chronicle was definitely of Hungarian provenance. In all probability, the prophetic message was another text that made its way from Hungary to Champagne.[8]

---

6. The English copies are in Matthew Paris's *Chronica maiora*, the *Annals of Dunstable*, a flyleaf of MS Cambridge, St. John's College 239, and MS BL Royal 13 E IX, f. 27ᵛ. I return to all these copies in detail in the following chapter.

7. MS Vat. lat. 3822, f. 6ᵛ, on which see Jeanne Bignami-Odier, "Notes sur deux manuscrits de la Bibliothèque du Vatican," *Mélanges d'archéologie et d'histoire*, 54 (1937), 211–241, with an edition of the prophecy in question (229).

8. Alberic of Trois-Fontaines, *Chronicon*, in MGH, *Scriptores*, 23, 949. Alberic's copy of the prophecy was first noticed by J. Van den Gheyn, "Note sur un manuscrit de l'*Excidium Aconis*, en 1291," *Revue de l'Orient Latin*, 6 (1898), 550–556 (at 553). On Alberic's connections with Hungary and his knowledge of Hungarian sources, see Bezzola, 60, who refers to the earlier literature.

Alberic entered the prophetic message in his chronicle for the year 1240, explaining that it was the result of a vision seen in a Cistercian monastery (left by him unnamed) "several years" earlier. The "several years" must be discounted: the prophet's knowledge of the coming of the Mongols could hardly have predated 1238, when Europeans first became aware of the Mongol menace. Most likely the backdating was done by Alberic or his source to enhance the appearance of miraculous clairvoyance. Alberic's copying of the prophecy under the year 1240, on the other hand, suggests that 1240 was when the text first arrived at Trois-Fontaines.[9] The Ottobeuren manuscript also dates the vision to 1240 and one English monastic copyist says explicitly that the prophecy arrived at his house in 1240.[10] The only different dating is given by two English chroniclers—Matthew Paris and an annalist of Dunstable—who report the miracle for 1239. Perhaps the text of the prophecy arrived at their houses as early as that year, but it is also possible that it reached them in 1240 and that they concluded independently (or from a common copy) that the miracle had transpired the year before.[11] In any event, the evidence leaves no doubt that the prophecy itself was written sometime between 1238 and 1240.

Only in Hungary was knowledge of the Mongol danger prevalent so early. Aside from the return of Julian with his bad news in late 1237, actual Mongol ambassadors reached Hungary in the period between 1237 and 1241. Batu Khan in fact complained in his letter brought back by Julian that King Bela had ignored thirty prior Mon-

9. Alberic's nineteenth-century editor, P. Scheffer-Boichorst, concluded that he wrote down entries year for year as they occurred and later—up to the conclusion of his work in 1251—made additions.

10. MS Cambridge, St. John's College 239, back flyleaf: "Anno Domini M°C°C quadrgesimo [sic] pervenit ad nos hec scriptura."

11. In neither of the works in question—Matthew Paris's *Chronica maiora* and the *Annals of Dunstable*—does the presence of an entry under a certain year prove it was written in that year. Richard Vaughan, *Matthew Paris* (Cambridge, 1958), 59–60, shows that Matthew Paris's treatment of the events of 1239 was only written in final form after November 1245 (Matthew probably worked from notes or earlier drafts). Similarly, C. R. Cheney, "Notes on the Making of the Dunstable Annals," *Essays . . . Wilkinson*, 79–98, shows that many entries in the Dunstable Annals were written later than the years under which they were entered.

gol legations, and, while this figure may be a rhetorical exaggeration, other sources confirm the fact that some Mongol embassies did get through to Bela before his defeat in the spring of 1241.[12] One can easily imagine the terror inspired by the appearance of dreadful oriental ambassadors bearing still more dreadful threats.[13]

From Hungary's vantage point around 1239, then, the future looked fearful, so fearful that someone sought solace by conceiving of the Mongol advance as part of the divine plan and by spreading his views in the form of a prophecy. According to the text that reached Swabia, Champagne, and England, the mysterious prophecy resulted from a miracle that transpired in a Cistercian cloister. Allegedly, a certain monk celebrating mass saw a hand writing out a prophetic message.[14] Of course it is impossible to prove that such a miracle did not happen as described, just as it is impossible to prove that a similar miracle did not transpire at Belshazzar's Feast. But the secular historian must follow Gibbon in assuming that the Deity has very seldom, since apostolic times, suspended the laws of nature for the service of religion. It will therefore be taken for granted that not the Lord but one of His creatures was the author of the prophecy.

Exactly who the author was will never be known, but we may assume he was a cleric, because in the earlier thirteenth century in northern Europe clerics were virtually alone in being able to write in Latin. This one was upset by news of the Mongols and sought to come to grips with the frightening events by finding eschatological sense

12. A circular letter of the Emperor Frederick II of 3 July 1241, recorded by Matthew Paris, *Chronica majora*, ed. H. R. Luard (RS 57; London, 1872–1884), IV, 112–119, blames Bela for ignoring "messengers and letters" from the Mongols, and Matthew himself (*Chronica majora*, III, 488) writes under the year 1238 (probably independently of Frederick's remark) of the Mongols having sent "threatening letters with dreadful legations." This passage, and Matthew Paris's interest in the Mongols in general, is treated by J. J. Saunders, "Matthew Paris and the Mongols," *Essays ... Wilkinson*, 116–132.

13. It is unclear exactly how much Bela did to defend himself, but at the very least he sent some scouts on exploratory missions in the direction of the advancing onslaught; see Bezzola, 53–57.

14. MS UB Innsbruck 187, f. 2^r: "Anno Domini M^{o}C^{o}Cxl^{mo} apud Snusnyacum monasterium Cysterciensis ordinis hec visio facta est cuidam monacho celebranti presentibus abbate et ministro. Apparuit quedam manus scribens in corporali verba hec" (the text of the prophecy follows). For MS variants see Appendix I.

in them. Other contemporaries were also looking for the deeper meaning of the Mongol advance, but our prophet went further by spreading his views as if they were supernaturally inspired. In order to assure himself an audience, he took the liberty of introducing his message with a fictitious account of a miracle modelled on Belshazzar's Feast and visions granted to saints during mass.[15] Since this deceit was not committed for the sake of personal recognition or even of enhancing the reputation of a local shrine, the author probably had no troubled conscience. On the contrary, he must have been happy to think of himself as God's intermediary, letting God's will be known in the most effective way possible.

This was his message:

> The high Cedar of Lebanon will be felled. Mars will prevail over Saturn and Jupiter. Saturn will waylay Jupiter in all things. Within eleven years there will be one God and one monarchy. The second god has gone. The sons of Israel will be liberated from captivity. A certain people called "without a head," or reputed to be wanderers, will come. Woe to the clergy! A new order thrives: if it should fall, woe to the Church! There will be many battles in the world. There will be mutations of faith, of laws, and of kingdoms. The land of the Saracens will be destroyed.[16]

The reader who finds that much of this seems more like balderdash than wisdom might like to hear that all the nonsense can be transformed into sense by the wand of scholarship. But such is surely not the case. Familiarity with medieval sources and ways of thinking can

15. In the standard thirteenth-century hagiographical compilation, *The Golden Legend*, prophetic miracles during mass are vouchsafed to SS. Gregory and Bernard: see *The Golden Legend of Jacobus de Voragine*, trans. G. Ryan and H. Ripperger (London, 1941; repr. 1969), 184, 476. Perhaps another model for the fiction was the "heavenly letter," supposedly placed on the altar of St. Peter's in Jerusalem by an angel. On this text, see Robert Priebsch, *Letter from Heaven on the Observance of the Lord's Day* (Oxford, 1936), and further literature cited by Martin Erbstösser, *Sozialreligiöse Strömungen im späten Mittelalter* (Berlin, 1970), 42–48.

16. My translation is based on a composite of the primitive copies, which can be found in Appendix I, A.

aid in understanding some of the text's allusions, but no one, no matter how learned, can ever hope to reenter fully into a medieval prophetic mind. Moreover, even if that were possible, all of the prophecy would probably still not be completely clear, because it was probably not meant to be completely clear in the first place. The author of the prophecy was supposedly God, and God, as anyone who read Ezechiel, Daniel, or Revelation knew, was not wont to reveal the future in the clearest terms. Since explicit prophecy could never have gained acceptance as being genuinely divine, the thirteenth-century prophet made his text designedly obscure—so much so that it was probably not even completely intelligible to himself. Nonetheless, he certainly did wish to communicate some urgent messages, and these appear to be clear enough.

The first words of the prophecy set a portentous mood and foretell imminent chastisement for the proud and sinful. Cedars of Lebanon grow thick in the Bible. As medieval commentators recognized, biblical cedars had both good and bad connotations. They could be fine, godly trees because of their great height, spreading foliage, perennial greenness, and durable wood, but the same qualities made them excellent symbols of pride before a fall.[17] Certainly the prophet had the latter meaning in mind because the Bible refers to the destruction of cedars to show how the Lord punishes the proud. In the Psalms, for example (Ps. 37:34–35), the Lord "cuts off the wicked" who spreads himself like a cedar, and in Ezechiel, chapter 31, He strikes down the vainglorious Assyrian, who is described as "a cedar in Lebanon" whose "height was exalted above all the trees of the field," and who was so fair "by the multitude of his branches . . . that

---

17. Jerome, *Comment. in Isaiam*, PL 24, 50–51, and Cassiodorus, *Institutiones*, I, chap. 15, par. 4—I use the translation by Leslie Webber Jones, *Cassiodorus Senator, An Introduction to Divine and Human Readings* (New York, 1946), 105. Medieval encyclopedists stressed the positive features of the cedar: see Isidore of Seville, *Etymologiarum . . . libri XX*, ed. W. M. Lindsay (Oxford, 1911), XVII, chap. 7, par. 33; Thomas of Cantimpré, *Liber de natura rerum* (Berlin, 1973), X, chap. 12, 318; and review of other evidence by Heimo Reinitzer, "Zeder und Aloe. Zur Herkunft des Bettes Salomos im 'Moritz von Craun,'" AfK, 58 (1976), 1–34 (at 3). The hymn to St. Augustine beginning *Cedrus alta Libani*, as printed in G. M. Dreves, *Analecta hymnica* (Leipzig, 1886ff.), XXXIV, 162, is unrelated to the vision under discussion.

all the trees of Eden that were in the garden of God envied him." [18]

The Book of Isaiah added an eschatological dimension to the image of the cedar's destruction. In some of the most famous words of Scripture, Isaiah foretold that in "the last days" men shall "beat their swords into plowshares and their spears into pruninghooks" (Isa. 2:4). At the same time the prophet warned that the Lord shall "rebuke many people," for "the day of the Lord of hosts shall be upon everyone that is proud and lofty, and upon everyone that is lifted up . . . and upon all the Cedars of Lebanon that are high and lifted up . . . and the loftiness of man shall be bowed down, and the haughtiness of men shall be made low" (Isa. 2:12–17). This passage was well known in the thirteenth century,[19] and the author of the prophecy clearly envisaged its fulfillment.

The prophecy's astrological references are similarly portentous. Although medieval astrology could often be very arcane, the major properties of Mars, Saturn, and Jupiter were easy to understand and probably as familiar to educated and half-educated people of the thirteenth century as verses from the Bible. The dominance of the fiery planet Mars in the skies meant war. Cicero expressed a common astrological view, reiterated in the Middle Ages, when he wrote of "the ruddy one, which you call Mars, dreaded on earth." [20] Saturn's

18. In keeping with such passages, the Cedar of Lebanon was used as an image of pride by St. Bernard: "Et quidem in schismate vidi impium superexaltatum, et elevatum sicut cedros Libani" (Epistola 914: PL 182, 552).

19. Innocent III, for example, cited the passage as a warning to the proud: see Lothario dei Segni (Pope Innocent III), *On the Misery of the Human Condition*, ed. Donald R. Howard and trans. M. M. Dietz (Indianapolis, 1969), II, chap. 33, 58. The standard commentaries of Jerome (PL 24, 42–43) and Haymo (PL 116, 729) opposed the chiliastic implications of Isaiah 2 by applying the prophecy of the "last days" to the first coming of Christ, but Joachim of Fiore and his followers placed Isaiah's prophecy in the future: see Joachim of Fiore, *Concordia Novi ac Veteris Testamenti* (Venice, 1519; repr. Frankfurt, 1964), f. 122c, and the pseudo-Joachite Isaiah commentary: *Abbatis Joachim Florensis Scriptum super Esaiam prophetam* (Venice, 1517), fos. 2ᵛ–3ᵛ. (A copy is in Yale University Library: MC35/J570/Ab 2/1516; Professor R. E. Kaske kindly lent me his microfilm.) The author of the vision did not have to be influenced by Joachim or Joachism to have read Isaiah eschatologically.

20. *Dream of Scipio*, chap. 5. I use the translation by W. H. Stahl of Macrobius, *Commentary on the Dream of Scipio* (New York, 1952), 73. Bartholomaeus Anglicanus's *De rerum proprietatibus*, (Frankfurt, 1601; repr. Frankfurt, 1964),

influence too was baleful. Saturn stood for trouble, vileness, and ma-
levolence, and was commonly linked by astrologers with Mars.[21] The
influence of Jupiter, on the contrary, was beneficent, having connotations that are still found in the adjective *jovial*. For Cicero, Jupiter
was "that brilliant orb, propitious and helpful to the human race."[22]
A prophecy, then, of Mars's prevalence over Saturn and Jupiter and
Saturn's triumph over Jupiter was a prophecy of disaster—the astrological equivalent of the felling of a high Cedar of Lebanon.

Of course astrological allusions hardly belonged in a God-sent
message. The Lord might have spoken in metaphors of fallen cedars,
but He should not have done so in the language of pagan astrology.
(The same Book of Isaiah that talks of cedars excoriates "astrologers
and star-gazers" [Isa. 47:13].) The astrological passage shows that the
author of the vision was naively invoking an alternate belief system
without recognizing its incongruity. (Some medieval theologians did
concede that the planets and the stars—themselves moved by God—
might reveal God's intentions in their motions, but even if heavenly
movements had predictive qualities, there was no need for the Deity
to issue a prediction of a prediction.)

The incongruous juxtaposition is best understood as an unso-
phisticated attempt to appeal to the authority of "science" within the
framework of miracle. After the revival of serious astrological study
in Western Europe in the twelfth century, owing primarily to the
translation of Arabic texts, astrology became, according to a con-

---

VIII, chap. 25, 402–403, an encyclopedia which dates from about the same time
as the Cistercian vision, also describes the "martial" qualities of Mars.

21. For example, passages cited in Raymond Klibansky, Erwin Panofsky, and
Fritz Saxl, *Saturn and Melancholy* (New York, 1964), such as *stellae vero Saturni
et Martis terribiles dicuntur* (182, n. 178, from a medieval commentary on Macrobius) and *Saturnini et martiales, quales gebellinos volunt, mali, maliciosi, iracundi,
superbi* (192, n. 203, from Coluccio Salutati). On Saturn's malevolent qualities,
see Klibansky et al., 187, citing Bartholomaeus Anglicanus.

22. Trans. Stahl, 73. On Jupiter's good qualities, see further Bartholomaeus
(ed. 1601), VIII, chap. 24, 401–402 and John of Paris, *Testimonia gentilium de
secta Christiana*, ed. Thomas A. Orlando (M.A. thesis: University of Virginia,
1973), 78 (from Book VI): "Ponunt [Ptolemy, Albumasar, Alcabicius] enim
ipsi Iovem et Venerem planetas esse benivolos et fortunatos, Saturnum et Martem
malivolos et infortunatos."

temporary encyclopedist, "the queen of the predictive sciences."[23] Astrology was studied in conjunction with astronomy and regarded as the practical, "applied," side of the new astral learning. As astronomers reduced the seemingly aimless wanderings of planets to order with the help of accurate calculations, so astrologers attempted to use astronomers' findings to reduce the seeming vagaries of human existence to similar order. And since astronomical reckonings were demonstrably predictive, astrological ones were accepted as such as well. Hence eschatological prophets were bound to avail themselves of astrology's language and prestige. The most popular predecessor of the "Cistercian vision," the late twelfth-century prophetic Toledo Letter, was expressed exclusively in terms of astrological certainty; although the Cistercian vision's astral allusions were less extensive, they similarly show how difficult it was to think of the future in the high Middle Ages without seeing stars.

After its general warnings, the prophecy proceeds to details. Its most difficult allusion is its reference to two gods, one of whom "has gone." Presumably the prophet was not a polytheist and was speaking metaphorically. Perhaps by the "second god" he meant Allah, the god of Islam. This hypothesis at first seems supported by the final line, which explicitly predicts the coming demise of the Saracens. But that prediction is given in the future tense while the sentence "the second god has gone" refers to the past. Mere erudition may never solve this problem. Assuming that the difficulty was not caused by an early textual corruption, we may be dealing here with an instance of prophetic gibberish—ominous-sounding but meaningless language that the prophet supplied solely for effect.

The allusion to the triumph of one God and one monarchy within eleven years sounds positive and was probably meant to be so. Hope for the coming of "one shepherd and one flock" (John 10:16), that is, for the union of the world under Christianity before the end of time,

23. Bernard Silvester, quoted by Brian Stock, *Myth and Science in the Twelfth Century* (Princeton, 1972), 28. On the importance of astrology in the high-medieval scientific scheme, see further Thorndike, II, 890–891; Charles Homer Haskins, *The Renaissance of the Twelfth Century* (Cambridge, Mass., 1927; repr. New York, 1957), 317; John E. Murdoch and Edith D. Sylla, eds., *The Cultural Context of Medieval Learning* (Dordrecht, 1975), 205, 214; and Hugh of St. Victor, *Didascalicon*, trans. Jerome Taylor (New York, 1961), 68.

was expressed continually throughout the high and later Middle Ages.[24] What is odd about the allusion in the vision is that it appears to be out of order, for the prophecy begins with dire warnings and proceeds immediately to others. If the line were moved to the end of the text it would make more sense: after eleven years of battles and mutations of faith, laws, and kingdoms, the Saracens will be converted and the world will be united for Christianity. (The license to move a line seems justified by the unmethodical nature of the text: a prophecy that mixes astrology with purported revelation could also offer predictions in scrambled chronological sequence.) Assuming that the prophecy was written in 1239, the choice of the exact figure of eleven years points to fulfillment in 1250, a year that was expected by other independent sources to be of great eschatological significance.[25]

The predicted liberation of the sons of Israel should be read together with the following lines about the coming of the people "without a head" as complementary ways of alluding to the advent of the Mongols. The "sons of Israel" would be the Mongols because a common European attempt to order the mysterious Asians within the realm of the known was to posit their descent from renegade Jews. Sometimes the Mongols were called Ishmaelites, or "sons of Ishmael,"[26] and sometimes they were considered to be descendants of

24. For examples see Lerner, "Refreshment of the Saints," 110–112, and passim. Here it suffices to cite the representative thirteenth-century *Compendium theologicae veritatis* of Hugo Ripelin (many early printed editions and two nineteenth-century ones in *Opera omnia* of St. Thomas and St. Bonaventure), VII, 13: "Judei vero tunc convertentur ad fidem et sancta ecclesia usque in finem mundi pacifica conquiescet."

25. The earliest form of the popular jingle *Cum fuerint anni transacti*, predicting the birth of Antichrist for any of a host of late-medieval years, made this prediction for 1250 and was apparently first coined in relation to the Mongol advance: see Reeves, *Influence of Prophecy*, citing Matthew Paris's *Additamenta*, and M. Haeusler, *Das Ende der Geschichte in der mittelalterlichen Weltchronistik* (Cologne, 1980), 60–61, who points to some of Matthew's own worries about 1250.

26. On the Mongols as Ishmaelites, or *filii Ismael*, see Bezzola, 41–43, and passim, and C. W. Connell, "Western Views of the Origin of the 'Tartars,'" *Journal of Medieval and Renaissance Studies*, 3 (1973), 128–129, who leaves out the earliest known published designation of them as such—that of Brother Julian. Unknown to previous scholars, the Mongols also appear as Ishmaelites in the un-

the Ten Lost Tribes. [27] The latter interpretation explained their sudden onslaught from the East, for according to medieval lore, the Ten Lost Tribes (sometimes confused with the peoples of Gog and Magog) had been shut up by Alexander the Great behind the Caspian Gates but would break loose in the last days.[28] This legend circulated widely in Europe before any news was heard of the Mongols and thereafter became an excellent way to account for their dramatic appearance.[29] The people "without a head" are clearly the Mongols as well because they are also referred to in the prophecy as wanderers; the Mongols were probably deemed "headless" because their swift armies appeared to terrified Westerners to be without a leader.[30]

In the prophet's mind, such terrible people would obviously be a scourge to the clergy. Apparently he thought the coming chastisement would be deserved because, as his next lines show, he vested his hopes in a "thriving" new order instead of the secular clergy or the old orders.[31] By the new order he meant either the Dominicans or the Franciscans, both at the height of their prestige around 1240. If the author was Hungarian, he probably meant the Dominicans because

---

published dialogue between "Alexander and Aristotle" in MS UB Innsbruck 187, f. 8ʳ (see n. 5 above). Haeusler, 59, points out that the *filii Israel* in the vision could perhaps be a mistake for *filii Ismael*, the latter a term that gained wide currency in the high-medieval West after its appearance in the *Revelations* of Pseudo-Methodius.

27. Bezzola, 102–103 and Connell, 129–132.

28. Andrew R. Anderson, *Alexander's Gate, Gog and Magog, and the Inclosed Nations* (Cambridge, Mass., 1932), esp. 58–86, and Cary (n. 5 above), 130–132.

29. The enclosure of the Ten Tribes appears in the twelfth-century *Historia Scholastica*, the standard medieval summary of biblical history and one of the most widely circulated books of the thirteenth century: see Anderson, 64–66. It appears too in Jacques de Vitry's *Historia Hierosolimitana (Historia orientalis)* of ca. 1230 in J. Bongars, ed., *Gesta Dei per Francos* (Hanau, 1611), I, 1095.

30. Later medieval glosses interpret *sine capite* to mean "leaderless" (see pp. 110 and 139 below). Some heretics too were deemed to be *sine capite* because they had no known founder: see Isidore of Seville, *Etymologies*, VIII, chap. 5, par. 66, a passage that reappeared in Gratian's *Decretum*, C. 24, q. 3, c. 39, par. 65, and was frequently copied throughout the Middle Ages.

31. Here I follow Töpfer, 145, and find no warrant for the translation of "Ve clero! Viget ordo novus; si ceciderit, ve ecclesie!" by Haeusler (n. 25 above), 62, as "Die neuen Orden schaden dem Klerus und sind Vorboten des Endes; wenn sie fallen, beginnt das Leid der ganze Christenheit."

they were displaying particular strength in Hungary. (The journeys of Brother Julian and the other Hungarian missionaries provide good examples of the vigorous activity of the Hungarian Dominicans around the time the prophecy was composed.)[32] Many observers in the second quarter of the thirteenth century believed that the two new orders together, or one of them alone, would play a special role in renewing the Church and in saving the world at the end of time.[33] The prophet, perhaps himself a Dominican or Franciscan, contemplated a double purification of the Church: by the Mongols externally and by one of the new orders internally. Assuming that his setting of the vision in a Cistercian cloister was fictional, he may have been making subtle reference to the superiority of one of the new mendicant orders to an older monastic one by having God inform a Cistercian about the central role of the mendicants in the divine plan.

The rest of the prophecy is self-explanatory. The coming of the headless will initiate a time of great turmoil—"battles[34] . . . mutations of faith, of laws, and of kingdoms"—that will culminate in the "subversion" of "the land of the Saracens." In associating the advent of the Mongols with the destruction of Islam, the prophet's hopes were typical. Even at the first rumors of Mongol armies in Turkestan around 1220, Western Christians hoped that the strangers would crush the Saracens.[35] Later, Matthew Paris reported that in 1238 a Saracen em-

---

32. On the early Dominicans in Hungary, Nikolaus Pfeiffer, *Die ungarische Dominikanerordensprovinz von ihrer Gründung 1221 bis zur Tartarenverwüstung 1241–42* (Zürich, 1913).

33. On the "senescence" of the "Church of the clergy" and the eschatological role of the two new orders in the pseudo-Joachite Jeremiah commentary, probably written before 1243, see Töpfer, 114, and 117, n. 75, and Reeves, *Influence of Prophecy*, 152. Other examples dating from around 1250 of the view that the two orders were to save the world at the end of time can be found in Reeves, 146–147. In my "Weltklerus und religiöse Bewegung im 13. Jahrhundert," AfK, 51, (1969), 100, n. 19, I give an early example (before 1236) of praise for the Dominicans for preaching in the evening of the world; for similar expressions concerning the Franciscans, see E. Randolph Daniel, *The Franciscan Concept of Mission* (Lexington, Kent., 1975), 28.

34. It is probably only coincidental that the prediction of coming *multa prelia* in the Cistercian vision also appears three times in the dialogue between Alexander and Aristotle about the horrors to be brought by the Mongols (n. 5 above).

35. Best on this is Bezzola, 13–28.

bassy came to the West asking for assistance against the "Tartar" fury. Allegedly, when this legation appeared at the English court, the bishop of Winchester interrupted the infidels' pleas for a common front by saying: "Let us leave these dogs to devour each other, that they may all be consumed and perish; and we, when we proceed against the enemies of Christ who remain, will slay them, and cleanse the face of the earth, so that all the world will be subject to the one Catholic Church."[36] The prophet, more realistically, has the Mongols attacking both Saracens and Christians, but he foresaw the same end: the defeat of Islam and the ultimate union of the world under "one God and one monarchy."

It is clear, then, that the vision is by no means purely pessimistic. It foretells great imminent upheavals and chastisements but also anticipates change for the better. The upheavals would bring suffering to many, but the prophet singles out only the clergy. Yet he does not condemn all the clergy but places his hopes for the Church in one of the new orders. Although there would be mutations of faith and of kingdoms, ultimately the Holy Land would be freed from the Saracens, and Christianity would prevail everywhere.

The author of the Cistercian vision was frightened by the Mongol advance but managed to allay his fears by finding in it a divinely ordained purpose.[37] Since he was sure that he had gained insight into God's plan, he could not rest content by remaining alone with his knowledge. His choice was to tell others about it in his own voice and risk indifference or obloquy, or to circulate his views as if they were the result of a miraculous message. In choosing the latter alternative he must have felt strengthened by his conviction that his insight really amounted to revelation. As we will see, it was quickly accepted as such by a large audience.

36. The incident is treated by Saunders (n. 12 above), 117–123.

37. A similarly chastising role for the Mongols was predicted by the troubadour Guilhem de Montanhagol. See his "Per lo mon fan li un dels autres rancura" of ca. 1257 in Peter T. Ricketts, ed., *Les Poésies de Guilhem de Montanhagol* (Toronto, 1964), 133, stanza 1, lines 6–9: "Mas ar venon sai deves Orien/li Tartari, si Dieus non o defen,/qu'ls faran totz estar d'una mensura." But Guilhem allowed the possibility that God might hold the Mongols back if men changed their ways.

Chapter II

THE TRANSMISSION OF
THE VISION

The Cistercian vision circulated rapidly and widely. The seven known surviving medieval copies reveal by their textual variants that many more copies are missing and show by their provenances that the vision travelled from its place of origin on the continent—probably Hungary—to at least Swabia, Champagne, Italy, and England. Remarkably, the prophecy's interest to contemporaries does not appear to stem from its warning about the Mongols, for only the Ottobeuren manuscript connected the text with the Mongol advance. Apparently, the relationship between the vision and the dramatic events in the East was quickly forgotten. Not obvious topicality but the striking story of the moving hand and the general edification provided by the message seem to have earned the vision its initial popularity. As we follow the text in its travels we can gain insight into the nature of its circulation and reception, and we can see how it became progressively altered the farther away it travelled from its origin in space and time.

The best copy of the vision is clearly that of the Ottobeuren manuscript.[1] This contains only one verifiable mistake, the inadver-

1. For editions of the copies of the Cistercian vision see Appendix I.

tent omission of a single word, and a probable one, the use of a present instead of a future tense. In the summer of 1241, the vision must have come with few intermediaries to the Swabian cloister, where a monk copied it carefully and without taking any conscious liberties.

Alberic of Trois-Fontaines in Champagne, on the other hand, provided a good text of the prophetic message but knowingly altered the covering miracle story. The two mistakes found in the text of his message are clearly inadvertent. Since they do not occur in any of the other surviving manuscripts, they may have been made by Alberic himself. If so, this would provide further support for the theory that Alberic received his text directly from a source in Hungary. But Alberic's version of the miracle story contains two unique conscious alterations. One is the backdating of the miracle by "several years" discussed in the first chapter. The other is a change in the rank of the message's recipient: in Alberic's version, an abbot receives the vision instead of a simple monk. Probably Alberic (or perhaps someone else before him) thought that God would have vouchsafed an urgent message only to the highest ranking member of a monastic community. In that case, Alberic probably thought that the text which had reached Trois-Fontaines was mistaken in this detail and corrected it on the assumption that he was describing the true course of events.

The last continental copy of the prophecy comes from an Italian prophetic anthology of the late thirteenth century.[2] This version omits the miracle story altogether, but its text of the prophecy is another fairly uncorrupted one. Perhaps it crossed the Alps together with the prefatory miracle story soon after the original composition, to be rediscovered by the copyist of the anthology a half century later. The anthologist may have thought that a miracle of 1240 was too dated to merit copying or deemed the prophecy alone appropriate for his collection.

Time's obliterations have effaced further traces of the prophecy's circulation in continental Europe, but the accidents of survival have spared four English copies. These show that the vision reached Eng-

2. The MS—Vat. lat. 3822—is described by Holder-Egger, 33, 97-105, and Jeanne Bignami-Odier, "Notes sur deux manuscrits de la Bibliothèque du Vatican," *Mélanges d'archéologie et d'histoire,* 54 (1937), 211-241. Holder-Egger, 97, argues for Roman Franciscan provenance.

land very shortly after its composition, no later than 1240, and that only one copy crossed the Channel. The mother text, which is not extant but whose existence is revealed by the texts of the four remaining copies, contained more mistakes than any of the surviving continental versions, but it was still a substantially faithful copy of the original vision. The four known English copies, however, all diverge from the mother text and vary widely from each other, leading to the conclusions that copies in England must have circulated extensively and that some English copyists took considerable liberties in recopying from their exemplars.

The surviving copy that is closest to the English original was entered by the noted thirteenth-century English chronicler, Matthew Paris, into his major work, the *Chronica maiora*. The fact that Matthew did not comment on the connection between the prophetic message and the Mongol invasions strongly suggests that he did not realize it had anything to do with them, because Matthew was otherwise extremely interested in Mongol affairs. Matthew gathered all the news about the Mongols that he could, down to the detail that their campaign of 1237–38 caused a panic that interrupted trade on the North Sea and thereby created a glut of herrings on the English market.[3] Matthew even reported that a short prophetic jingle about the birth of Antichrist was inspired by the Mongol advance.[4] If he made this connection for one prophecy, it is reasonable to assume that he would have made it for another had he recognized it. Thus his silence strongly suggests that the copy of the vision arrived in England without any accompanying statement about the grounds for its original conception. Judging from the silence of the other English copies, the connection between the prophecy and the Mongol advance was never drawn in Britain.

Although Matthew Paris's copy is closer to the English original than any of the others, it still contains many unique variants.[5] Specifi-

---

3. J. J. Saunders, "Matthew Paris and the Mongols," *Essays . . . Wilkinson*, 116–132 (at 117–119), who quotes Gibbon's wry observation on the whimsicality of the relationship between the orders of a Mongol Khan on the borders of China and the glut of herrings in England.

4. See Chapter One, n. 25.

5. Matthew Paris, *Chronica majora*, ed. H. R. Luard, (RS 57; London, 1872–

cally, it not only alters the sense of a passage that was corrupt in the mother copy, but it also abridges part of the introduction, transposes elements of one phrase, deletes another phrase, and includes minor stylistic alterations, such as adding the word *indeed*.

There are three reasons for believing that Matthew Paris made most or all of these changes himself. One is that he worked at Saint Albans. Since this monastery was close to London and to fresh sources of continental information, Matthew was likely to have obtained a copy that was close to the English original. A second reason is that none of his variants appear in any of the other three surviving English copies: thus no intermediary phase could have been responsible for a common number of divergences. Finally, it is known that Matthew habitually tampered with the language of other texts he copied, even texts of official documents.[6]

Assuming that Matthew made most or all of the changes described, the question of his rationale arises. At first it might seem as if his attitude toward his text was strangely nonchalant. He could not have thought that the vision was a hoax because he reported it as fact. (We know that Matthew was otherwise credulous.)[7] But if he believed that the message came from God, should he not have left every word in place? Were not his liberties equivalent to polishing the language of the Ten Commandments?

One possible answer is that Matthew conceived of himself to be correcting the vagaries of human transmission. Certainly he knew that he had not obtained the divine message from the lips of the Cistercian monk himself but was faced with a text that had gathered

---

1884), III, 538. A translation is by J. A. Giles, *Matthew Paris's English History* (London, 1852-1854), I, 171. Brief treatments of the prophecy as it appears in Matthew Paris and the Annals of Dunstable (see below) are in Davide Bigalli, *I Tartari et l'Apocalisse* (Florence 1971), 137-139, and Bernard McGinn, *Visions of the End* (New York, 1979), 150. Martin Haeusler, *Das Ende der Geschichte in der mittelalterlichen Weltchronistik* (Cologne, 1980), 59, attempts without warrant to relate Matthew's report of the vision to his preoccupation with the Mongols and reports mistakenly (62) that the vision had already appeared in the chronicle of Roger of Wendover.

6. Richard Vaughan, *Matthew Paris* (Cambridge, 1958), 132–135.

7. For example, *Chronica majora*, III, 367–368, 415; IV, 249.

the excrescences of human mistakes after its miraculous descent. Since scribes inevitably made copying errors, Matthew may have thought it his right, even duty, to rectify obvious corruptions.[8] Although a scrupulous modern editor would presume to alter only the most obvious mistakes, Matthew might then have gone on to take the principle of possible corruption as a license to emend at will.

But it seems more likely that Matthew really knew he was revising and nonetheless ignored the implicit presumptuousness of his actions. Chances are that he, and many other scribes who tampered with the Cistercian vision or other supposedly God-sent prophetic texts, simply felt certain he knew what was right while engaged in the act of copying. While performing his work his subjectivity overwhelmed his objectivity even though afterwards he might have agreed that presuming to act as copy editor for God was sacrilegious.

Around the time that Matthew Paris received his copy at Saint Albans, another copy of the prophecy arrived at the nearby Augustinian priory of Dunstable, only 17 kilometers to the northwest of Saint Albans on Watling Street, one of the busiest thoroughfares of medieval England.[9] It might have been thought that the copy which arrived at Dunstable came from Saint Albans, but the surviving texts show that it was derived from another source, because the Dunstable copy does not repeat any of Matthew Paris's variants. It does contain several variants found in the two remaining English copies, but the Dunstable copy was not itself the source for either of these. Hence other lost copies came between the English original and the Dunstable one. Perhaps the original text arrived first in London and was then

8. Medieval readers and authors were keenly aware of the prevalence of scribal copying errors. Among ample testimonies to this fact are Cassiodorus, *Institutiones*, I, chap. 15—see the translation by Leslie Webber Jones, *Cassiodorus Senator, An Introduction to Divine and Human Readings* (New York, 1946), 103–112; Abelard, prologue to *Sic et Non*, PL 178, 1339–1349; Pierre Dubois, *The Recovery of the Holy Land*, trans. Walther I. Brandt (New York, 1956), 106; the lament of Thomas Waleys quoted by Beryl Smalley, *English Friars and Antiquity in the Early Fourteenth Century* (New York, 1960), 81; and the observations of John of Rupescissa, reported by Bignami-Odier, *Rupescissa*, 64.

9. *Annales Prioratus de Dunstaplia*, in *Annales Monastici*, ed. H. R. Luard (RS 36; London, 1864–1869), III, 151. On the location, see C. R. Cheney, "Notes on the Making of the Dunstable Annals," *Essays . . . Wilkinson*, 97–98.

carried from there directly or by means of a good copy to Saint Albans while copies from which the other surviving English versions descend were being made in London.

Unlike most of the variants found in Matthew Paris's text, many that cropped up in the course of the transmission to Dunstable were simple copying mistakes or the products of misunderstandings.[10] Instead of having the world united under one God within eleven years, the Dunstable text has it united in nine, probably as the result of a confusion of Roman xi with Roman ix. It also has the "second god" dying instead of going away (*obiit* for *abiit*), and it fully obscures the original allusion to the Mongols by leaving out the word *wandering* (*vagans*) originally used to describe the terrible invaders.

One change made before the prophecy reached Dunstable altered its meaning considerably. The original text contained the warning *Ve clero* ("Woe to the clergy"), but one copyist turned the *V* into a *D* and thus created the sentence: "A new order out of the clergy thrives" (*De clero viget ordo novus*). This too might have been a simple copying error—thirteenth-century minuscule *v*'s and *d*'s can be confused by someone working carelessly. It seems more likely, however, that this is one example of conscious editorial change. Probably some copyist was offended by the anticlericalism of the original prophecy and decided to make the vision credit the clergy with the creation of a flourishing new order instead of warning of imminent chastisement. Whatever the cause, the most threatening line in the original text was thereby removed.

The change from *Ve* to *De* makes it clear that the text of the Cistercian vision was transmitted in writing and not by word of mouth. The consonants *v* and *d* do not sound alike and *Ve clero!* calls for a completely different spoken intonation than *De clero* ... Therefore it is inconceivable that someone would have confused *Ve clero! Viget ordo novus* with *De clero viget ordo novus* because he was hard of hearing or because he was listening to someone else with a speech defect. The change could only have come from paleographical error

10. According to Cheney, the surviving MS of the Dunstable Annals—BL Cotton Tiberius A. x—is a fair copy of the original. Some errors could have been made in the process of recopying, but, if so, they were probably minimal since the surviving copy was otherwise a very careful one.

or conscious decision at a writing desk. Numerous other examples that will appear throughout this study confirm the conclusion that the Cistercian vision and its more widely circulated later avatars were disseminated by means of parchment or paper and that constant alterations in the text were the result of decisions made by readers and writers, not hearers.[11]

In addition to all the variants lodged in a common ancestor, the surviving Dunstable copy contains some changes that are unique. Whether these were made before the prophecy reached Dunstable or by the Dunstable annalist himself, the surviving text is very different from the one that first circulated on the European continent. The annalist, of course, had no way of knowing that. For him the miracle story and the message were the only ones he knew, and they remained sufficiently portentous to be included in his record of great events. Certainly by that time some passages had become so corrupt that he could not possibly have understood them, but that fact may only have served to make the prophecy appear all the more awesome.

Similar conclusions apply to a third English copy, one that survives on a flyleaf of a thirteenth-century manuscript Bible written at a Gilbertine house in Yorkshire or Lincolnshire.[12] Like the Dunstable copy, the Gilbertine text is several steps removed from the English original. These steps must have followed each other in quick temporal succession, for the Gilbertine copy states that the prophecy arrived

11. Of course news of the most sensational contents of a prophecy could always have passed by word of mouth. For an actual example of the oral transmission in 1318 of a prophecy's major contents, see Jean Duvernoy, *Le Registre d'inquisition de Jacques Fournier* (Toulouse, 1965), I, 160–161. A written prophecy was behind the oral rumors relayed here: most likely it was an early copy of the fictive letter of the Grandmaster of the Hospitallers that is still unedited but is referred to in Lerner, "Refreshment of the Saints," 139, and Roberto Rusconi, *L'Attesa della fine* (Rome, 1979), 138–139.

12. The MS—which I have not been able to examine firsthand—is Cambridge, St. John's College 239. See the description by M. R. James, *A Descriptive Catalogue of the Manuscripts in the Library of St. John's College, Cambridge* (Cambridge, 1913), 277–278. Gilbertine provenance is indicated by a calendar in the MS; location in either Yorkshire or Lincolnshire is determined by the facts that most Gilbertine houses were located in those counties and that Yorkshire and Lincolnshire saints appear prominently in the calendar. Frau Waltraud Huber kindly called my attention to this copy of the vision.

at the house in 1240, and we know that the original could not have arrived in England any earlier than 1239. Like the Dunstable version, the Gilbertine text contains both common variants and unique ones that carry it far away from its continental progenitor. One noteworthy omission is the lack of reference to the miracle having transpired in a Cistercian cloister. This was probably intentional: possibly a Gilbertine copyist was loath to give favorable publicity to a rival order. The Gilbertine text further adds some unrelated and (in the surviving form) incomprehensible words about poverty and possessions, showing that somewhere along the line someone with preoccupations of his own tried his hand at some gnomic additions.[13]

The Gilbertine copyist's decision to preserve the prophecy on a flyleaf was typical of a procedure followed by numerous other copyists of short eschatological texts. When monasteries were not regularly recording history in chronicle form, there was no given place to set down important news for enduring consideration other than in the blank spaces of books. Flyleaves were particularly suitable because they came easiest to hand and because prophecies inscribed on them could not easily be overlooked by subsequent users of the manuscript. The rear flyleaf of the Gilbertine Bible was blank when a canon in 1240 felt compelled to set down the text of the vision for the sake of his contemporaries and of posterity. After that, six different hands added six different short entries, two more of which were mid-thirteenth-century prophecies.[14] Such a leaf half-covered with prophetic

---

13. Namely, "Paupertas est odibile bonum. Curarum [?] remocio [?]. Possessio sine calumpnia." I cannot tell whether this is related to the incipit of an anonymous treatise against *falsi religiosi* as in MS Padua, Biblioteca Antoniana 9 Scaff. I (14th/15th centuries), fos. 303ᵛ–318ᵛ: "Paupertas est parvi possessio. Honesta res est laeta paupertas. Illa vero non est paupertas si laeta est."

14. The first is a copy of the popular jingle on the birth of Antichrist—*Cum fuerint* . . . (first reported by Matthew Paris, see Chapter One, n. 25)—in this version ascribed to Joachim of Fiore and issued for the year 1260. See the James catalogue and Reeves, *Influence of Prophecy*, 49, which both print the full three lines of the Gilbertine text. (For other, later, copies of *Cum fuerint* see Reeves, 50, n. 3; and Lerner, "Refreshment of the Saints," 138, n. 133.) The other short prophecy in the Gilbertine MS is another pseudo-Joachite text—*Corruent nobiles* —issued for the years between 1250 and 1265. See Reeves, *Influence of Prophecy*, 50–51, who does not mention this copy. Both of these prophecies were probably entered into the MS in the 1250s.

messages impressively displays the sense of seriousness with which new prophecies were received in monastic communities.

The last English version is a most bizarre one that appears at the end of a pastiche of prophecies about English politics. This survives in a manuscript written at Saint Albans under the direction of the chronicler Thomas Walsingham during the last decade of the fourteenth century. Although Walsingham endeavored to pick up the historiographical standard once borne at Saint Albans by Matthew Paris, the copy of the vision in the pastiche bears no relation to the text earlier produced by Matthew but belongs instead to a branch of the Dunstable-Gilbertine family.[15] It is useless to speculate about how it may have reached Walsingham since there is no way of learning about its fortunes during some 150 years. All that can be said is that in its present form it appears as the highly inappropriate ending of a long prophetic text about England, purportedly written by Merlin and miraculously revealed to King Edward III. Possibly Walsingham himself was the author, but, from the internal evidence of the surviving manuscript, it seems more likely that it was copied from a fourteenth-century exemplar and that Walsingham merely presided over the gathering and recopying of preexisting prophecies.[16]

Since the copy of the vision in the Saint Albans pastiche is the

15. The MS is BL Royal 13 E IX, and the prophetic pastiche appears on f. 27[r-v]. For the provenance and dating of the MS, see V. H. Galbraith, "Thomas Walsingham and the St. Albans Chronicle, 1272–1422," *English Historical Review*, 47 (1932), 12–30, and Galbraith, *The St. Albans Chronicle 1406–1420* (Oxford, 1937), xxxviii–xl, xlvii–li.

16. The pastiche begins with the prophecy *Sicut rubeum draconem*, a text also found in MS BL Arundel 66, f. 291[v] (15th century). (The rubric in the Royal MS which states that the pastiche was a prophecy of Merlin's revealed to Edward III is also found in the Arundel MS, f. 291[v], but with somewhat different wording and introducing a different prophecy—*Arbor fertilis*.) Following *Sicut rubeum draconem* in the St. Albans's pastiche is another originally separate prophecy, *Mortuo leone iusticie*, (see Ward, I, 293–295). Since neither the *Mortuo* nor the *Cedrus* texts are set off by paragraph markings, but one paragraph marking does otherwise appear in a mistaken location, it seems probable that the pastiche underwent some copyists' alterations before the present copy. Another argument for a somewhat earlier fabrication is the fact that the pastiche is surrounded by copies of other prophecies, which suggests that Walsingham put together an anthology from different prophetic sources rather than fabricating a pastiche on his own.

latest one known, it is not surprising that it reads like the outcome of a game of "telephone." The introduction about the miracle in a Cistercian cloister is missing, either because it had disappeared by then or because the fabricator thought it had no place within the body of a prophecy ascribed to Merlin. Most of the miraculous message remains but is frightfully garbled. Not only do many phrases appear in the wrong order, but certain passages often bear only scant resemblance to their originals. For example, the phrase "people called 'without a head,' or reputed to be wanderers" appears in the pastiche as a "repudiated people without a veil," and the prediction that there will be "mutations of faith, laws, and kingdoms" becomes a prediction of "faith, laws, and munitions." One can observe the "telephone" process most clearly at work in the change from the original warning to the clergy (*Ve clero*), to the alteration that made a new order come from the clergy (*De clero*), to this text's statement that a new order comes from heaven (*De celo*)! The entire product of Saint Albans was so obscure that it seemed adequately suited to terminate a prophetic pastiche about dragons, lions, eaglets, and other exotic fauna, whose comings and goings supposedly alluded to the history of England.[17]

Taken together, the astonishingly large number of variants found in the four English copies of the vision make it possible to draw several conclusions about the reception of the text. The most obvious is that many copies once circulated that no longer survive. Another is that the meaning of many passages of the prophecy in its different lines of descent could not have been clear to medieval readers. We can see how scribes sometimes "corrected" the text on the assumption that the passage in front of them was so inexplicable it must have been faulty, and we can see how their "corrections" sometimes made the text even more inexplicable than it had been before.

"Correction" of the text on the grounds that it must have been faulty was just one kind of scribal alteration. Other alterations came

17. Ward, I, 314, followed by Rupert Taylor, *The Political Prophecy in England* (New York, 1911), 86, and Erwin Herrmann, "Spätmittelalterliche englische Pseudoprophetien," AfK, 57 (1975), 87–116 (at 98), mistakenly described the prophecy as relating to the reign of Richard I, perhaps because he thought the crusading King was in some way invoked by the line about the subversion of the Saracens.

about from sheer inadvertence, and others arose from conscious decision—sometimes tendentious willfulness—in places where there could not have been any reasonable doubt about the accuracy of the exemplar. The last class of alterations is the most intriguing and the most difficult to explain. Some scribes conceivably rationalized their willful changes on the grounds that prior copying errors must have been present even in places where errors might not have seemed to be present. But it seems more likely that scribes like Matthew Paris, or the scribe in the Gilbertine line of transmission who deleted the reference to the *Cistercian* cloister, knew at the moment they made changes that they were really making them on their own license. In that case, they must have made the subjective decision that they knew what was right without facing the objective reality that they were altering a text which had supposedly descended from heaven.

Why was a prophecy that progressively made less and less sense copied and recopied so often? No answers can be offered with certainty, but it would seem that one reason why the story of the vision spread so quickly in chronicles and on flyleaves was that the miracle was an exciting and memorable event in and of itself. The miracle of the moving hand was no more difficult to believe than many other prodigies that were accepted without cavil by thirteenth-century observers, and, if God was really speaking to his creatures, it was surely worthwhile recording what He said. Furthermore, even though parts of the message were incomprehensible, the overall purport of the text remained clear. Readers might not know who the "people without a head" and later "without a veil" were, but they assuredly could still tell that the moving hand warned of coming troubles yet promised ultimate victory over Christianity's main external enemy, the Saracens. In its broad outlines, this was a message that many expected to hear.[18] Thus the overall purport of the prophecy was acceptable and its obscurities were no insuperable obstacle to circulation because God was supposed to speak obscurely, and many readers loved to scratch their heads over dark images.

The report of the prophetic miracle, however, did not circulate for long. Of the seven surviving copies, five were written in the first year of the prophecy's existence and the later two owed their survival

18. See Conclusions for support for this assertion.

only to their appearance in prophetic compendia. It is as difficult to say why a prophecy did not endure as it is to explain why it circulated rapidly to begin with, but perhaps the explanation for the Cistercian vision's evanescence is that the miracle of 1239 or 1240 did not seem like exciting news in later years and that without the interest of the miracle story the prophetic message itself had too little topical applicability to attract attention on its own. But the vision did not die entirely. In the late thirteenth century, an inspired reviser reconceived and transformed it in a way that would give it an entirely new life.

Chapter III

FROM SNUSNYACUM TO
TRIPOLI

The thorough transformation of the Cistercian vision was inspired by events as shocking to Western Christians as the earlier dramatic appearance of the Mongols. By the late thirteenth century, the Mongols were no longer a threat: in 1289 the Il-Khan of Persia, a third cousin of the terrible Batu, named his son Nicholas after the reigning Roman pope and sent legations to Europe not to demand submission but to propose a united venture against the Saracens.[1] Those very Saracens, however, had reemerged as mighty opponents of Christianity. After turning back the Mongols in 1260, the Mamlukes of Egypt became strong enough toward the end of the century to move against the last remnants of the Crusading States in the Holy Land. In 1278 they took Lattakieh, in 1289 Syrian Tripoli, and in 1291 Acre, the first city of the kingdom of Jerusalem. After the fall of Acre, the remaining Christian outposts on the mainland surrendered without a fight; the Mamluke Sultan then ordered the razing of all the fallen fortresses to make sure that there would be no Christian resurgence. Westerners

1. A. Moestaert and F. W. Cleaves, *Les Lettres de 1289 et 1305 des ilkhans Airun et Oljetu à Philippe le Bel* (Cambridge, Mass., 1962) and Jean Richard, *La Papauté et les missions d'orient au moyen âge (XIIIe–XVe siècles)* (Rome, 1977), 103.

were not to return to the Holy Land as rulers until after the victories of General Allenby in 1917.[2]

Unlike the Mongol invasions, the fall of Tripoli and Acre posed no threat to the security of Europe, but the news of their loss was nonetheless greeted in the West with horror. Not only was it now clear that Christians were further from reconquering Jerusalem (lost in 1244) than ever, but the defeats were regarded as a sign of divine displeasure. Subsequent events made matters even worse. Pope Nicholas IV had tried to raise funds and troops for a new crusade even before the fall of Acre. When he learned of the calamity, he continued his efforts and ordered all Western archbishops to hold provincial councils to confer on how to retake the city.[3] But the pope died in April of 1292 while answers were still coming in, and afterwards the papal see remained vacant for a prolonged and dispiriting interregnum of over two years. No crusaders left for the East during that time; nor did any depart during the subsequent turbulent pontificates of Celestine V (1294) and Boniface VIII (1294–1303), when the papacy was preoccupied by concerns that lay closer to home. The unprecedented Roman Jubilee of 1300 was a tacit recognition of the fact that pilgrimage ardor would have to be redirected from the Holy Land to the Eternal City.

The sense of personal loss that some pious Christians experienced at the fall of the Holy Land was profound. Just as Abbot Samson of Bury put on haircloth and abstained from meat when Jerusalem fell

2. Erwin Stickel, *Der Fall von Akkon: Untersuchungen zum Abklingen des Kreuzzugsgedankens am Ende des 13. Jahrhunderts* (Bern, 1975), 1–88. In English see Steven Runciman, "The Crusader States, 1243–1291," in Kenneth M. Setton, ed., *A History of the Crusades,* 2d ed. (Madison, Wisc., 1969), II, 557–598. After this book had gone to press I learned of Charles Samaran, "Projets français de croisades de Philippe le Bel à Philippe de Valois," *Histoire littéraire de la France,* 41 (1981), 33–74. This does not bear directly on the material in this chapter but provides valuable background information. Samaran cites a Cambridge University doctoral dissertation of 1977 by Sylvie Schein, "The West and the Crusades (1291–1314)," that I have not seen.

3. Ernest Langlois, ed., *Les Registres de Nicholas IV* (Paris, 1886–1905), II, 902–903 (nos. 6791–6792). On the councils themselves, see Bartholomew Cotton, *Historia Anglicana,* ed. H. R. Luard (RS 16; London, 1869), 199–215; C. J. Hefele and H. Leclercq, *Histoire des conciles* (Paris, 1907–1921), VI, 1, 326–28; and Franz Heidelberger, *Kreuzzugsversuche um die Wende des 13. Jahrhunderts* (Basel, 1911), 5.

in 1187, so around 1300 an Italian friar named John wrote that on the vigil of Ascension of 1292, while he was reciting the Psalm, "Oh God, the heathen are come into thine inheritance; thy holy temple have they defiled ...," he felt a terrible pain in his heart at "that lamentable death" that had transpired overseas. This caused him such tears that he could not finish reciting; instead he prayed to the Lord to have mercy on His people.[4]

Personal insights like this one are not often granted to the medievalist, but Friar John's reaction could not have been unusual, for news of the fall of the Holy Land was recorded with dismay in chronicles throughout Europe. Further manifestations of grief were expressed in Nicholas IV's description of the events as a "doleful cup of bitterness," and an English council's call for prayers, vigils, and fasts. Later, in 1298, an Italian traveller in the East, Ricoldo of Monte-Croce, wrote five letters bitterly lamenting the fall of the Holy Land, and as late as 1305, an Italian preacher assured his flock that the losses of Tripoli and Acre should not cause a loss of faith because they were condign punishments meted out by God.[5]

Given the political situation of the years after 1291, it was unrealistic to expect that Western forces would retake the recently lost fortresses, let alone Jerusalem, but pious souls could always hope for

---

4. The only edition of the Latin text can be found in Donckel, "Visio" (see list of abbreviations). The text, discussed further below, is fictional, but the description of the friar's anguish at the loss of Acre must have been rooted in actual experience. On the history of scholarly treatments of the text, see the Introduction, n. 6.

5. The chronicles are listed by Reinhold Röhricht, "Die Eroberung 'Akkâs durch die Muslimen (1291)," *Forschungen zur deutschen Geschichte*, 20 (1880), 93–126. Also see Harry Rothwell, ed., *The Chronicle of Walter of Guisborough*, Camden Series, no. 89 (London, 1957), 228, which follows the continuation of Martin of Poland in invoking Jeremiah. Nicholas's laments can be found in Langlois, 901–903 (nos. 6782–6805). Ricoldo's letters are edited by R. Röhricht, "Lettres de Ricoldo de Monte-Croce," *Archives de l'Orient Latin*, 2 (1884), 258–296. See, e.g., 291: "Heu mihi, quia video tantam deiectionem fidei christiane! Ubi est Tripolis, ubi est Accon, ubi sunt ecclesie christianorum, que ibi erant ... ? " The Italian preacher is Giordano of Rivalto. For his sermon see Alexander Murray, "Piety and Impiety in Thirteenth-Century Italy," *Studies in Church History*, 8 (1972), 83–106 (at 102–103). Further evidence of the impact of the fall of Acre on contemporaries can be found in J. N. Hillgarth, *Ramon Lull and Lullism in Fourteenth-Century France* (Oxford, 1971), 50, and 73–74.

miracles. Several independent prophecies written before and after 1300 reflect such hopes. A short prophetic text beginning *Ve mundo in centum annis* ("Woe to the world in one hundred years"), written between 1291 and 1301, probably in Catalonia, "predicted" the fall of the Christian cities in Syria and their continued loss until the coming of a "new David."[6] Another prophecy, by a certain "Brother Columbinus," written a few years after 1300, probably in France, "predicted" that a time of great tribulations would begin with the birth of Antichrist in 1287, that shortly afterwards Acre would be destroyed by the power of the Sultan, that a pope would lament its fall and call kings and princes for a crusade, but that such would not transpire because God would not ordain it. Only after the coming of many other terrible events culminating in Antichrist's open reign in 1316 would the Lord in 1320 slay Antichrist and the whole world be converted to Christianity.[7] A third prophecy that followed similar lines

6. Printed editions are in Hugo de Novocastro, II, 36, and Pou y Marti, 54–55. The prophecy is also described and partially edited by Heinrich Finke, *Aus den Tagen Bonifaz VIII* (Münster, 1902), 218–221. The *terminus post quem* is based on the knowledge of the fall of the Christian cities and the *terminus ante quem* on the appearance of the *Ve mundo* prophecy in Arnold of Villanova's *Tractatus de mysterio cimbalorum ecclesie*, written before the end of 1301 (see Maier, 56). Arnold's *De mysterio* appears to have been the ultimate source for all later copies of this subsequently extremely popular prophecy. Arnold states that he learned of it from an inspired *vir fere illiteratus*. If this was a real person (as I am inclined to believe) and not just Arnold's alter ego (as Hillgarth, 152, n. 13), he was probably a Catalan because Arnold himself came from Catalonia and because the prophecy climaxes with reference to Spanish events. Moreover, it seems likely that the prophecy's victor in climactic Iberian civil wars and subsequent conqueror of the African Moors was meant to be a king of Aragon because the hero is described as a "bat" and the bat was an Aragonese armorial emblem: on the bat surmounting the Aragonese royal crest, see A. Morel-Fatio, "Souhaits de bienvenue, adressées à Ferdinand le Catholique par un poète Barcelonais, en 1473," *Romania*, 11 (1882), 333–356 (at 348), and confirmation for the mid-fourteenth century in a passage from John of Rupescissa described by Bignami-Odier, *Rupescissa*, 137.

7. A curtailed version of the "Columbinus" prophecy can be found in E. Boutaric, ed., "Notices et extraits de documents inédits relatifs à l'histoire de France sous Philippe le Bel," *Notices et extraits des manuscrits de la Bibliothèque Impériale*, 20, pt. 2 (1862), 235–237, but instead see the full text in MS BL Cotton Cleopatra C. x, fos. 157ʳ–158ʳ (There are many other MSS, but this is the best copy so far known to me). The prophecy seems to be French because it emphasizes French politics. Its reference to Flemish wars and troubles for the king of France suggests a date after the battle of Courtrai of 1302. The *terminus ante*

is that of the Italian Friar John who felt the fall of Acre like a wound in his heart. Supposedly in the midst of his lamentations, a strange old man appeared to him to say that the loss of the Holy Land was an act of God and that many other dreadful trials were soon to follow. But when John, in complete despair, asked whether God really meant to destroy the faith, the old man assured him that ultimately a wondrous time would come when the infidels would be defeated.[8]

These prophecies resemble the original Cistercian vision in attempting to come to terms with catastrophe by seeing it as part of a larger divine plan. They all regard the fall of the Holy Land as a just punishment for human sins and predict still more dreadful trials to come. But they all foretell the ultimate miraculous triumph of the faith. Just as the author of the Cistercian vision refused to believe that the Mongol onslaught would result in the utter destruction of Christendom and dreamed of ultimate victory, so the three later prophets, working independently, arrived at similar conclusions regarding the fall of the Christian outposts in Palestine. None was influenced by the earlier vision: their reactions were molded by a common Christian expectation of eschatological persecutions and the ultimate conversion of the world.

Another European, however, discovered the Cistercian vision while he was brooding about the events overseas and saved himself the trouble of composing a completely new prophecy by resurrecting and renovating the old one. This person must have worked between the summer of 1289 and the summer of 1291 because he knew of the fall of Tripoli but not yet of the fall of Acre.[9] Almost certainly he was a German because, as we will see, he predicted the return to Germany of the Emperor Frederick II.

The transformation of the Cistercian vision was done with great care and deliberation. Since we possess the text (although not the exact copy) that our craftsman remodelled, it is possible to peer over

---

quem must be 1312 because the prophecy falsely predicts the election of a third Frederick for that year.

8. Donckel, "Visio."

9. This dating revises that which I offered in "Medieval Prophecy and Religious Dissent," *Past and Present*, 72 (August 1976), 3–24 (at 12), when I had not yet realized that the original reviser was ignorant of the fall of Acre.

his shoulder and watch him work.[10] His first deft alteration was to provide a dramatic setting for the miraculous vision. The original text told of a miracle in an imaginary Cistercian cloister called Snusnyacum or in a Cistercian cloister with no name at all. Not content with this vagueness, the reviser moved his miracle to a Cistercian cloister in Tripoli and then changed the year of the miracle to 1287. The result was to conjure up a miracle in doomed surroundings. As everyone who would read the prophecy knew, Tripoli actually fell shortly after 1287; there could thus have been no better place for seeing something like handwriting on a wall. What the fabricator did not know, however, was that there was no Cistercian cloister in Tripoli. The nearest one to Tripoli had been at Belmont, about 17 kilometers away, but that house had been abandoned before 1287.[11] The locale, then, was dramatic, but purely imaginary.

In addition to changing the place and date, the remodeller also improved upon some of the details of the original miracle. He specified that the prophetic vision was seen by a Cistercian monk who was celebrating mass, between the oblation and communion. Whereas the original text reported that the monk saw a hand writing a message bodily (*in corporali*), the reviser turned this into a hand writing on the corporal cloth (*super corporale*) covering the altar. Clearly the words *in corporali* suggested to him the idea of having handwrit-

10. For the text of his product see Appendix II. I explain there the grounds for my reconstruction of the original version of the Tripoli prophecy.

11. The matter has caused perplexity to modern Cistercian researchers, who have mistakenly accepted the historicity of the vision. Leopold Janauschek, *Originum Cisterciensium* (Vienna, 1877; repr. Ridgewood, N.J., 1964), I, 139, knew that there was no Cistercian monastery in Tripoli and thought that the vision must have taken place in Belmont. Frédéric Van der Meer, *Atlas de l'ordre Cistercien* (Paris, 1965), 272, lists Belmont as being abandoned in 1289, presumably on the strength of the date in the vision, but D. H. Williams, "Cistercian Settlement in the Lebanon," *Cîteaux*, 25 (1974), 61–74 (at 71), shows that the last definite mention of Belmont was in 1282. Williams rejects the evidence of the vision not because he recognizes it as a fabrication but because he mistakenly thinks that the words *in claustro grisei ordinis Tripolis* referred to a Franciscan house. In fact, there was no Franciscan house in Syrian Tripoli either, and the term *gray order* was often used to apply to the Cistercians. Certainly the fabricator meant a Cistercian house since he was following his exemplar in this (later MS copies also recognized it as such).

ing appear on the cloth. The combined effect of these revisions provided a semblance of concreteness that the original lacked.

After recreating the miracle, the author of what will now be called the Tripoli prophecy rewrote the prophetic message as follows:

> The high Cedar of Lebanon will be felled, and Tripoli will soon be destroyed. Mars will overcome Saturn, and Saturn will waylay Jupiter. The bat will subjugate the lord of the bees. Within fifteen years there will be one god and one faith. The other god has vanished. The sons of Israel will be liberated from captivity. A certain people who are called without a head will come. Woe then to the clergy, and to you Christianity! The ship of Peter will be tossed in manifold waves,[12] but will escape and dominate in the last days. There will be many battles in the world, and many massacres, and severe famines, and plagues in many places, and mutations of kingdoms. The land of the barbarians will be destroyed. The mendicant orders and many other sects will be annihilated. Then the lion will arise out of mountain caverns and cross the mountains and slay the other lion. The beast of the West and the lion of the East will subjugate the whole world. And then there will be peace in the whole world and copious fruit and an abundance of all things for fifteen years. Then there will be a common passage beyond the congregated waters to the Holy Land, and the city of Jerusalem will be glorified, and all the cities of Judea will be rebuilt. The Holy Sepulchre will be honored by all. And in such tranquillity news will be heard of Antichrist and of all marvels. Blessed is he who will then overcome, for he shall not suffer perpetual death. Be vigilant!

12. Or *great waves*. The surviving witnesses to the earliest form of the prophecy (see Appendix II) differ on whether to provide *variis fluctibus* (the John of Paris text) or *validis fluctibus* (Bodl., Bodley 140, and BN lat. 16021). It is impossible to tell which is the original and which the variant form because the same disagreement crops up in early witnesses to the next phase of the prophecy (see Appendix III: *variis* in Bloemhof; *validis* in the others). It seems more likely that two different scribes independently corrected *variis* with *validis* than the other way around because *variis* made less sense and because the same word appears in the prophecy a few lines later (*fames valida*). But the possibility of the replacement of *validis* with *variis* cannot be excluded: see Chapter Six, n. 28.

A reductionist paraphrase of these vatic lines is rather simple. Like "Brother Columbinus," the author of the Tripoli prophecy believed that Antichrist had been born in 1287 and that within thirty years he would come to reign openly. This was part and parcel of medieval Antichrist lore which assumed that, since Antichrist's life would be a hideous parody of the life of Christ, Antichrist would live for thirty years in obscurity, just as Christ did, before appearing openly in a three-and-a-half-year ministry.[13] The first fifteen years of the thirty-year span would be dreadful: Tripoli would fall, the clergy would be persecuted, and wars and plagues would rage. But in the following fifteen years there would be peace, plenty, and a successful crusade until "news of Antichrist" would be heard.

As simple as these outlines are, however, the prophecy is certainly not simple if read line for line, partly because the author preferred some degree of opacity, and partly because he chose wherever possible to avoid using his own words. Even at first glance it can easily be seen how the first half of the Tripoli prophecy was woven from the warp of the old Cistercian vision and the woof of the later writer's own concerns.

The original first line about the felling of the cedar of Lebanon was ideal for an opening because it now seemed to relate perfectly to the disastrous events in the Levant. Indeed, in all likelihood, the striking new applicability of the incipit must have been the reason why the remodeller was attracted to the old vision in the first place. Lest there be any doubt about what the felling of the cedar meant in its new context, the author—we will call him the Tripoli prophet— went on to "predict" explicitly the imminent destruction of Tripoli. This is an example of prophecy *ex eventu*—a safe "prediction" of an event that had already happened. Usually predictions *ex eventu* appear at the beginnings of medieval prophetic messages in order to lend persuasiveness to what follows. Certainly that was the purpose in the present case.

13. See, e.g., the popular life of Antichrist, probably written in the late thirteenth century or fourteenth century, beginning "de Antichristo et eius adventu, hoc tenendum est, quod nascetur ultra mare," in, e.g., MS Eichstätt 698 (old 269), 383ᵇ–384ᵃ (at 383ᵇ):". . . in etate tringinta annorum incipiet predicare in Ierusalem. . . ."

The woof having been thrown in, the Tripoli prophet could go back to the old warp about Mars, Saturn, and Jupiter. Presumably he retained these lines because he believed astrology offered "scientific" corroboration of prophecy. Yet if the planets had really formed a baleful configuration shortly after 1239, it was unlikely that they would form the same one shortly after 1287. A true devotee of astrology would have offered a new and accurate planetary forecast for the changed times, but this amateur was content to copy what he had already found.

After that repetition, he again wove in a new woof: "The bat will subjugate the lord of the bees." Perhaps this cryptic line was inspired by a line in another obscure prophetic text, namely the mid-thirteenth-century prophecy of the "Erythrean Sibyl," which states that "the bat will devour the prince of the bees."[14] But even if this were our author's source, the identification would still not help our interpretation, because the Erythrean Sibyl's prophecy about the "bat" and the "prince of the bees" was meant to apply to Italian politics directly after the death of Frederick II, a subject unrelated to the later author's concerns.

Most likely the Tripoli prophecy's warning about the bat and the lord of the bees was meant to reiterate the initial warnings of coming disaster. In Leviticus 11:19–20, the bat was counted among the "creeping fowls" that "shall be an abomination," and medieval commentators conceived of the bat as a "vile animal" that flees light. Most relevant to our context is Saint Jerome's view that the bat, which makes a strident noise and cannot bear the sun, may aptly be compared to heathen idols.[15] Bees, on the other hand, were beloved to medieval

14. MS UB Breslau (Wrocław) Rehdiger 280, f. 19rb: *Vespertilio vorabit principem apum.* (This line is not found in the edition in Holder-Egger, 30, 328–335: more work needs to be done in comparing the numerous copies of this popular prophetic text.)

15. Commentary on Isaiah, PL, 24, 54–55. See also Isidore of Seville, *Etymologiarum . . . libri* XX, ed. W. M. Lindsay (Oxford, 1911), XII, chap. 7, par. 36; Bartholomaeus Anglicanus, *De rerum proprietatibus* (Frankfurt, 1601; repr. Frankfurt, 1964), XII, chap. 38; and Thomas of Cantimpré, *Liber de natura rerum* (Berlin, 1973), V, chap. 116, 228–229. Albertus Magnus, writing a few decades before the Tripoli prophet, conceived bats to be like thieves or deceivers who come in the night: see his *Postilla super Isaiam*, in *Opera omnia*, XIX (Münster, 1952), 46–47. I consider unlikely the possibility that the prophet might have

writers because of their presumed virginity, order, industry, and sweet productivity. One thirteenth-century moral treatise was entitled *The Universal Good of Bees*.[16] Probably the victory of the bat over the lord of the bees is the victory of the Saracen over the Christian; if not, it is surely a prediction of some other imminent woe. The margin of doubt may have been intentional: the prophet who began with portentous biblical imagery and astrological allusions rounded these out with emblems from nature not because he thought they would help his audience understand his precise meaning but because animal imagery was a traditional form of expressing prophecy. Not surprisingly, the dark words about the bat and the lord of the bees bewildered even the prophet's contemporaries,[17] but that very bewilderment may have enhanced their assurance that the prophecy was genuinely divine.

Having provided the requisite animal imagery, the author returned once more to the language of the Cistercian vision, changing as little as possible. He had to alter the "eleven years" given in his exemplar because he was no longer concerned with a span pointing from 1239 to 1250, and he changed the "eleven" to "fifteen" so that he could have two congruent fifteen-year spans adding up to Antichrist's hidden life of thirty. Aside from that, the only divergences from the old Cistercian vision in the next few lines are minor. Possibly the change, for example, from "one god and one monarchy" to "one god and one faith," had some arcane significance, but it is best not to be oversubtle in straining for exegetical gnats, partly because the Tripoli prophet may have made certain minor changes on whim and

---

conceived of the "bat" as a king of Aragon despite the likelihood that the "bat" in the contemporary *Ve mundo* prophecy is a king of Aragon (see n. 6 above), because there is otherwise no evidence of Aragonese or Spanish orientation in the Tripoli prophecy. But some Ghibelline expression at a time when the Aragonese were at war with the Angevins cannot be entirely excluded.

16. Thomas of Cantimpré's *Bonum universale de apibus*. A survey of various positive allegorical treatments of bees in the Middle Ages is Manfred Misch, *Apis est animal—apis est ecclesia. Ein Beitrag zum Verhältnis von Naturkunde und Theologie in spätantiker und mittelalterlicher Literatur* (Bern, 1974). Misch overlooks an interesting twelfth-century encyclopedic treatment: Alexander Neckam, *De naturis rerum*, ed. T. Wright (RS 34; London, 1863), 268–269.

17. See below pp. 77 and 82.

partly because we cannot even be certain that he made every last change himself. In other words, since we possess neither the exact copy of the Cistercian vision with which the Tripoli prophet worked, nor the autograph of his own product, we do not even know whether all the alterations found in the earliest copies were the work of a single reviser or the sum total of scribal changes and mistakes made in unknown intermediate lines of transmission.

Putting aside the meaning of the small changes, it also cannot be told exactly how the prophet interpreted the string of lines he copied more or less faithfully from his exemplar, for although we can figuratively look over his shoulder and watch him writing, we cannot easily enter his mind. What did he understand by the disappearance of "the other god"? Did he have his own clear understanding of the identity of "the sons of Israel" or "the people without a head"? Although assurance in these matters is impossible, probably the difficult lines from the earlier prophecy made no particular sense to him. Most likely he repeated them just because they were there and sounded suitably doleful. The first fifteen years of Antichrist's nurturing were to be terrible and the string of inherited lines made that point sufficiently clear.

Yet this is by no means to say that the Tripoli prophet copied blindly. He clearly understood the meaning of imminent "woe to the clergy" because it was expressed in plain Latin, and he copied that prediction as he did what came before. But then he stopped short and omitted the lines that read "a new order thrives: if it should fall, woe to the Church!" This was his first full deletion from his exemplar and reflects his own decided point of view. Clearly the prophet cut out the line because he hated the mendicants, an antipathy he expressed in his own words later in his text. The change in attitude was in keeping with widespread changes in European attitudes towards the mendicants that developed between the second and the last quarters of the thirteenth century. Around 1239 a writer could hope that the Church might be renewed through the achievements of one of the new mendicant orders; around 1290, when the mendicants had lost their pristine vigor, such hopes were flagging or abandoned.[18]

18. The striking change in attitudes toward the mendicants in the two versions of the prophecy was already noticed by Töpfer, 145–146.

Instead of writing, "Woe to the clergy! A new order thrives: if it should fall, woe to the Church!", the Tripoli prophet supplied, "Woe then to the clergy, and to you Christianity!" Not just the omission of the reference to the "new order" but the extension of the threat of woe to all Christianity is noteworthy. The author of ca. 1290 did not intend his new prophecy to be a limitedly anticlerical jeremiad. For him the whole Christian flock had to be purified before there could be a better world.

The next lines were original and show once more that the author was not inveterately hostile to the Church and its hierarchy. In his view, the "ship of Peter" would certainly be tossed, but it would ultimately emerge from danger and prevail in the last days. The "ship of Peter" in high-medieval texts means the Church governed by the papacy. Two passages in the gospels gave rise to the frequent medieval employment of the image of Peter's ship. One, Luke 5:1–11, tells of how Christ taught from Peter's ship, endowed it with "a great multitude of fishes," and then told Peter that henceforth he would "catch men." In medieval exegesis this text became a basis of support for claims of papal primacy. The ship in Luke was not tossed in the waves, but another in Matthew 14:22–33 was so tossed until Jesus bade Peter walk on water and then calmed the winds. Since this vessel held all the apostles led by Peter, medieval exegesis took it too to be Peter's ship, or the papally guided Church, which "might be tossed but would not sink."[19]

The author of the Tripoli prophecy may have been moved by current events to predict the imminent "tossing" of the papal barque. Whereas he hated the mendicants the reigning pope, Nicholas IV (1288–1292), was the first Franciscan to have been raised to the papal see. Worse, Nicholas had been helpless to prevent the fall of Tripoli and was dedicated to the cause of prosecuting the narrowly political War of the Sicilian Vespers, even at the cost of delaying a great crusade.[20]

19. Hugo Rahner, "Navicula Petri: Zur Symbolgeschichte des römischen Primats," *Zeitschrift für katholische Theologie* 69 (1949), 1–35. Rahner, 4, points out that the Vulgate uses *navis* and the diminutive *navicula* interchangeably.

20. See Steven Runciman, *The Sicilian Vespers* (Cambridge, 1958), 266, and Otto Schiff, *Studien zur Geschichte Papst Nikolaus IV* (Berlin, 1897).

Nonetheless the prophet had no animus against the institution of the papal Church as such, as can be seen from his prediction of the ultimate triumph of Peter's ship at the end of time. This prediction was a medieval commonplace. Numerous medieval commentators had pointed out that the Church had already been tossed but had not yet sunk,[21] and some placed further tossing in the future. The twelfth-century German Gerhoch of Reichersberg predicted that the Church would be threatened at the end of time by rough waves that would be miraculously calmed before the Last Judgment, and thirteenth-century pro-papal verses predicted that, although Frederick II would try to capsize the ship of Peter, it would be tossed but never sink.[22]

Later, Giotto's *Navicella* mosaic, done at the behest of a cardinal for the interior of Saint Peter's in Rome, represented the literal biblical scene and a greater figurative one.[23] The *Navicella*, which dominated the entrance hall of the Vatican basilica after its execution in the early years of the fourteenth century (but is now known only from fragments and copies), showed Christ supporting a kneeling Saint Peter—both miraculously buoyed by the water—while the other apostles look on in various attitudes of fear and wonder. Giotto may

21. Rahner, passim.

22. The passage in Gerhoch appears in his *De quarta vigilia noctis*, in MGH, *Libelli de lite*, III, 513. The pro-papal verses can be found in Holder-Egger, 30, 364; see also the commentary by Hans Martin Schaller, "Das letzte Rundschreiben Gregors IX. gegen Friedrich II.," *Festschrift Percy Ernst Schramm zu seinem siebzigsten Geburtstag* (Wiesbaden, 1964), I, 309–321 (at 313–314). (The similarity between these verses and the passage in the Tripoli prophecy was already noticed by Töpfer, 145, n. 229.) The twelfth-century canonist Huguccio also cited the maxim that "Peter's ship may be tossed but will never sink" (*Fluctuare potest petri navicula sed non submergi*): see Brian Tierney, " 'Only the Truth Has Authority': The Problem of 'Reception' in the Decretists and in Johannes de Turrecremata," in K. Pennington and R. Somerville, eds., *Law, Church, and Society: Essays in Honor of Stephan Kuttner* (Philadelphia, 1977), 69–99 (at 89), citing *Summa ad 9, q. 3, c. 17*. References to the *navicula Petri* in Joachite literature can be found in Joachim of Fiore, *De prophetia ignota*, in B. McGinn, ed., "Joachim and the Sibyl," *Cîteaux*, 24 (1973), 136, and in the pseudo-Joachite Isaiah commentary: *Super Esaiam Prophetam* (Venice, 1517), fos. 20ᵛ, 28ᵛ, 58ᵛ. None can be seen as a direct source for the Tripoli prophecy.

23. See the description and reproduction of a later copy in Cesare Gnudi, *Giotto* (Milan, 1958), 175–180, and fig. 145a. On dating, see Alastair Smart, *The Assisi Problem and the Art of Giotto* (Oxford, 1971), 71, and Julian Gardner, "The Stefaneschi Altarpiece," JWCI, 37 (1974), 98.

also have shown a pope kneeling in a corner beneath Christ; even if he did not, he surely meant to depict Christ's approbation of the papacy and the Church's powers of endurance. Legend has it that when Saint Catherine of Siena was praying before this mosaic in 1380, during the time of the Great Schism, she felt the weight of Giotto's ship come down so heavily on her shoulders that she fell crushed to the floor.[24] The Tripoli prophet might have been moved by Giotto's work as well (though perhaps not quite so intensely) had he been able to view it.

Almost predictably, having used his own language, the prophet returned once more to words taken from the original text of a half century earlier: the prediction of many battles to come. Then he elaborated, drawing this time on another source, Christ's eschatological sermon in Matthew, chapter 24, and Luke, chapter 21. Since Christ warned of coming wars, as the Cistercian vision had done, and then went on to warn of famines and plagues in diverse places, the prophet also went on to warn of coming famines and plagues in diverse places. The Tripoli prophet did not copy from the gospels verbatim because that might have seemed too blatant a borrowing, but he did help himself to enough words to make his source clear.[25]

Then he returned to the original vision yet again. The words "mutations of kingdoms" came directly from his model, and the prediction that "the land of the barbarians" will be destroyed was only a slight alteration of the original "the land of the Saracens" will be destroyed. The reason for this change probably lay in the fact that the prophet did not yet want to predict a victorious crusade (which comes at the end of his prophecy) but also did not want to abandon the line. Whether he had a clear notion of exactly who the "barbarians" were cannot be said; maybe he thought they were relatives of "the sons of Israel" or "the people without a head."

Since the old vision ended with the words *terra sarracenorum*

---

24. Millard Meiss, *Painting in Florence and Siena After the Black Death* (Princeton, N.J., 1951; repr. New York, 1964), 107. (Meiss, figs. 1 and 97, gives reproductions of tossed ships, modelled on Giotto's, by Orcagna and Andrea da Firenze.)

25. Cf. the Tripoli prophet's *et fames valida, et hominum mortalitas per loca* with Matt. 24:7: *et erunt pestilencie et fames et terremotus per loca.*

subvertetur, the Tripoli prophet was thereafter on his own. Freed from the dictates of his exemplar, he proceeded to express some of his most passionate hopes, beginning with his prediction of the annihilation of the mendicant orders and many other "sects." The very designation of the mendicant orders as "sects" shows the author's great hostility insofar as the word *sect* was usually applied to heretics. Of course the prophet knew that the friars were not heterodox, but he could tar them with that brush because their profession of mendicancy and preaching bore resemblance to the practices of evangelical heretics. (When the first Franciscans appeared in Germany around 1219, they were taken for heretics and set upon by the populace.)[26] The friars had always had their opponents, but opposition to them was becoming particularly pronounced by the end of the thirteenth century when the privileges they had received from the papacy were becoming an ever greater threat to the jurisdictional powers of bishops and the authority and income of parish priests. This opposition peaked between 1282, when Martin IV gave the friars unrestricted rights to preach and hear confessions at the expense of the parish clergy, and 1300, when Boniface VIII limited those rights.[27] Considering that the mendicant orders were concurrently losing much of their pristine *esprit* and beginning to quarrel with each other and among themselves, it is no wonder that resentment toward them was becoming more intense and widespread. The prophet's hostility is easily intelligible in this context and suggests that he was a secular cleric or monk. (His Latin literacy makes it highly unlikely that he was a layman.)

Although the annihilation of the mendicant orders was a consummation the Tripoli prophet devoutly wished for, it still appears in the context of the first fifteen years of terrible upheavals. Peace comes about only as the result of political developments launched by the emergence of the "lion" from mountainous caverns to cross the

26. Jordan of Giano, *Chronica*, ed. Heinrich Boehmer (Paris, 1908), 4. See further John B. Freed, *The Friars and German Society in the Thirteenth Century* (Cambridge, Mass., 1977), 26, 88–89.

27. See P. Glorieux, "Prélats français contre religieux mendiants," *Revue d'histoire de l'église de France*, 11 (1925), 309–331, 471–495, and Ludwig Hödl, *Johannes Quidort von Paris, "De confessionibus audiendis"* (Munich, 1962), 6–8.

mountains and slay the "other lion." The rampant lion is clearly the
Emperor Frederick II, who was called a lion in other prophetic texts,[28]
and who was believed in the decades after his death to be hiding in
Mount Etna in Sicily.[29] The prediction of the emergence of the lion
in the Tripoli prophecy is the earliest German evidence for the belief
that Frederick was hiding in a mountain. It also shows that Germans
believed that he was in a mountain in Italy (thereby corresponding
to the Etna legend) and would soon cross over the Alps.[30] Although

28. Namely, Frederick's open letter of 1240, *Collegerunt pontifices*, which
ends with a prediction that he would roar forth like a lion— *leo fortissimus*—to
put the Church in order, and the prophetic *Dicta Merlini*, written after Frederick's death, which also allude to him as *leo rugiens*. For the former, see J. L. A.
Huillard-Bréholles, *Historia diplomatica Friderici Secundi* (Paris, 1852–1861;
repr. Turin, 1963), V, pt. 1, 309–312, and the commentary thereon by Hans
Martin Schaller, "Die Antwort Gregors IX. auf Petrus de Vinea I, 1 'Collegerunt
pontifices,'" *Deutsches Archiv für Erforschung des Mittelalters*, 11 (1954/55),
140–165 (at 148–150). For the latter, Holder-Egger, 15, 174–177, and the version
given in the chronicle of Salimbene, MGH, *Scriptores*, 32, 359–360. It is true that
Frederick II was more often called an eagle than a lion in later prophetic
literature, but it would hardly have been fitting to have had an eagle asleep in a
mountain.

29. Töpfer, 164–166. See further Fedor Schneider, "Kaiser Friedrich II. und
seine Bedeutung für das Elsass," *Elsass-lothringisches Jahrbuch*, 9 (1930), 128–
155 (at 149–155) (repr. Schneider, *Ausgewählte Aufsätze*, ed. Gerd Tellenbach
[Aalen, 1974], 431–458 [at 452–458]), and Schneider, "Untersuchungen zur
italienischen Verfassungsgeschichte: III. Ein Schreiben Manfreds über den Pseu-
dofriedrich," *Quellen und Forschungen aus italienischen Archiven und Biblio-
theken*, 18 (1926), 213–218 (repr. *Ausgewählte Aufsätze*, 58–63). Professor Dr.
H. M. Schaller kindly called my attention to the latter article.

30. Scholars have wondered about the similarity between the thirteenth-
century Etna legend and the later "Kyffhäuser" legend that Frederick II was
sleeping in the Kyffhäuser mountain in Thuringia. Franz Kampers, *Vom Werde-
gang der abendländischen Kaisermystik* (Leipzig, 1924), 140, was convinced that
there must have been some direct connection between the two legends and could
only speculate that the Etna one was brought to Germany by wandering min-
strels or knights; Töpfer, 177, n. 107, dubious about such speculations, argued
that the Kyffhäuser variant must have had strictly German origins. The Tripoli
prophecy provides a crucial missing link, revealing that some Germans in the
late thirteenth century knew the Italian legend; later on the detail that Frederick
was asleep in an Italian mountain must have been forgotten and the Kyffhäuser
locale supplied in its place. On the German legend, see further Peter Munz,
Frederick Barbarossa (Ithaca, N.Y., 1969), 3–22, who cites further literature and
makes the important point (11, n. 6) that the earliest reference to the ruler in

the prophecy is a unique thirteenth-century German testimony to these legends, it is by no means the only evidence for late thirteenth-century German hopes that Frederick II would soon return. Quite to the contrary, such hopes were so strong that between 1283 and 1295 there was "a true epidemic of false Fredericks" in Germany, some of whom gained mass support.[31] Several later versions of the Frederick II dream specified that the returned Frederick would persecute the clergy and redress economic inequalities, but no hint of these expectations is found in the Tripoli prophecy. Economic or social reform simply was not on the prophet's mind.

Instead, his text goes on to predict that Frederick would slay the "other lion," Rudolf of Habsburg, and then, as the undisputed "lion of the East," unite with the "beast of the West" to subjugate the whole world. The "beast of the West" is either a ruler from Spain or, far more likely, the king of France, the strongest European ruler of his day. Assuming that the prophet meant the king of France, the prediction of Franco-German world conquest represents a compromise between two different prophetic traditions. In the second half of the thirteenth century, Germans and Italian Ghibellines minted and circulated several prophecies to the effect that a great new Emperor—usually expected to be an heir of Frederick II—would defeat the papacy, chastize the clergy, and conquer the world.[32] In opposition, followers of the French Guelf champion, Charles of Anjou, put forth a prophecy that a certain Charles "from the royal house of France" would become the last Emperor of the world, rule over all of Europe, and reform the Church.[33] This prophecy was issued before 1281, when Charles of Anjou was at the height of his power.

---

the Kyffhäuser need not have been meant to apply to Frederick II's grandson Friedrich der Freidige.

31. On the many false Fredericks, see Töpfer, 175–176, who cites further literature. My quotation is from Schneider, "Kaiser Friedrich II," 129 (repr. *Ausgewählte Aufsätze*, 432).

32. For example, the prophecies *Regnabit Menfridus* and *Gallorum levitas* described by Reeves, *Influence of Prophecy*, 311–312, and Töpfer, 169–170, 185–186 (on a new copy of *Regnabit Menfridus*, see n. 38 below).

33. Alexander von Roes, *Memoriale*, eds. Herbert Grundmann and H. Heimpel, in MGH, *Staatsschriften des späteren Mittelalters*, I, pt. 1, 136.

After 1282, when Charles had been crippled by the Sicilian Vespers, the prophecy became unrealistic, but around the time of the composition of the Tripoli prophecy, at least one other version was advanced to apply to the French king, Philip the Fair.[34] The German author of the Tripoli prophecy might have wished that a German alone would conquer the world, but, unlike some of his contemporaries, he seems to have recognized that German power was not what it had been and that even a miraculously risen Frederick II could not conquer the world on his own. Whether he was conscious of it or not, his prediction of East-West unity also gave his prophecy a multinational appeal.

With such unity established, the age-old dream of peace and plenty would be realized. The most influential sources for this theme in the Middle Ages were the extremely popular prophecies of the "Tiburtine Sibyl" and Pseudo-Methodius.[35] Both of these works, written originally in Greek and Syriac in the fourth and seventh centuries respectively and accessible in the medieval West in Latin translations, predicted that sometime before the triumph of Anti-

34. Dietrich Kurze, "Nationale Regungen in der spätmittelalterlichen Prophetie," *Historische Zeitschrift*, 202 (1966), 1–23 (at 8–9); Kurze, *Johannes Lichtenberger* (Lübeck and Hamburg, 1960), 23 with n. 137; and Herbert Grundmann, "Liber de Flore," *Historisches Jahrbuch*, 49 (1929), 33–91 (at 71) (repr. Grundmann, *Ausgewählte Aufsätze*, II [Stuttgart, 1977], at 141). The problem of possible prophetic allusions to Philip the Fair is too complicated to discuss in detail here, but it should be noted that in the single firmest source, the *Liber de Flore* of 1304, the French king "from the line of Pippin" with the initial "P" is described as being two-headed (*bicephalus*) because he has power over east and west; this "P" thus is a French-oriented equivalent of the jointly-ruling "lion of the East" and "beast of the West" in the Tripoli prophecy. An eschatological union between Germany and France was independently predicted by a third contemporary text, the vision of Friar John: see Donckel, "Visio," 376–377.

35. Early Latin versions of both of these works are edited by Ernst Sackur, *Sibyllinische Texte und Forschungen* (Halle, 1898; repr. Turin, 1963), 59–96, 177–187. The more widely circulated short version of Pseudo-Methodius was edited independently by Charlotte D'Evelyn, "The Middle English Metrical Version of the *Revelationes* of Methodius," *Publications of the Modern Language Society of America*, 33 (1918), 135–203 (at 191–203), and K. Rudolf, "Des Pseudo-Methodius 'Revelationes' (Fassung B) und ihre deutsche Uebersetzung in der Brüsseler Handschrift Eghenvelders," *Zeitschrift für deutsche Philologie*, 95 (1976), 68–91 (at 77–91). For a recent survey of literature pertaining to both texts and partial translations of both, see Bernard McGinn, *Visions of the End* (New York, 1979), 43–50, 70–76.

christ a last great Christian ruler would inaugurate a marvelous regime of happiness. According to the Tiburtine Sibyl, near the end of time a messianic Roman Emperor of splendid appearance would reign for a number of years (the number varies in different manuscripts) when there would be plenty throughout the world and the price of wheat, wine, and oil would be miraculously low. Similarly, Pseudo-Methodius predicted that a last great Roman Emperor would bring such unprecedented peace and tranquillity to the world that people would have no fear or worry in their hearts and would give themselves over to "eating, drinking, and marrying." These texts influenced numerous subsequent prophecies, including—directly or indirectly—the Tripoli prophet's prediction of "world peace, copious fruits, and an abundance of all things" under the reign of the conquering heroes.

Unquestionably, from the strictly theological point of view, the expected time of peace and plenty before Antichrist was not supposed to be prized but was merely a delusory calm before the storm. Patristic authority in general insisted that after the Incarnation humanity had no real betterment to look forward to on earth other than Christ's Second Coming, and if the Tiburtine Sibyl and Pseudo-Methodius allowed some exception to this, it was only a small one. Indeed Pseudo-Methodius himself knew that the final time of peace should not be portrayed too positively, and hence his very words about "eating, drinking, and marrying" were taken from Christ's eschatological sermon wherein the Lord warns that men would be caught unawares by the coming of the Son of Man in the last days just as they had been caught off guard by the Flood in the days of Noah (Matt. 24:37–39). Moreover, Pseudo-Methodius also cited in the same context the lines of Saint Paul: "The day of the Lord so cometh as a thief in the night. For when they shall say 'peace and safety,' then sudden destruction cometh upon them" (1 Thess. 5:2–3). Similarly, much later a formal theologian like the Tripoli prophet's near contemporary Hugh of Novocastro might follow Pseudo-Methodius on the time of peace before Antichrist but in so doing would make the time seem almost more of an episode of divinely ordained trickery than one of rewards.[36]

---

36. Hugo de Novocastro, bk. I, chap. 10 (the edition is unfoliated). On the Franciscan *doctor scholasticus* Hugh of Novocastro (the place-name could be

Unlike Hugh of Novocastro, however, the Tripoli prophet was not constrained by theological niceties because he worked anonymously, and his text shows that, although he knew the peace before Antichrist was merely a lull, he clearly looked forward to it. Thus he drew no appalling comparisons to the days before the Flood, and whereas Pseudo-Methodius and Hugh of Novocastro had the final peace broken by a terrible onslaught of Gog and Magog, the Tripoli prophet placed his equivalent of such persecutions before the fifteen years of peace rather than after. But the most telling argument in favor of the Tripoli prophet's more positive conception of the final time is the fact that his portrayal of it culminates in a successful "common passage" or crusade.

Like the triumph of the messianic rulers and the time of peace, the crusade theme in the Tripoli prophecy was not new. It too owed its origins to a Sibylline-Methodian germ that flowered profusely in the high Middle Ages. Specifically, while both the Tiburtine Sibyl and Pseudo-Methodius told of a great messianic ruler laying down his crown in Jerusalem in expectation of Antichrist, high-medieval prophets transmuted this abdication into a successful crusade that was to be the messianic ruler's final and greatest accomplishment.[37] Since pseudonymous prophetic texts that included such predictions abounded in the thirteenth century, the Tripoli prophet did not have to rely entirely on his own words in telling of the wondrous eschatological crusading victory, and thus, once more, we find him plagiarizing.

His borrowing here was only of a few words, but it does show that the "prophet" was writing with several different earlier texts at his disposal. The one now in question was a prophecy that arrived in

---

either Newcastle or, more likely, Neufchâtel), see the entry by C.-V. Langlois in the *Histoire littéraire de la France*, 36 (1927), 342-349. The printed edition gives the year of composition of Hugh's Antichrist tract as 1319 (see the end of bk. II, chap. 26), but the evidence of bk. II, chap. 28 shows that the work had to have been written between the death of Clement V in April 1314 and the accession of John XXII in August 1316. In corroboration, a year of composition of 1315 is given by two independent MS witnesses: see Mainz, Stadtbibliothek 151 (old 247), f. 14ʳ, and Aquila, Archivio di Stato cod. S. 58, f. 196ʳ.

37. For the origins of the transmutation, see Carl Erdmann, "Endkaiserglaube und Kreuzzugsgedanke im 11. Jahrhundert," *Zeitschrift für Kirchengeschichte* 51 (1932), 384-414.

Germany from Italy in 1269 and foretold the imminent establishment of a reign of concord by the young Hohenstaufen heir, Friedrich der Freidige, Landgrave of Thuringia. Hitherto, the only known version of this prophecy was one ending with an allusion to this Fredrick's triumph over France, but a thirteenth-century copy in an Austrian manuscript presents a different and apparently more authentic ending that promises a final wondrous time in the Holy Land when "the Holy Sepulchre will be marvelously honored."[38]

Undoubtedly, the Tripoli prophet's prediction that "the Holy Sepulchre will be honored by all" was taken from this text, and for all we know, his accompanying lines describing the glorification of Jerusalem and the rebuilding of the cities of Judea may have been taken from another text no longer identifiable. Yet the mere fact that the prophet borrowed does not mean that his heart was not in what he wrote. Since he was unaware that there was no Cistercian cloister in Tripoli, he probably had never been to the Holy Land himself, but he surely had a vision of it in his mind's eye. For him the "glorification of Jerusalem" was the inevitable culmination of the wonders beginning with the emergence of the triumphant "lion" and the final apotheosis of earthly history before the last act of the eschatological drama began.

That act had to open with the manifest appearance of Antichrist, and since the prophet preferred not to use his own words when he did not have to, he took the statement that in the final tranquillity "news will be heard of Antichrist" from still another source. Specifically, a prophecy for the years 1250 to 1265 beginning *Corruent nobiles* ends with the words "then news will be heard of the preaching of Antichrist."[39] Although surviving copies of this text have so

38. The prior known version of this prophecy, beginning *Regnabit Menfridus*, appears in the *Chronica minor auctore Minorita Erphordiensi*, in MGH, *Scriptores*, 24, 207, and is best analyzed by Töpfer, 169–170. The new version, discovered and called to my attention by Dr. Alexander Patschovsky, appears in a codex of the Austrian Benedictine monastery of Admont as a thirteenth-century addition, probably written in Admont, to a twelfth-century MS. See MS Admont 326, f. 230ᵛ, and compare this version's "Ipsius eciam temporibus terra sancta et sepulchrum Domini mirifice honorabitur" with the Tripoli prophecy's "Sepulchrum Domini ab omnibus honorabitur."

39. The *Corruent nobiles* prophecy is edited by Reeves, *Influence of Prophecy*, 50, from MS BL Royal 8 C IV. Reeves does not mention two other early copies—

far been found only in English and Irish manuscripts, it almost certainly was written on the continent and must have circulated there as well.[40] In the thirteenth-century English Gilbertine manuscript discussed in the previous chapter, the prophecy is found on the same leaf as the original Cistercian vision (although copied in a different hand), suggesting that the Tripoli prophet himself might have seen the two texts in close proximity. Whatever the case, he surely had the *Corruent nobiles* text nearby while he was at work and turned to it toward the end of his labors.

As terrible as the reign of Antichrist would certainly be, it is noteworthy that the Tripoli prophet does not dilate on it. Rather, for him it was only an entr'acte between two great final acts of divine beneficence—the "glorification" of Jerusalem and the Judgment. Hence after predicting "news" of Antichrist and all sorts of marvels (Antichrist was expected to win many over to his side by performing blasphemous miracles), the prophet proceeded to his conclusion that those who would live to overcome the onslaught of Antichrist would not suffer eternal death. It went without saying that the fortunate ones would be those who survived Antichrist's persecutions and resisted his blandishments. Implicitly, the prophet alluded to the

---

Cambridge, St. John's College 239, end flyleaf (the Gilbertine MS discussed in Chapter Two) and Dublin, Trinity College 347, fos. 388ᵛ–389ʳ (from the Irish Franciscan house of Multyfarnham). I learned of the Dublin copy from a draft catalogue of the medieval Latin manuscripts of Trinity College prepared by Professor Marvin L. Colker; see Professor Colker's description of this MS in *Speculum*, 54 (1979), 719–720. Both of these copies have the reading *tunc audientur nova de predicacione Antichristi*. Fourteenth-century versions (several of which are listed in Reeves, *Influence of Prophecy*, 51, n. 1) leave out the word *predicacione*, thereby presenting a sentence that is identical to the one in the Tripoli prophecy (the fourteenth-century reading very likely derives from a mid-thirteenth-century exemplar).

40. My reasons for assuming a continental origin are: (1) the first prediction in the text alludes *ex eventu* to the failure of the first crusade of Louis IX of France, a disaster more likely to have been deeply upsetting in France than elsewhere; (2) the text also predicts a papal schism with a "just" pope remaining in Lyons—another sign of likely French authorship; (3) the text's spurious ascription to Joachim of Fiore and specific knowledge of Joachim's *Liber Concordie* would more likely have arisen on the continent than in England at so early a date as ca. 1251; (4) the copy in the Multyfarnham MS appears between other material of probable continental provenance (the testament of St. Francis and another pseudo-Joachite prophecy).

medieval expectation that some would be deluded by Antichrist but others would withstand him and live through his three-and-a-half-year reign to see the Second Coming and Judgment. These steadfast Christians would be granted eternal life. The last words of the prophecy promising that "blessed is he who will then overcome, for he shall not suffer perpetual death" were taken verbatim from the Book of Revelation (2:11), and in closing with them the prophet who began by enumerating so many coming disasters ended affirmatively with an explicit biblical reminder of God's justice and grandeur.

God's providential grandeur, indeed, was the major theme of the entire prophecy. The miraculous moving hand tells the Cistercian of Tripoli, and through him the whole Christian world, that Tripoli will fall and that there will be terrible days of rage but that ulti-mately right order will prevail. The clergy will be chastised, the Christian Church itself almost destroyed, and the mendicant orders annihilated. But good men need not despair, for God will still be in His heaven and bring redemption out of His purifying fire. When the Lord wishes, He will turn war and famine into peace and plenty, redress the loss of Tripoli by the reconquest and glorification of the Holy Land, and grant eternal life to those who survive the purifying trials and resist the wiles of Antichrist.

The Tripoli prophet's concept of right order was conservative. Although he foresaw the chastisement of the clergy and the annihila-tion of the mendicants, he looked forward to the ultimate triumph of the papacy. He also longed for strong rulers, hoping that peace and plenty would be brought to the world by the unchallenged rule of two mighty monarchs. For him, that peace would culminate not in a new way of life, or even in a new stage of spiritual illumination, but in a successful reconquest of the Holy Land—the old crusade idea in a new dress. A subtitle of the Tripoli prophecy could well be "Jerusalem Delivered."

This is not to say that nothing in the Tripoli prophecy would have sounded threatening to the rulers of Church and world. Two lines in particular would have been insurrectionary had they been in-cluded in a manifesto for direct action. The prediction of the return of Frederick II to slay the "other lion" was in effect one of regicide, produced by and appealing to contemporary discontent. Still, the prophet's hope was not for social revolution; rather, he longed for the reappearance of an autocratic Emperor, long dead, to reverse the political eclipse of Germany. Similarly, the predicted annihilation of the mendicants was really a reactionary hope. In the thirteenth century, secular clerics and members of the older orders considered the mendicant way of life to be an unprecedented novelty: for them, a world without friars would be a good old world.

Since the Tripoli prophet was certain that the divine wrath he perceived was well founded, he was perforce a critic of his times, but his criticisms were superficial and prejudiced. Germany could have gained little by the mere replacement of one ruler with another, and the mendicants were no more corrupt than any of the other orders. The prophet, almost certainly a cleric himself, was displeased by clerical rivals and disconcerted by the weakness and corruption he saw around him, but he was too much a part of his age to conceive of thoroughgoing change. Moreover, he did not write primarily to present a list of grievances, let alone a call to arms. Instead, he hoped to account for disaster and to console himself and his readers by showing that disaster was part of a beneficent divine plan. Although he did foresee a better time in the future, he was not a theoretician engaged in drawing detailed blueprints for that better time. In interpreting God's ways to man, he wished primarily to bring comfort and thereby to shore up the faith.

How could someone who wished to shore up faith have been so deceitful? Not only did the prophet fabricate a vision, but he also resorted to *ex eventu* deception and plagiarism. Far from imagining him writing in a rapt trance, we must picture him seated at a desk, methodically piecing together his own words and somebody else's and pondering borrowings from several different sources. To modern sensibilities such methods seem cynical, but it is doubtful that the Tripoli prophet had a troubled conscience, for he knew that he was conveying inspired truth in order to instill faith and hope. No doubt he felt that by inventing a miracle, using old prophetic language, and providing *ex eventu* details, he would assure greater confidence in his prophecy than if he relied on forthright self-identification. Since he had some burning messages to communicate, he decided to express them as best he could.

To be sure, by modern standards his attitude toward the original vision was inconsistent. Presumably he realized that the alleged miracle of 1239 or 1240 never really happened, and presumably he did not consider all of the original message unalterably true, or else he would not have tampered with it so extensively. Yet he must have found some core of veracity in the original words since he used so many of them in his own recreation. In their original context they were wrong, but related to the contemporary crisis they were right. Together with his own lines and some other borrowed ones, they formed the best way for expressing the certain plan of Providence.

Chapter IV

THE TRIPOLI PROPHECY
IN ITS FIRST GENERATION

The contemporary success of the Tripoli prophecy was resounding. Soon after the prophecy's composition, while shock at the loss of the Holy Land was intense, the prophetic message circulated widely throughout northern Europe. Within roughly a decade it appeared in a Parisian scholastic treatise, in chronicles written in Friesland, Bavaria, and Austria, in flyleaves of manuscripts copied in Bavaria, Lincolnshire, and Chartres, and in a vernacular translation written in northeastern or eastern France. These surviving copies show that there were numerous others which have subsequently disappeared or still lie unnoticed: texts of the prophecy must have circulated by the scores, perhaps by the hundreds.

The reasons for the prophecy's early popularity are not hard to find. Although readers of the Cistercian vision around 1240 apparently did not connect the meaning of that prophecy with its catalyst —the Mongol onslaught—those who read and circulated the Tripoli prophecy in the 1290s could not have failed to have connected it with the recent Christian defeats in the Holy Land because the prophecy supposedly came from the Holy Land and explicitly "predicted" the fall of Tripoli. Moreover, an early revision, which almost completely supplanted the original, went further and "predicted" the fall of Acre as well. Accordingly, the prophecy alluded clearly to current events that were very much on peoples' minds and no doubt helped readers to place those dismaying events within a larger, more intelligible context.

The scholastic treatise that contains the Tripoli prophecy is John of Paris's *De Antichristo* of 1300, a work which comments explicitly on the value of the prophecy and reveals how it was regarded by a leading thinker of the age. John, a Dominican theologian active in Paris from about 1280 to his death in 1306, was sometimes called "Quidort"—"the sleeper"—but there was nothing somnolent about the intellect reflected in his writings. John's most remarkable work, his political treatise of 1302, *On Royal and Papal Power*, has earned justified praise for its "concise and trenchant argumentation," its "dispassionate analysis," and its rare "intellectual chastity and integrity." One modern expert has even called it "perhaps the greatest of all the works of political theory written at this time."[1]

John's characteristic coolness, lucidity, and spirit of moderation are also present in his treatise *On Antichrist*, but, since the nature of the subject matter is less "rational," it has attracted far less modern attention.[2] John was moved to write on eschatology by a controversy

1. Quotations from Walter Ullmann, *A History of Political Thought: The Middle Ages* (Baltimore, Md., 1965), 200, 204, and Brian Tierney, *The Crisis of Church and State, 1050–1300* (Englewood Cliffs, N.J., 1964), 195–196. The treatise is available in two English translations: *On Royal and Papal Power*, trans. John A. Watt (Toronto, 1971) and, same title, trans. A. P. Monahan (New York, 1974). General estimations of John's work are offered in Martin Grabmann, "Studien zu Johannes Quidort von Paris, O. Pr.," SbM, 1922, no. 3, 1–60, and, with primary reference to his theology, Frederick J. Roensch, *Early Thomistic School* (Dubuque, Iowa, 1964), 98–104, 275–289. Roensch comments, with warrant, that John's nonpolitical work "deserves more attention than it has been given."

2. The only published edition dates from the sixteenth century: *Expositio . . . Joachim* (see list of abbreviations), fos. 44ʳ–51ᵛ. There is a brief summary in Heinrich Denifle, "Der Plagiator Nicolaus von Strassburg," *Archiv für Literatur- und Kirchengeschichte des Mittelalters*, 4 (1888), 312–329 (at 322–328), and a brief distorted treatment by Alois Dempf, *Sacrum Imperium* (Munich and Berlin, 1929), 430, but the only extensive modern discussion is by Pelster (see list of abbreviations), 36–41. A token of modern indifference to the *De Antichristo* is its absence from the consideration of John's works by Fritz Bleienstein, *Johannes Quidort von Paris, Ueber königliche und päpstliche Gewalt* (Stuttgart, 1969),

centering around the layman Arnold of Villanova, a physician for kings and popes who found a second calling as an evangelist. Arnold had become certain from his biblical studies that there was important news to communicate about the coming of Antichrist and the end of the world. In his view, a passage in Daniel revealed that Antichrist would appear around the year 1376 and that afterwards the world could not last for more than half a century. Since Arnold felt that all Christians should be apprised of this urgent truth, he submitted his statement of it, *On the Time of the Coming of Antichrist and the End of the World,* to the members of the theological faculty of Paris in 1299 while he was on a diplomatic mission for his lord and patient, King James I of Aragon.[3] Arnold hoped that approval of his treatise by the experts at the leading university of Christendom would ensure the widest respect for it, but that approval was not forthcoming. Instead, the Parisian theologians condemned his views and the bishop of Paris had him arrested in violation of his diplomatic immunity. Although Arnold gained his freedom soon afterwards and appealed his case to the papal court (where it dragged on for several years), the incident became a *cause célèbre* which elicited several other eschatological treatises.[4]

John of Paris's *De Antichristo*, completed in 1300, was written

---

10–12. A critical edition of the text is currently being prepared as a Cornell University doctoral dissertation by Mrs. Sara Clark.

3. The contents of the tract are summarized by Pelster, 33–35, and by Harold Lee, "*Scrutamini Scripturas*: Joachimist Themes and *Figurae* in the Early Religious Writings of Arnold of Villanova," JWCI, 37 (1974), 33–56 (at 35–42), both of whom worked without knowledge of Maier's important article (see list of abbreviations), which shows that the best surviving MS of Arnold's treatise *On the Time of the Coming of Antichrist* is Vat. Borgh. 205 (fos. 26ʳ–48ʳ), and that in this MS the year given by Arnold for Antichrist's advent is 1376. There has been much confusion about this date, but 1376 coincides not only with independent information about Arnold's reckoning given in the fourteenth century by Friar Gentilis (see Maier), but also with other independent evidence given by Pierre d'Ailly in his *Tractatus et sermones* (Strassburg, 1490), sig. t4ᵛᵃ–t5ʳᵃ (Serm. 3 de adv. Domini). (Since John of Paris gave Arnold's date as 1366, it is likely that Arnold himself altered the date in different versions of his work.)

4. The entire incident and the resulting theological treatments of eschatology are discussed by Pelster. On Arnold's conservative stance in opposition to Scholastic Dominican theologians, see Franz Ehrle, "Arnaldo de Villanova ed i 'Thomatiste,'" *Gregorianum*, 1 (1920), 475–501.

in an attempt to mediate between Arnold and Arnold's Parisian theological opponents. John could play this role well because he was an expert theologian of the illustrious Dominican order but had not yet become a regent master of theology and had played no part in Arnold's condemnation. Simply stated, his compromise was twofold. With regard to Arnold's conclusions, he rejected the specific computation of Antichrist's advent around 1376 but accepted Arnold's general argument that the time of Antichrist was not far off. With regard to Arnold's methods, he replaced the idiosyncratic reading of a single scriptural passage with the cool analysis of a wide array of eschatological information transmitted by the "saints," the Bible, and natural philosophy. (In relying on the Bible alone, the "visionary" Arnold was methodologically more traditional than the Scholastic John.) Arnold of Villanova had provoked the wrath of the Parisian masters not only by advancing a bold, unprecedented reading of Daniel, but still more by invading the preserve of the experts at a time when laymen did not write on theology; John of Paris agreed with Arnold's major finding that Antichrist would probably come soon (a common view) and tried to make it respectable by supporting it with the rigorous methods of contemporary theological science.

A treatise with such "scientific" aspirations would seem to be an unlikely vehicle for an early copy and consideration of the Tripoli prophecy, but here modern assumptions and medieval realities diverge. John of Paris accepted the text of the prophecy without wondering whether it might have been a fabrication. Although it was of no hallowed antiquity, indeed could not have reached Paris more than a decade earlier than the time when John wrote, he included it among the expressions of "saints" who had the "spirit of prophecy." Moreover, after copying the entire text into his treatise, he proceeded to comment that insofar as it clearly predicted the fall of Tripoli it was already "verified in part."

John, however, could not go any further in interpreting the text for two reasons. One was that the copy which came his way contained a scribal alteration that deprived the prophecy of some of its clearest import. Whereas the original alluded to a period of trials of fifteen years, for some inexplicable reason the version that John inherited gave three years, with the result that the original prediction of an overall total of thirty years until the coming of Antichrist could no longer be perceived.[5] In other words, because of the deficiencies of his text, John could not possibly see that the moving hand was stating that Antichrist had been born in 1287 and would come to reign openly in 1317. Hence he was unable to relate the Tripoli prophecy to the main subject of his treatise—information concerning the date of Antichrist's appearance.

Someone else might have proceeded to gloss the prophecy even with its inexplicable eighteen instead of thirty years, but the other reason why John offered no further interpretation was that his was an atypical intellect. As we will see, many late-medieval readers had no hesitation about reading the cryptic lines of the Tripoli prophecy more or less any way they wished, but John of Paris, "the most solemn theologian of his day,"[6] was more restrained. Thus after writing that the prophecy was "verified in part" by the fall of Tripoli, he went on to confess that he found the rest "obscure" because the meaning of its names was "uncertain" and because he could not tell when the predicted events would happen.[7] What he did not say, but presumably felt, was that subsequent events might later "verify" and make comprehensible more of the prophecy. The Tripoli verification, at any rate, attested to the prophecy's inspiration and justified its inclusion *in extenso* in John's treatise, where others could make of it what they would.

5. The "John of Paris" version diverges from the reconstructed original primarily in having *infra tres annos unus deus* . . . in place of *infra quindecim annos erit unus deus* . . . and in adding *et omnis terra turbabitur* within the sequence "in mundo erunt multa prelia, et multe strages, *et omnis terra turbabitur*, et fames valida, et hominum mortalitas per loca." The first change may have arisen from a mistake in reading roman numerals or was perhaps a way of implicitly predicting the fall of Acre in 1291 as well as the fall of Tripoli. The addition of earthquakes to wars, famines, and plagues has the logic of following Matt. 24:7 and Luke 21:11 even more to the letter than the original did.

6. The judgment of the fifteenth-century *Miroir historial abrégé de France*, in Paul Saenger, ed., "John of Paris, Principal Author of the *Quaestio de potestate papae* (*Rex pacificus*)," *Speculum*, 56 (1981), 41–55 (at 55).

7. MS Bodl., Canon. Pat. lat. 19 (early 14th century), fos. 22ᵛ–23ʳ: "Hec autem prophecia licet sit verificata in parte, scilicet quam ad ea que predixit de Tripoli, tamen quam ad residuum (MS: residium) est obscura, quia dubium est quid significent nomina et utrum vel alia omnia simul vel distanter vel in quanta distancia sint futura."

Unbeknownst to John, about twice as many late-medieval readers as usual would be able to consider his treatise because it was soon afterwards plagiarized by another Dominican, Nicholas of Strassburg. Nicholas, chiefly remembered as a defender of Meister Eckhart in 1327, had studied in Paris in the years before 1320 and returned to Germany shortly thereafter to become lector of the Dominican house at Cologne. In 1326, while exercising this office, he dedicated three treatises united under a collective heading, *On the Advent of Christ*, to Archbishop Baldwin of Trier as a token of his admiration and in thanks for innumerable "benefits."[8] Whatever these benefits may have been, Nicholas must have hoped for more because Baldwin, uncle of the king of Bohemia, was a mighty prince of the Church. Nicholas wrote humbly that he was only offering treatises because "silver and gold [were not] his"; but at least two of the three works he offered were not really his either: in fact he plagiarized both from the works of John of Paris. The alert nineteenth-century scholar Heinrich Denifle was the first to recognize that Nicholas must have used his time in Paris to copy out John's treatises *On the Advent of Christ in the Flesh*[9] and *De Antichristo* for his own subsequent use; now it can be stated that Nicholas probably copied them from a

---

8. See Eugen Hillenbrand, *Nikolaus von Strassburg, Religiöse Bewegung und Dominikanische Theologie im 14. Jahrhundert* (Freiburg/Br., 1968). The dating of the dedication to Baldwin of Trier is not certain. Hillenbrand, 32, 56–57, gives 1323 but was unaware that several MSS of the version of Nicholas's work dedicated to Baldwin give 1326 as the *annus presens*: e.g., Bodl., Bodley 140, fos. 60r–96r, and UB Utrecht 386, fos. 190r–199r. The weight of this evidence makes me prefer 1326, but it is still unclear why Nicholas called himself simply *lector Coloniensis* when he had a claim to higher titles by that time. A thorough study of all the surviving Nicholas MSS might throw further light on this problem.

9. Ironically, much of this treatise rests heavily on the *Metaphysica* of Roger Bacon. Nonetheless, doubts about John's authorship of the *De adventu Christi secundum carnem*, otherwise known as the *Testimonia gentilium de secta Christiana*, as most recently expressed by Thomas A. Orlando, "Roger Bacon and the 'Testimonia gentilium de secta Christiana,'" *Recherches de théologie ancienne et médiévale*, 43 (1976), 202–218, are unwarranted and should be completely removed by the early fourteenth-century attribution of the treatise to *frater Johannes de Parisius in quadam collectione quam fecit amore regine Navarre* in MS BN lat. 15450, f. 453vb, reported by J. N. Hillgarth, *Ramon Lull and Lullism in Fourteenth-Century France* (Oxford, 1971), 244, and ignored by Orlando. An edition is by Orlando, *Testimonia gentilium de secta Christiana* (M.A. thesis: University of Virginia, 1973).

manuscript he found in the library of Saint-Germain-des-Prés in the Latin Quarter.[10] The only changes Nicholas made in John's *De Antichristo* were to curtail the original prologue, add some extra considerations at the end, alter the dates that referred to the "present year," and divide the work into chapters. All else was mere penmanship.

As a crowning audacity, Nicholas rededicated the same three treatises to a new patron in the same year. This time he wanted to thank Pope John XXII for naming him to a high Dominican office. A more talented man might have risen to the occasion with a new treatise; a less ambitious one might have expressed his thanks with a letter. But Nicholas dashed off copies of the same works he had sent to Baldwin with a new dedication explaining that he had written them expressly for the pope. Such conduct was brazen even by medieval standards. It was common to insert borrowed passages into one's own work without attribution, and it was not unheard of to dedicate one's own work on different occasions to different recipients, but it was most unusual to pass off entire treatises as one's own twice.[11] Yet no one in the Middle Ages seems to have recognized the deception. John of Paris's *De Antichristo* survives in at least nine fourteenth- and fifteenth-century copies, and Nicholas's plagiarized *De Antichristo* was copied separately a few more times than that, but apparently no one matched up the two works.[12]

10. For full demonstration of the plagiarism, see Denifle (n. 2 above). The MS that Nicholas probably used is now BN lat. 13781, formerly from St.-Germain-des-Prés (ownership mark f. 1ʳ). This is an early fourteenth-century MS that contains in sequence both of the treatises that Nicholas appropriated; study of the texts of the Tripoli prophecy shows that the St.-Germain MS contains readings different from those found in other John of Paris MSS but which reappear in the Nicholas of Strassburg copies (see Appendix II). Since a Parisian MS (Arsenal 78) names Nicholas of Lyra, a slightly later Parisian contemporary of John of Paris, as the author of the third treatise that Nicholas sent to Archbishop Baldwin, it seems very likely that Nicholas of Strassburg plagiarized this work as well; cf. Hillenbrand, 32–33.

11. Denifle gives Nicholas no quarter, concluding with some bile that "if Nicholas was one of the most eminent theologians of the [Dominican] order in Germany in the first half of the fourteenth century, it is clear that the order then had no eminent theologians in Germany."

12. See Appendix II. Before Denifle's discovery, Karl Schmidt, *Johannes Tauler von Strassburg* (Hamburg, 1841), 6, praised Nicholas of Strassburg's judg-

Embedded within the many copies of the Antichrist treatise, the Tripoli prophecy led its own mutable life, for some scribes were too puzzled or intrigued by the prophecy and others too familiar with it to copy it as they found it. Scribes who were puzzled by incomprehensible passages in the prophecy changed them at will,[13] and several scribes also took the more arbitrary liberty of altering dates and numbers. A fourteenth-century copy of John's treatise makes the miracle in Tripoli transpire in 1075 (an historical impossibility), and several copies of Nicholas's version have it transpiring in 1266, even though Nicholas himself copied the correct date of 1287.[14] There are no obvious explanations for these changes, but the change in one of the copies of the plagiarism to the effect that "one god and one faith" would come in 1335 most likely came from eschatological reckonings taken from Dan. 12:12: "Blessed is he that waiteth and cometh to the thousand three hundred and five and thirty days."[15] Various manuscripts also display the desire to lengthen the predicted time of wondrous abundance: whereas the original text limits this to fifteen years, a marginal addition in an early John of Paris manuscript presents an alternate reading of thirty years, and the copyist of the Saint-Germain manuscript most likely used by Nicholas of Strassburg made it twenty-five years.[16] Since Nicholas retained this latter change, it passed into numerous other copies.

In addition to changes caused by incomprehension or arbitrary

---

ment and learning without realizing that John of Paris was the one who really deserved this praise.

13. For example, BN lat. 13781, f. 86ᵛ: *Ve . . . toti Christianitati* for *Ve . . . tibi Christianitas*; UB Frankfurt, Barth. 141, f. 148ᵛ: *Vespertilio dominum apum superabit vel fulgabit* for the Nicholas of Strassburg original *Vespertilio dominum apum superabit vel fugabit.*

14. 1075 in MS Milan, Ambrosiana I. 227 Inf., f. 33ʳ; 1266 in the two MSS reported by Denifle, 325, n. 8, as well as in UB Utrecht 386, f. 193ᵛ. The fact that Nicholas himself copied 1287 is shown by the preservation of that date in at least four copies of the Nicholas MSS (see Appendix II). The mistaken date of 1277 in UB Frankfurt, Barth. 141, f. 148ᵛ, is clearly the product of a copyist's error.

15. The date 1335 appears in MS Bodl., Bodley 140, f. 87ʳ.

16. Thirty years in Bodl. Canon. Pat. lat. 19, f. 22ᵛ, written by a later hand; twenty-five years in BN lat. 13781, f. 86ᵛ, followed by Laon 275, f. 5ʳ, Cues, Hospital 57, f. 99ʳ, Vat. Pal. lat. 924, f. 233ʳ (which mistakenly has twenty-six years), and by all of the Nicholas of Strassburg MSS I have seen.

desires to improve, three different transmissions of the prophecy reveal the presence of what textual critics call "contamination." The pejorative connotation of this term applies only to textual criticism: when a scribe "contaminates" he does not really pollute his manuscript but supplies a variant reading from another copy. Such "contaminations" impede the work of the editor looking for straight lines of manuscript descent, but they can be quite illuminating for the cultural historian.

In the first case, the Saint-Germain-des-Prés copy of John of Paris's *De Antichristo* shows that the scribe who copied the message of the moving hand added a variant reading from a completely different manuscript tradition of the prophecy. Where John's version has the sentence, "The bat will overcome [*superabit*] the lord of the bees," a variant from a completely different line of transmission reads, "The bat will drive away [*fugabit*] the lord of the bees." Remarkably, the Saint-Germain copyist knew this variant and presented it as an alternate reading in his margin. From there it was incorporated by a group of derivative John of Paris manuscripts and also by Nicholas of Strassburg to read, "The bat will overcome or drive away [*superabit vel fugabit*] the lord of the bees." Since the Saint-Germain copy was made before 1320, the marginal addition shows that an independent copy of the Tripoli prophecy had become known to the Parisian copyist by that time. It also shows that the prophecy must have made a vivid impression on him: while copying theological treatises by John of Paris, he came to a prophecy within one of them that he already knew and provided an alternate reading by referring to another manuscript at his disposal. (The alternative, that he read the other copy of the Tripoli prophecy after he finished copying the treatise and went to the trouble of going back to it to add the marginal variant, seems less likely.)

The Saint-Germain copy contains only one "contaminated" reading, but a family of John of Paris manuscripts contains a larger number. This family descends from a missing fourteenth-century copy almost certainly of Italian provenance.[17] Quite clearly, the

17. The surviving MSS in the family are: Avignon, Bibliothèque Calvet 1087, fos. 206ʳ–219ʳ (ca. 1400); Milan, Ambrosiana I. 227 Inf., fos. 31ᵛ–35ᵛ (14th century); Turin, Biblioteca Nazionale Universitaria G. IV. 8, fos. 24ᵛ–35ʳ (mid-15th

scribe of that missing copy recognized the text of the Tripoli prophecy in the midst of his main work, found another copy that had circulated independently of John of Paris, and used it to "correct" the text John of Paris had offered.[18] Although this scribe's changes brought the product further away from, rather than nearer to, the text of the original, it is nonetheless remarkable that he recognized the prophecy when he saw it in the *De Antichristo* and equally remarkable that he had another independent copy at his reach. Remarkable too is the fact that he cared enough about his work to go to the trouble of "correcting" the copy he found in the body of John of Paris's treatise.

The best "contamination" of the Tripoli prophecy, if one can use this seeming contradiction in terms, appears in a manuscript of Nicholas of Strassburg's plagiarism transcribed in the second half of the fourteenth century in an English Dominican cloister, most likely Saint Clement's, Leicester. This copy reveals a very thoughtful line-by-line comparison with a second text of the prophecy that had independently reached the same Dominican house.[19] The second text was a very early pristine one and hence much superior to the one embedded within Nicholas of Strassburg's *De Antichristo*. Clearly the Dominican scribe realized this fact himself. In the midst of copying Nicholas of Strassburg's treatise, he recognized that he had a better

century); Venice, San Marco III. 177, fos. 35ᵛ-42ᵛ (1469). All, except the Avignon MS, are definitely of Italian provenance, and the Avignon MS might be Italian as well—it came to the Bibliothèque Calvet from the Celestinian cloister of Avignon, but that cloister was founded in 1395 and many of its MSS were obtained as gifts or brought to it from other monasteries of the order. Moreover, even if the Avignon copy had originally been made in Avignon, it could have been copied from an Italian exemplar. The independent copy of a version of the Tripoli prophecy that points to an exemplar used for the contamination is also Italian: Vat. lat. 793, f. 96ᵛ.

18. All the MSS listed above contain the following variants: *visio Tripoli* for *visio Tripolis*; *Nam apparuit* for *apparuit*; the addition of the words *corpus Domini* (at the end of the prologue); and *magnis fluctibus* for *variis fluctibus*.

19. Bodl., Bodley 140, f. 87ʳ⁻ᵛ. A description of the MS is given by F. Madan and H. H. E. Craster, *A Summary Catalogue of Western Manuscripts in the Bodleian Library at Oxford* (Oxford, 1922-1953), II, 112-113, who have it "written chiefly by William of Glen Magna." The variants in the Bodleian copy are related to the variants in an independent copy of the earliest version of the Tripoli prophecy: see Appendix II.

copy of the Tripoli prophecy at his disposal, interrupted his process of mechanical transcription, and brought the better copy to his desk. Then, every time he noticed variant readings, he considered his alternatives and copied the ones he preferred. Two erasures show that he even changed his mind twice, eliminated the reading he found in one copy, and replaced it with a better one from the other.

It would be hard to find clearer evidence of how familiar the Tripoli prophecy was to fourteenth-century readers and of how seriously they took it than the three independent cases of scribal contamination. All three scribes recognized the text of the prophecy when they saw it in a larger context and knew where to locate other copies for comparison. All of them cared so much about producing better texts of the prophecy that they interrupted their main work to improve the texts bequeathed to them by John of Paris or Nicholas of Strassburg. The fourteenth-century English Dominican, in particular, took great pains to embark on a close comparison and then a reconsideration of his alternatives. For all three, the Tripoli prophecy was apparently an old friend, and they wanted to do it as much justice as they could.

Having seen how the Tripoli prophecy circulated by means of the treatises of John of Paris and Nicholas of Strassburg, we can return to the earliest phases of its life. The text that was copied in 1300 by John of Paris is one of four known witnesses to the pristine form of the Tripoli prophecy that was written around 1290. A second witness is the sum of variants in the fourteenth-century English Dominican copy of Nicholas of Strassburg just discussed, and the third and fourth are fifteenth-century Italian copies, which are more appropriately introduced later.[20]

There are also scores of other copies of the Tripoli prophecy, but they all descend from an early revision made shortly after 1291. The revision in question had to have been composed after August of 1291 because it explicitly "predicted" the loss of Acre as well as Tripoli, and news of Acre's fall first reached the West at that time. Clearly someone with the loss of the Holy Land on his mind read the prophecy, decided that the prescient moving hand must have known

20. BN lat. 16021, f. 19^{r-v}, on which see pp. 91–92 below, and Vat. lat. 793, on which see pp. 128–129 below.

about the more important fall of Acre as well as the fall of Tripoli, and added the linked prediction with a clear conscience.

In addition to predicting the fall of Acre, the reviser's other major change was to delete the whole sentence about the miraculous return of the "lion," Frederick II. The best explanation for this is that the reviser was a German and took out the prediction about the lion's return because he found it politically offensive. The surviving manuscript evidence favors the hypothesis that the revision was German insofar as the earliest and least corrupt copies come from within the territory of the medieval German Empire. And there is certainly no doubt that the line about the risen lion would have been regarded by many as offensive. In predicting that a "lion" would rise up out of mountain caverns, cross the mountains, and slay the "other lion," the Tripoli prophet was in effect foretelling the elimination of the reigning German ruler and thereby appealing to subversive sentiments. Similar expectations and prophecies of Frederick II's return had in fact called forth several bold imposters, one of whom had held court in the Rhineland in 1284–85, received foreign ambassadors, and summoned the Emperor Rudolf to appear before him. Altogether there were at least five such false Fredericks who appeared throughout Germany between 1283 and 1295; all were finally apprehended, but only after they had created difficulties for the governing authorities.[21] Evidence exists that such pretenders were supported by the lower classes in the towns, and it is known that shortly after 1300 some Germans expected that the returning Frederick II would "drive out the priests."[22] Most likely the post-Acre reviser did not want to encourage such hopes and divested the Tripoli prophecy of its most insurrectionary line out of political tendentiousness. Since his revision quickly became the predominant form of the prophecy, the line thereafter passed out of currency.[23]

The only other substantive changes the post-Acre reviser made

---

21. On the many false Fredericks, see Töpfer, 175–176, who cites further literature. An English account is Norman Cohn, *The Pursuit of the Millennium*, 3d ed. (New York, 1970), 113–115.

22. Töpfer, 176.

23. It was independently deleted for unknown reasons in BN lat. 16021, f. 19ʳ and retained with major alterations in Vat. lat. 793, f. 96ᵛ.

muted the exemplar's exultation about better times to come. Although he retained the fifteen years of peace, he toned down the original description of them by deleting the reference to an "abundance of all things." Similarly, in telling of the wondrous final Christian occupation of the Holy Land, he toned down the original description by deleting the prediction of the "rebuilding of all the cities of Judea." Finally, he omitted the original last line, which told of the "blessing" of those who would overcome Antichrist's persecutions. While all these changes certainly muted the optimism of the original, they by no means left a text that was completely gloomy, for the remainder still predicted the coming of universal peace and copious fruit, a successful crusade, and the "glorification of Jerusalem."

Since the post-Acre revision carried the day and contained several minor changes that are not worth discussing individually, a translation of it (minus the introduction, which is more or less unchanged) is in order before continuing.[24]

> The high Cedar of Lebanon will be felled, and Tripoli will soon be destroyed, and Acre captured. Mars will overcome Saturn, and Saturn will waylay Jupiter. The bat will subjugate the lord of the bees. Within fifteen years there will be one god and one faith. The other god will vanish. The sons of Israel will be liberated from captivity. A certain people who are called without a head will come. Woe then to the clergy, and to you Christianity! The ship of Peter will be tossed in manifold waves, but will escape and dominate in the last days. There will be many battles in the world, and great massacres, and severe famines, and plagues in many places, and mutations of kingdoms. The land of the barbarians will be converted. The mendicant orders and many other sects will be annihilated. The beast of the West and the lion of the East will subjugate the whole world. And then there will be peace in the whole world and copious fruit for fifteen years. Then there will be a common passage by all the faithful beyond the congregated waters to the Holy Land, and they will triumph. And the city of Jerusalem will be glorified, and the Holy Sepulchre will be honored by all. And in such tranquillity news will be heard of Antichrist and of other marvels of God. Therefore be vigilant.

24. See Appendix III for the Latin text. I refrain from commenting on this reviser's self-estimation of his work because it was probably similar to that of others discussed—namely, an inner-directed sense that he knew better what the prophecy *should* have said than the textual tradition itself revealed.

Textual analysis of the surviving manuscripts reveals that the revision was transmitted in numerous phases before it reached its earliest identifiable copyists. One early text, probably the earliest version extant, appears in a continuation of the chronicle of Bloemhof in Wittewierum—a Premonstratensian abbey in West Friesland—for the years from 1272 to 1296.[25] This chronicle continuation does not follow strict chronological order in its entries, but it does reveal some chronological progression. Since the compiler states that the miracle of the moving hand transpired in Tripoli in 1287 but enters the event between others of 1291 and 1296, the report probably arrived in Wittewierum between those years. Almost certainly it arrived there before 1296 because that is the date of the last entry in the compilation.

Although the Bloemhof copy is very early, its numerous variants show that it is still several steps removed from the autograph of the post-Acre revision. After the promulgation of the revision, an unknown copyist added to the prologue the detail that the monk saw the divine message written "in golden letters." Either that scribe or another made the more substantive change that the "sons of Jerusalem," rather than the "sons of Israel," would be liberated from captivity. These and two other smaller changes appear in the Bloemhof copy and also in other manuscripts, showing that all of them were not made at Bloemhof because the other manuscripts do not descend from the Bloemhof one.[26] In addition, three more minor variants are unique to the Bloemhof copy.[27]

25. The best edition is in MGH, *Scriptores*, 23, 454–572 (at 567–568). (The MGH edition rests on the only surviving MS, which unfortunately dates from the sixteenth century.) The continuation in question is treated by Victor Le Clerc in *Histoire littéraire de la France*, 21 (Paris, 1847; repr. 1896), 67–71. This includes a text of the Tripoli prophecy (and Le Clerc's French translation thereof) that is taken from a faulty eighteenth-century edition of the Wittewierum chronicle. I have not seen Johann Gelhorn, *Die Chronik Emos und Menkos* (Danzig, 1872).

26. The Bloemhof variants—*litteris aureis, filii Ierusalem, in fine* for *in fine dierum*, and *ordines mendicorum* for *ordines mendicancium*—are all found, for example, in MS BL Royal 9 B IX, f. 2ʳ, which definitely did not descend from the Bloemhof text. Because of the extraordinarily complex manuscript traditions and the likelihood of contaminations, it has proven impossible for me to count the minimum number of intervening steps between the original revision and any given surviving copy, although I have whiled away some fine hours trying to do so.

27. They are *dominum apostolicum* for *dominum apum, ab omnibus finibus*

Aside from its numerous variants, a noteworthy fact about the Bloemhof copy of the Tripoli prophecy is that it appeared in the Bloemhof chronicle at all. Wittewierum in West Friesland was so far removed from the main communication networks of Europe that the continuation of the Bloemhof chronicle was devoted almost exclusively to local affairs. Apparently the Tripoli prophecy was one of the few items of distant news that made its way to the backwaters of Friesland. Its appearance in the Bloemhof chronicle is thus a good indication of its wide circulation.

Other tokens of wide circulation are two early copies made in Bavaria, which like Friesland lay within the borders of the medieval German Empire, but at West Friesland's farthest extreme. The less easily datable of the two transmits one of the earliest stages of the text known to survive from Germany proper. By about 1500 at the latest, this copy was housed in the monastery of Sankt Mang's near Füssen, at the foot of the Bavarian Alps, and must have been executed about two hundred years earlier not too far from there. Aside from paleographical arguments for a dating shortly after 1300, an early dating seems most probable from the context in which the copy of the prophecy appears. Specifically, since it was added by a different hand to the blank space at the end of an unrelated manuscript—the metrical *Summula pauperum* or *Summula Raymundi* (a mnemonic guide to morality written in Bavaria between 1235 and 1272)—it seems likely that it was copied around the time of the Tripoli prophecy's original circulation when a scribe was most likely to have seized on any blank space to preserve some dramatic news.[28]

---

for *ab omnibus fidelibus*, and *miracula* for *mirabilia*. The possibility cannot be excluded that the first of these errors was made by the sixteenth-century copyist of the Bloemhof continuation as a result of misreading abbreviations that may have been something like $\overline{dmm}$ $\overline{apm}$.

28. The copy, now UB Augsburg, Oettingen-Wallerstein'sche Bibliothek (formerly housed in Maihingen and Schloss Harburg), I, 2, 4°, 28, fos. 85ᵛ–86ʳ, was kindly called to my attention by Professor Dr. Peter Dinzelbacher, Augsburg. The present MS was bound around 1500 in St. Mang's, Füssen, from different component parts, the relevant one being the *Summula pauperum* with appended Tripoli prophecy running on two quires from fos. 69 to 86. Dr. Alexander Patschovsky, who generously examined the whole MS for me, reports that f. 86 was clearly once the rear flyleaf of an independent MS fascicle. (Dr. Patschovsky prefers a dating for the copy of the prophecy between ca. 1330 and

But even though this Bavarian copy was probably an early one, and indubitably was very pristine, it bears evidence that readers from the start had trouble making sense of all the text: namely, while displaying no tendentious tampering and very little stylistic "touching up," it contains one change showing that an early scribe simply could not believe that it said what it said. Whereas the original contains the incomprehensible prediction that "the bat will subjugate [*subiugabit*] the lord of the bees," an alteration first identifiable here, and repeated widely afterwards, makes this "the bat will chase away [*fugabit*] the lord of the bees." This, of course, was really no improvement insofar as it left the line just as incomprehensible as it was before, but it shows that contemporary readers were struggling to make sense where none could actually be found.

The other Bavarian copy is roughly datable because it appears in a set of annals—those of Eberhard of Regensburg covering the years from 1273 to 1305.[29] Since Eberhard, archdeacon of the Regensburg cathedral chapter, placed his transcription of the Tripoli prophecy at the end of a documentary appendix rather than in the body of his annals proper, he probably copied it in 1305, the year of his last annalistic entry. But it is uncertain whether his exemplar reached Regensburg in that year or earlier because other documents in his appendix date from 1292 and must have lain among the papers of the Regensburg cathedral chapter from their arrival until 1305 when

---

ca. 1350 on grounds that are too complicated to relate here.) I take the entire fascicle with near certainty to be originally Bavarian not just because of its earliest known occurrence in Füssen, but also because its text of the Tripoli prophecy is related to the second early Bavarian one (in the annals of Eberhard of Regensburg) and because the *Summula pauperum*, composed by the Bavarian Adam Teutonicus, circulated most widely between ca. 1272 and ca. 1350 in Bavaria: see Fernando Valls Taberner, "La 'Summula Pauperum' de Adam de Aldersbach," *Spanische Forschungen der Görresgesellschaft*, 1st ser., 7 (1938), 69–83.

29. MGH, *Scriptores*, 17, 591–605 (at 605). Its composition is analyzed by Paul Kehr, *Hermann von Altaich und seine Fortsetzer* (diss., University of Göttingen; Altenburg, 1883), 69–81. According to Kehr, 80, the last part of the annals was written no later than 1305. The only surviving MS of Eberhard's annals dates from the fifteenth century, but this does not create any difficulties because Eberhard's text of the Tripoli prophecy was recopied in the annals of Weichard of Polhaim (see directly below) and also later in the fourteenth century (see p. 88 below).

Eberhard recopied them. Since these letters pertain to the fall of Acre, it is possible that Eberhard copied out the Tripoli prophecy in the same appendix with them because he recognized a thematic connection.[30] Whatever the case, within two years after 1305, Eberhard's annals were used as a source by Weichard of Polhaim, a canon of Salzburg cathedral, who borrowed the complete Tripoli prophecy from Eberhard.[31] Weichard's only change was to enter the text in proper chronological order under the year 1286 (a mistake for 1287 inherited from Eberhard), showing that he believed a prophetic miracle had really happened in that year.

In addition to reaching the farthest extremes of the German Empire, the post-Acre Tripoli prophecy also crossed the English Channel and arrived in the Benedictine monastery of Bardney in Lincolnshire, where it was copied on the flyleaf of a previously completed manuscript before 1300.[32] As the Bardney witness shows, in this direction, as elsewhere, early scribes were inveterately intent on "improvements."[33] One of these modestly endeavored to rectify a pas-

---

30. Even if Eberhard's exemplar reached Regensburg as early as ca. 1292, it already contained several alterations testifying to earlier layers, such as the *fugabit* for *subiugabit* found also in the Füssen MS. The most evident mistake in Eberhard's copy, the provision of the year 1286 instead of 1287, may possibly have been made by Eberhard himself since it is only found elsewhere in copies definitely or possibly descending from Eberhard.

31. MGH, *Scriptores*, 9, 810–818 (at 811). Weichard's last annalistic entries were for 1307.

32. BL Royal 9 B IX, f. 2^r. See the description by George F. Warner and J. P. Gilson, *Catalogue of Western Manuscripts in the Old Royal and King's Collections (British Museum)*, I (London, 1921), 289–290. I conclude that the Tripoli prophecy in the Bardney MS was copied before 1300 because it appears before a prediction of the birth of Antichrist for 1300 which would hardly have been copied after 1300.

33. Some of these variants also appear in the Bloemhof text (see n. 26 above). Others, *ab omnibus Christi fidelibus* for *ab omnibus fidelibus*, *visitabitur* for *honorabitur*, and the omission of *secte* do not appear in the Bloemhof copy but do appear in MS Cambridge, Corpus Christi College 404, f. 100^v (on which see pp. 93–101), a copy that definitely did not descend from the Bardney MS. All these common variants and the deletion of *hominum* in *hominum mortalitas* and *congregandis* for *congregatas* are shared by the Bardney MS and the twin copies in BL Harley 485 and Bodl., Bodley 158, which also did not descend from the Bardney MS (for these copies see pp. 106–108).

sage that was inexplicable in the original—the strange reference to "congregated waters."[34] But others were obviously tendentious. Thus the deletion of the word *sect* from the prediction of the annihilation of the mendicants clearly aimed at toning down the original antifraternal animus. The Tripoli prophet hated the mendicants so much that he not only predicted their annihilation but implied that they were heretics; by omitting the word *sect*, the inventor of this change removed the latter implication. Similarly, instead of setting the vision in the cloister of the gray (Cistercian) order, the Bardney version sets it in the cloister of the black (Benedictine) order. This change could not have been intended to improve upon verisimilitude because there was no Benedictine monastery in Tripoli, just as there was no Cistercian one there. Rather, rivalry of orders was surely at work: since Bardney was a Benedictine house, either the Bardney copyist, or perhaps one before him at a sister monastery, must have decided to alter the locale of the vision in order to gain credit for his own order.

The Bardney scribe certainly attached great importance to the prophecy. It may be assumed that his exemplar was not his to keep: perhaps it was the property of a passing traveller, or perhaps it came to Bardney by means of a monastic interlibrary loan. However it reached Bardney, the copyist decided that it was too important merely to read and surrender and that it had to be preserved so that he and fellow monks could read and ponder it as they wished. So he copied it out in the most accessible blank space he could find: a flyleaf of a completely unrelated text, a thirteenth-century copy of Peter Lombard's *Sentences*. Shortly afterwards another eschatological prophecy —a mid-thirteenth-century jingle about the birth of Antichrist, revised to predict Antichrist's birth for 1300—came his way, so he copied that too. Later two other fourteenth-century hands added to the flyleaf two additional eschatological texts.[35] At Bardney the Tripoli

34. *Aquas congregatas* made as little sense to scribes as the line about the "bat" and the "lord of the bees." For other independent attempts at "correction," see the readings of the 1396 version, Villola, Peter of Aragon, the 1347 version, the French family, and the 1387 version, all in Appendix III.

35. On the jingle predicting Antichrist's birth, see above p. 21 with n. 25, and p. 32 with n. 14. The version for 1300 on the Bardney flyleaf also appears in John of Paris's *De Antichristo* (see the published version in *Expositio . . . Joachim*, f. 47ʳ). I conclude that the jingle in the Bardney MS was copied slightly

prophecy certainly had its intended effect of making readers consider the future.

Another flyleaf copy of the Tripoli prophecy was one added to a legal manuscript from the cathedral chapter of Chartres. This entire codex was burned to a char in an allied bombing raid in June 1944, but fortunately the text of the prophecy was published in the nineteenth-century catalogue of the Chartres manuscript holdings.[36] Taken together with three other copies to be treated in later chapters, the Chartres text reveals the existence of a discrete family of variants that will be referred to as the "French family" because three of the four surviving specimens were of French origin.[37] The common variants in the French family probably multiplied over the course of copying evolution. Some of them were editorial changes designed to make the prophecy read more smoothly, others were changes introduced to clarify obscure passages, and a few seemed designed to change undesired meaning. Prominent among the last class was the omission of the assurance that the papacy would "dominate" at the end of days. The French family also avoids the implication that the mendicants were sects by deleting the whole phrase that refers to "many other sects" being annihilated.

Predictably, the Chartres copy also contained some changes that were unique. The most substantive of these were the transformation

---

later than the Tripoli prophecy because it is written by the same hand but on a different slant. On the margin above the prophecy an early fourteenth-century hand copied a short eschatological statement attributed there to St. Bernard: "Ut ait beatus Bernardus: Non erit pilus in panno. . . ." (Mr. J. W. Roumen of the Kartoteek Bernard-Konkordans kindly tried to locate this passage among the genuine works of St. Bernard for me, but without success.) Below the Tripoli prophecy and the Antichrist jingle, a fourteenth-century hand added the verse prophecy *Regnum scottorum*, on which see Rupert Taylor, *The Political Prophecy in England* (New York, 1911), 72, and other MSS listed by Warner and Gilson (n. 32 above). (A hitherto unnoticed fourteenth-century copy of *Regnum scottorum* is in MS Huntington Library HM 1345, f. 46ᵛ.)

36. MS 322, described in *Catalogue générale des manuscrits des bibliothèques publiques de France: départements*, 11 (Paris, 1890), 155–156. The loss is described and listed in *Catalogue générale*, 53 (Paris, 1962), 3, 11. M. de Cozeneuve of the Chartres Bibliothèque municipale confirmed the complete destruction of MS 322 to me by letter.

37. For more details on the French family, see Appendix III.

of the "beast of the West" into the "beast of the South" and the introduction of a Greek word, *ancefala*, to replace the Latin "people without a head" (*gens que vocatur ancefala et prevalebit*). The new beast must have been some real or expected "southern" political hero, and using the Greek word was pure pretentiousness: a self-satisfied copyist could not resist showing off his own knowledge and thus made God amusingly bilingual.

Although the nineteenth-century catalogue provided the text of the Chartres copy, its dating was vague, offering only "14th century" for the entire manuscript. Yet it seems most likely that the Tripoli prophecy arrived at Chartres very early in the fourteenth century because other flyleaf copies of prophecies were customarily made in the years when the given prophecy first circulated. Certainly the prophecy was added to the flyleaf after the main text was completed because the manuscript in question was the second of two volumes of Hostiensis's commentary on the Decretals, copied straight through before the prophecy was added to the extra space. The legal text of Hostiensis had nothing to do with eschatological revelations, but someone in the Chartres cathedral chapter thought that the revelations were so important that they had to be set down in the nearest blank space to be found.

The most urgent commitment to communicating the Tripoli prophecy was shown by an early reader who translated it into a northeastern dialect of French. This person must have completed his work very shortly after the post-Acre revision because the sole surviving copy of his translation—from the Benedictine monastery of Saint Jacques at Liège—must have been made in the years immediately following the fall of Acre in 1291.[38] This can be concluded from the facts that the main text of the manuscript is the *Excidium Aconis*, a Latin narrative of the fall of Acre, and that the translation of the Tripoli prophecy immediately follows, with the altered date of 1291 given for the miracle of the moving hand. Clearly the narrative and the prophecy were copied together under the immediate impress of

38. The MS is described by J. Van den Gheyn, *Catalogue des manuscrits de la Bibliothèque Royale de Belgique* (Brussels, 1901–1948), XI, 298, and the text is edited by Van den Gheyn, "Note sur un manuscrit de l'*Excidium Aconis*, en 1291," *Revue de l'Orient Latin*, 6 (1898), 550–556. (I reprint it in Appendix III.)

Acre's fall and the miracle redated to make it seem particularly focused on the loss of Acre. An unforeseen result, however, was to have
the moving hand "predicting" the loss of Tripoli for 1291, although
this event actually transpired in 1289.

The French translation was definitely made from a Latin text
not identical to any of the extant ones. The Latin words that lay
behind the existing French cannot always be determined, but certainly
the translation must have taken the bat's *chasing* (instead of subjugat-
ing) and the ship's tossing in *great* waves (instead of manifold waves)
from an ancestor common to both it and the early German texts.
Nonetheless, the translation bears other signs which show that it did
not descend from any single known extant copy, such as the appearance of a strange "god of his powers" (*le dieu de se oes*) in place of
the "lord of the bees," which must have arisen from an earlier Latin
corruption of *dominum opum* for *dominum apum*. Discounting any
such variants for which the translator was not responsible, he took
few, if any, conscious liberties of his own. His knowledge of Latin,
however, seems to have been somewhat shaky because in three places
he confused singulars and plurals of nouns.[39]

The most remarkable fact about the French translation of the
Tripoli prophecy is its very existence, for it was unusual for Latin
eschatological prophecies to be translated into the vernacular as early
as the late thirteenth century. So far as can be told in the current absence of a thorough study, the only vernacular translations of Latin
prophecies that may have predated this one were two different French
translations of the Tiburtine Sibyl, but since these were made in verse
they arose at least in part from literary motives.[40] The translator of
the Tripoli prophecy had no poetic intentions whatsoever. His sole
aim was to make the portentous message of the moving hand accessi-

---

39. Viz.: *li autre dieu* for *alter deus*, *les bestes doccident* for *bestia occidentalis*,
and *sens testes* for *sine capite*. I am greatly endebted to Professor William D.
Paden for lending his expertise in helping me to study this text.

40. See the twelfth-century Anglo-Norman translation of the Tiburtine Sibyl,
ed. Hugh Shields, *Le Livre de Sibile by Philippe de Thaon*, Anglo-Norman Text
Society, no. 37 (London, 1979). I am not aware whether students of Old-French
literature have yet taken cognizance of the translation of the Tiburtina in BN
franç. 375, fos. 27ʳ–28ʳ, a copy which appears to date from the later thirteenth
century.

ble to as wide an audience as possible, in other words to the literate laity who could not read Latin and perhaps also to the laity who could not read at all but might listen. But he was clearly ahead of his time, for his translation was not widely recopied. Only in the fifteenth century, when lay literacy was more widespread, would the laity begin to circulate vernacular eschatological prophecies among themselves in the way that the clergy had done before them.[41]

Short of widespread vernacular circulation, the success of the Tripoli prophecy in its first few years was unqualified. All told, the surviving versions attest to the penetration of the text into many different parts of northern Europe and the proliferation of numerous copies. Part of this success must have stemmed from the prophecy's accurate "prediction" of the fall of the Holy Land: if even John of Paris believed that the beginning of the prophecy had been confirmed by events, surely many others believed the same thing. As long as it seemed clear that the prophecy's opening was truly prophetic, readers must have concluded that the rest of the events it predicted were bound to follow. Unquestionably many of the prophecy's succeeding lines were obscure, but the obscurities merited puzzling over and the main course of future events—a series of trials, the reconquest of the Holy Land, and the coming of Antichrist—were sufficiently clear. The last words of the prophecy told readers to be "vigilant," and untold numbers were at least vigilant enough in response to recopy the moving hand's predictions, reconceive some of them, and pass them on.

41. One test of when vernacular eschatological prophecies really became abundant is to see when there were enough of them to comprise the bulk of material in large prophetic anthologies. The earliest large vernacular prophetic anthologies that I know of were compiled in the 1460s: namely, BN Allemand 129 and UB Munich 2° 684.

Chapter V

TRUTH, THE DAUGHTER OF TIME: FOURTEENTH- AND FIFTEENTH-CENTURY COPIES OF THE TRIPOLI PROPHECY

The major difference in the fortunes of the original Cistercian vision and the Tripoli prophecy is that the former sunk into virtual oblivion after its first rapid circulation whereas the latter retained its popularity with its increasing age. Five of the seven surviving copies of the Cistercian vision date from its first years of life, but the majority of the surviving copies of the Tripoli prophecy were made after its first decade or two of circulation. This tenacious hold the text exerted on late-medieval imaginations hardly seems credible. An old miracle story should no longer have been regarded as "news," and the passage of time should have shown that events were not transpiring as the miraculous message predicted. By any critical consideration, "one god and one faith" had not come fifteen years after 1287, and no reliable news had yet been heard of Antichrist. Why then was the prophecy incessantly copied long after it was written?

In attempting to answer this difficult question, we might first divide the surviving manuscripts in which later copies of the Tripoli prophecy appear into four classes. Some of the relevant manuscripts are historical compilations, others prophetic anthologies, one a scientific treatise, and the remainder manuscripts in which the prophecy appears without any immediately apparent relationship to the rest of the manuscript's context. The writers who produced these different classes of copies had different motives for their decision to copy out the old message of the moving hand, but we will also see that they shared some basic reactions to it.

For three historians, the miracle in Tripoli was no longer "news," but it nonetheless belonged in their compilations because it was a noteworthy event from the past. The earliest of the three was Gilles Li Muisis, abbot of the Benedictine monastery of Saint Martin's of Tournai, who began his historiographical work in 1347 at the advanced age of seventy-five.[1] Because cataracts were making him blind and hindering him from the performance of active duties, he decided to pass his time as usefully as possible by dictating his memoirs to an assistant. Although most of Gilles's work consists of personal recollections, he felt bound not only to record his memoirs but also to write a full-scale history that included events from the distant past. Accordingly, one section of his history, composed between 1347 and 1349, is made up of short entries running from the deeds of Abraham to events of 1294. No doubt in helping prepare this section Gilles's aide was occupied more as a research assistant than as an amanuensis.

Within this purely annalistic part of Gilles Li Muisis's work, an entry pertaining to the Tripoli prophecy runs as follows: "In the year 1288 [*sic*] a Cistercian monk saying mass saw a hand writing on the corporal cloth in golden letters. Among other things it wrote that Tripoli would soon be captured and also that Acre would be captured afterwards."[2] It can be seen immediately that much of the language

1. On him and his work, see Albert D'Haenens, "Gilles Li Muisis, historien," *Revue Bénédictine*, 69 (1959), 258–286, and D'Haenens, "Gilles Li Muisis," *Biographie Nationale . . . de Belgique*, 32, supp. 4 (Brussels, 1964), 528–540.

2. From Li Muisis, *Tractatus tertius, pars prima*, in J.-J. de Smet, ed., *Corpus chronicorum Flandriae* (Brussels, 1841), II, 151. For the Latin, see Appendix III.

of this abbreviated version is identical to that of other written transmissions. The nearest relative of Gilles's report is the copy of the Tripoli prophecy in the Bloemhof chronicle made around 1296: both copies provide the detail that the hand wrote in golden letters, and both are unique in predicting that Tripoli will be captured (all other copies have it being destroyed).[3] In all likelihood, around the time that one early copy of the Tripoli prophecy arrived at Bloemhof, another came to Saint Martin's of Tournai and remained there until it was drawn upon by abbot Gilles in the middle of the fourteenth century.

The one obvious difference between Gilles Li Muisis's copy and the others is that Gilles's report breaks off after the prediction of events that were already known to have happened. This was a way of commenting implicitly on how well the message had already proven accurate. Gilles seems to have agreed with John of Paris in judging that the rest of the prophecy was too obscure to be readily comprehensible; certainly he could not have thought that it had been disproven by events because he then would have rejected the whole account. For his purposes as a chronicler the abbreviation sufficed, whereas the whole text might have confused his readers. For Gilles, the miracle of the moving hand was an edifying event worthy of record, and the fact that the opening had proven true was confirmation of its divine origin.

What Li Muisis left implicit, a second historian who alluded to the Tripoli prophecy made explicit. This writer was the north German schoolmaster, Dietrich Engelhus, who compiled a world chronicle for school use while teaching in Göttingen and its vicinity in the

---

The more modern edition of Li Muisis's *Tractatus tertius* by H. Lemaître, *Chronique et Annales de Gilles Li Muisis* (Paris, 1906), omits the *pars prima* because it is not an original historical source. The original MS in which this text is found—now Courtrai, Bibliothèque publique MS 135—is a contemporary fourteenth-century copy from St. Martin's.

3. On the Bloemhof text, see above pp. 75–76. The date of 1288 given by Gilles probably resulted from simple paleographical error in the process of transmission. The same mistaken date appears in the copy made by Henry of Kirkestede treated later in this chapter, and, taken with another variant—the use of the word *Cistercian* instead of *gray order*—shows that Henry's exemplar came from a family that bore some relations to Gilles's.

1420s.[4] Engelhus organized his chronicle by the reigns of popes and emperors and entered his report of the miracle in Tripoli as the first item under the pontificate of Honorius IV—that is, for the period from April 1285 to April 1287. According to him:

> At that time a certain monk in Tripoli, celebrating in the presence of his abbot, saw a hand writing bodily these words: "The high Cedar of Lebanon will be felled. Tripoli will be destroyed, Acre captured. Mars will overcome Saturn, Saturn will waylay Jupiter. The bat will drive away the god of the bees. Woe then to the clergy, and to the land of Christianity! Therefore be vigilant.

Had Engelhus stopped there his report would have been quite similar to that of Li Muisis, but immediately thereupon he proceeded to state that "not long afterwards, in 1289, Tripoli was captured, and Acre, the most renowned city then held by the Christians, was destroyed by the Sultan . . . and 30,000 Christians there were killed."[5] Obviously, then, for him the first part of the message was fully borne out by the subsequent events. Whether he had any notion of what the "bat driving away the god of the bees" was supposed to mean is impossible to say, though it may be he thought the prediction applied in some way to the last event he reported in sequence under Honorius IV's pontificate, a Mongol victory in Hungary during the reign of Ladislaus IV (1272–1290) that purportedly cost 80,000 Christian lives. In any event, it seems sufficiently clear that Engelhus

---

4. See on him the entry in *Die deutsche Literatur des Mittelalters: Verfasserlexikon*, 2d ed., II (Berlin, 1980), 556–557, which cites further literature. The only full edition of Engelhus's chronicle is the antiquated one by G. W. Leibniz, *Scriptores rerum Brunsvicensium*, II (Hannover, 1710), 977–1143, where the prophecy appears at 1121. Being unable to go back to the several different MS versions of Engelhus, I reproduce in Appendix III Leibniz's edition. No careful work has yet been done on Engelhus's sources and it remains possible that his knowledge of the Tripoli prophecy came from some as yet unidentified chronicle intermediary. Whatever the case, his truncated text is most closely related to what I have designated as the German family.

5. Leibniz, 1121: "Non diu igitur posthaec, anno Domini 1289, Tripolis capta est: et Accaron, civitas famosissima tunc Christianorum, destructa est a Soldano, Elfe nominato, et occisi sunt ibidem Christiani XXXM. utriusque sexus. Tartari etiam in Ungaria interfecerunt LXXX millia Christianorum, tempore Ladislai filii Stephani, Regis Ungariae, multis in captivitatem abductis."

omitted reporting the bulk of the Tripoli prophecy for the same reason Li Muisis did, a disinclination to distract from the true miracle of a heavenly message predicting the Holy Land's fall.

There was, however, at least one historian who thought that the entire prophetic text was worthy of record, namely an anonymous Benedictine of Sankt Emmeram's, Regensburg, who compiled a set of annals, mostly about local affairs, having the terminal date of 1388.[6] The Benedictine's source for his copy of the Tripoli prophecy was unquestionably the earlier annals of Eberhard of Regensburg, written in the same locality, for his copy is identical to Eberhard's text (aside from negligible copying alterations) and another of his entries is also taken from Eberhard.[7] Eberhard's annals, however, were just one source the anonymous monk used. The fact that he fastened on the miracle at Tripoli and chose to copy out the entire prophetic message even though his primary concern was Bavarian history shows that the miracle and the complete message as well appeared to him to be of major importance.

A formula that unites all three historiographical inclusions of the Tripoli prophecy is what William J. Brandt calls the "principle of interest."[8] All three chroniclers believed in the historicity of the miracle in Tripoli and all included reports of it because it was sufficiently "interesting," that is, because it illustrated the awesome, miraculous ways of God. They differed only in their emphases. Li Muisis and Engelhus wanted to call attention to the prophetic miracle, so they truncated the text of the prophecy in order to focus on how it had already proven true; the anonymous monk, on the other hand,

6. The compilation is found in MS Clm 14594 (late 14th century—prov. St. Emmeram's), fos. 51ʳ–81ᵛ. It was very poorly edited in the eighteenth century as "Anonymi Monachi Bavari compilatio chronologica rerum Boicarum" by Andreas Felix Oefele, *Rerum Boicarum scriptores* (Augsburg, 1763), II, 332–344. Oefele used a copy made by the early seventeenth-century antiquarian C. Gewold from the St. Emmeram MS—see on this Martin Mayr, "Wiener Handschriften zur bayerischen Geschichte," NA, 5 (1880), 119–148 (at 133).

7. For the Latin of the anonymous monk's text from Clm 14594, f. 78ʳ, see Appendix III. The only variants from Eberhard of Regensburg's text are minor orthographical ones and the omission of an *et*. The other match between Clm 14594 and Eberhard is an entry for 1277 (in Clm 14594, f. 76ʳ).

8. William J. Brandt, *The Shape of Medieval History, Studies in Modes of Perception* (New Haven, Conn., 1966), 47.

thought that the entire text of the prophecy was as important for his readers to have as an account of the miracle that produced it, so he copied it all. Although the unproven parts of the prophecy should have raised problems, none of the three alluded to any such thing, no doubt because the proven miracle was all they needed to inspire their faith.

The same "principle of interest" can be invoked to explain the frequent presence of the Tripoli prophecy in a neglected medieval genre, the prophetic anthology. Dozens of late-medieval manuscripts were devoted wholly or largely to the assemblage of assorted prophetic texts. Such anthologies bore similarities to annalistic compilations insofar as both were collections of noteworthy entries, often gathered from diverse sources. Both also served to edify their readers about God's works and plans. For the medieval reader, history and prophecy helped equally to interpret current events because the present was part of a plan that included past and future. The genres of historical and prophetic anthology overlapped at just the point represented by the Tripoli prophecy: the narrative of the miracle joined with the message could appear in a history mainly because it told of a past miracle, or it could appear in a prophetic anthology because it contained a prophecy.

The close relationship between historical compilation and prophetic anthology is further illustrated by the fact that some medieval chronicles were in part little more than collections of prophecies. An example is the vernacular Bolognese chronicle of Pietro da Villola, a parchment maker and stationer of Bologna who compiled a history of his own time in the middle of the fourteenth century.[9] Instead of beginning his history with chronologically arranged entries, Villola opened his work with a number of prophecies. Although he presented these without comment, it can be assumed that he copied them because they satisfied the same instincts that led him to write history, namely, the desire to report novelties and manifestations of the divine will.

9. See Albano Sorbelli, *Le Croniche Bolognesi del secolo XIV* (Bologna, 1900), 61–80, and Roberto Rusconi, *L'Attesa della fine* (Rome, 1979), 139. Pietro's work, which he began in 1342, was continued by his son, Floriano, in 1362. Other late-medieval chronicles that open with texts of prophecies are those of Jean de Venette and Pietro di Mattiolo of Bologna.

Presumably he thought his readers would be as much edified by his prophetic anthology as by the main historical compilation that followed.

The first prophetic text Villola chose for presentation was none other than the Tripoli prophecy, minus the introductory account of the moving hand.[10] Villola surely did not delete the introductory story himself because he presented introductory attributions for other prophecies he included. Assuming that he knew nothing about the miracle story, he could not have known that it was supposedly revealed to a monk in 1287. Nonetheless, he should have recognized that it was more than a half-century old because it "predicted" the fall of Tripoli and Acre. Hence, had he read the text with a critical spirit, he should have had some doubts about the rest of it. But Villola was a gatherer rather than a critic: not only did he place the Tripoli prophecy at the head of his collection without expressing any reservations, but he also included a prophecy about popes that was far more obviously discredited by the course of events.[11] No doubt he believed that the prophecies he found and presented were all divinely inspired, despite whatever difficulties of interpretation they may have presented on a literal reading.

Another northern Italian prophetic anthology that included the

10. A. Sorbelli, ed., *Corpus Chronicorum Bononiensium* (*Rerum Italicarum Scriptores*, XVIII, pt. 1; Città di Castello, 1905), 4–5, from MS Bologna, Biblioteca Universitaria 1456. I reprint this in Appendix III. Villola's copy is related to the German family, but contains numerous variants that were made either in the course of transmission or by Villola himself. Most of these were the results of crude copying errors, but at least two seem to have been conscious alterations in places where scribes were prone to try "improvements" on the received text. One is the omission of the word *bees* to yield "the bat will chase away the lord"; the other tendentiously changed "the mendicant orders and many other sects will be annihilated" to "the mendicant order and others will be annulled."

11. Sorbelli, *Corpus chronicorum Bononiensium*, 16: "Post Celestinum regnabit papa superbus, post superbum katolicus, post katollicum hereticus, post hereticum nullus." This prediction of the demise of the papacy three pontificates after Celestine IV (1241) or Celestine V (1294) was proven wrong at the latest after the death of John XXII in 1334. On this prophecy, see Leone Tondelli, "Profezia Gioachimita del secolo XIII delle regioni venete," *Romana deputazione di storia patria per l'Emilia e la Romagna, sezione di Modena, studi e documenti*, 4 (1940), 3–9, who identifies the Celestine as Celestine IV. Another, hitherto unnoticed, version is in MS BL Cotton Cleopatra C x, f. 158r.

Tripoli prophecy was compiled a century later, specifically around 1470, almost certainly by someone in the service of Margrave Lodovico Gonzaga of Mantua.[12] This collection is noteworthy for its equation of prophecy with science. It contains a large number of prophecies, such as those of the Erythrean and Tiburtine Sibyls, John of Rupescissa, the pseudonymous "Telesphorus," and "the response of a demon to questions posed to him in Greece during the time of Pope Eugenius IV by a certain magician who held him captive."[13]

12. BN lat. 16021, briefly referred to by Emil Donckel, "Studien über die Prophezeiung des Fr. Telesforus von Cosenza, O.F.M. (1365–1386)," *Archivum Franciscanum historicum*, 26 (1933), 29–104, 282–314 (at 38) and Bignami-Odier, *Rupescissa*, 252, but never adequately studied or described. Northern Italian provenance is beyond doubt. The watermark on fos. 13 and 70, an arbalest within a circle, is similar to Briquet 739, 744–745, 747 (Venice and Treviso, late 15th and early 16th centuries) and is probably from a Venetian papermill. (There are other, more unusual, watermarks in the MS that I was unable to identify.) An inscription on the top of f. 1ʳ—*Ill(ustrissi)mi Domini march. Mantue*—is in a hand of about 1500 and could not have been written later than 1530 when the margraves of Mantua were raised to the rank of dukes. The MS almost certainly was copied in Mantua under the direction of someone associated with the Gonzaga court because, in addition to the inscription, the MS includes (fos. 10ᵛ–11ᵛ) a letter on Halley's comet by the astronomer Antonius de Camera, dated 21 June 1456, addressed to Margrave Lodovico Gonzaga, and not known in any other copy (on Antonius, see Thorndike, IV, 438). The compiler must have ordered the recopying of a text that was already in the Gonzaga collection. My dating of ca. 1470 comes from internal textual evidence. The latest texts in the MS are a prophecy for 1465 (f. 37ʳ⁻ᵛ), and an epitome of John of Rupescissa's *Vade mecum* predicting disasters for the 1470s (fos. 5ᵛ–6ʳ). Above all, f. 32ᵛ: "Sequita una prophetia che al mondo canta come nelli anni del sesanta," indicates that the 1460s had recently passed. I am extremely grateful to Mlle Marie-Thérèse d'Alverny for helping me appraise this MS.

13. Erythrean Sibyl, fos. 1ʳ–4ᵛ; Tiburtine Sibyl, fos. 15ᵛ–18ᵛ; Rupescissa, fos. 5ᵛ–6ʳ (as Bignami-Odier, *Rupescissa*, 252) and 37ᵛ (an extract from the *Vade mecum—Intentio XV* concerning Italy—overlooked by Bignami-Odier, perhaps because it is falsely identified as having been written by a Carthusian in 1459); Telesphorus, fos. 38ʳ–55ʳ (as Donckel, "Telesforus," 38. But note the additional presence in this MS of Rusticianus's letter concerning Telesphorus [fos. 6ʳ–7ᵛ] overlooked by Donckel. This copy should be of importance for future studies of Rusticianus; its separate presence here may also be another confirmation of Mantuan origins for the MS because Rusticianus was a member of the Dominican convent of Mantua in 1439: see R. Creytens, "Les 'Consilia' de S. Antonin de Florence, O.P.," *Archivum Fratrum Praedicatorum*, 37 [1967], 263–342 [at 284–290]); "Responsio demonis ad interrogacionem sibi factam in partibus Grecie ibi detenti ab quodam nigromante . . . tempore quo vivebat Eugenius quartus

But it also includes treatments of the appearance of Halley's comet in 1456 and an earthquake that shook the kingdom of Naples in December of the same year.[14] Quite clearly the director of the compilation (several hands did the actual copying) considered as grist for his mill all natural and supernatural portents he thought could tell him in any way about the condition and future of Italy.

Within this mélange appears a badly corrupted copy of the Tripoli prophecy in its original, pre-Acre form. Quite oddly it is introduced as a "Prophecy of Abbot Joachim," an ascription that makes no sense at all because the text immediately goes on to refer to a vision experienced by a Cistercian monk in 1287.[15] Whoever selected the text for inclusion, however, like Pietro da Villola, was less a critic than a packrat. Whatever Joachim may have had to do with the Cistercian monk did not concern him, nor does his manuscript explain how a prophecy of 1287 related to affairs in Italy in the late fifteenth century. All he wished was to compile texts that might have helped explain the present and future, and the Tripoli prophecy struck him as being as valid for inclusion in his anthology as were numerous other similar prophetic texts.

Three other relevant late-medieval prophetic anthologies were all copied on the island of Britain, where "Cedars of Lebanon," despite the climate, always seem to have flourished. One, a Welsh anthology of the mid-fifteenth century, reveals practically nothing about why the prophecy was copied so long after its initial circulation: all that can be said is that the anonymous anthologist expressed no doubts about its veracity.[16] But the other two allow us to look further into the mentalities and motives of their compilers.

...," incipit: "Veniet draco contra grecorum imperium." This is not yet an exhaustive listing of all the prophecies in the collection, some of which are in Italian verse and several of which remain to be identified.

14. Fos. 9ʳ–13ᵛ. On both comet and earthquake, see Thorndike, IV, 413–417. The first text in the group, incipit: *Stelle cum caudis secundum Ptolomeum* . . . , is by Pietro Bono Avogaro, an astrologer of Ferrara: see Thorndike IV, 464, who knew the work but thought it lost. Thorndike otherwise does not refer to any of the texts in the group.

15. F. 19ʳ–ᵛ: "Prophetia Abbatis Ioachim. Anno 1287 quidam monachus ordinis grisorum dixit missam. . . ." For the full text, see Appendix II.

16. MS Aberystwyth Peniarth 50, pp. 245–246. The MS is described by J.

The first anthology was put together in the abbey of Bury Saint Edmunds by the fourteenth-century monk, Henry of Kirkestede, who wrote his name at the head of the table of contents.[17] Recent research has shown that Henry of Kirkestede was an administrator at Bury and an expert librarian and bibliographer.[18] Ordained in 1338, he was a monk at Bury by 1346 and was made subprior before 1361. He also served as master of novices and, for most of his monastic career, as chief librarian of Bury. In the last capacity he became an avid bibliographer, devising a system of classmarks for all of Bury's books, and travelling to other monastic libraries to examine their holdings. The fruit of his labors was a large "medieval bio-bibliographic union catalogue," which listed authors, titles, and libraries where the works in question could be found. The date of Henry's death is uncertain, but it definitely came after 1378, probably after 1381.[19]

Gwenogvryn Evans, *Report on Manuscripts in the Welsh Language* (London, 1898–1910), I, pt. 2, 389–399, and V. J. Scattergood, *Politics and Poetry in the Fifteenth Century* (London, 1971), 392. It is composed of many different prophetic pieces written by at least three different hands of the second and third quarters of the fifteenth century, perhaps working in the Cistercian cloister of Neath. A photographic reproduction of pp. 4–7 (a different hand from that which copied the Tripoli prophecy) is in Reinhard Haferkorn, *When Rome is Removed into England: Eine politische Prophezeiung des 14. Jahrhunderts* (Leipzig, 1932), plate II. I have not examined the whole MS and cannot say how much of it was copied in the hand that copied the Tripoli prophecy. The copy of the prophecy gives a wrong date for the miracle, 1277 instead of 1287, and contains numerous other errors, omissions, and major alterations in the order of the predictions. Only one change introduces intelligible new sense: "Unus deus erit et una fides et dii gencium evanescent." For the full text, see Appendix III.

17. MS Cambridge, Corpus Christi College 404, described in Montague R. James, *A Descriptive Catalogue of the Manuscripts in the Library of Corpus Christi College, Cambridge* (Cambridge, 1912), II, 269–277, and Reeves, *Influence of Prophecy*, 539. I have not seen the MS myself but have studied a complete photocopy.

18. Except where noted, everything that follows on Henry's career and bibliographical work derives from the extraordinary study by Richard H. Rouse, "Bostonus Buriensis and the Author of the *Catalogus Scriptorum Ecclesiae*," *Speculum*, 41 (1966), 471–499. Rouse reproduces Henry's table of contents for his prophetic anthology, plate I.

19. The quotation is from Rouse, 472. Rouse, 494, points to the recording in Henry's hand of Pope Gregory XI's death in 1378 in the Cambridge MS, f. 94[v]. A passage in a prophecy copied by Henry on f. 97[v] in his late hand appears to

Henry's prophetic anthology was just as much a monument of erudition and energy as his library catalogue. Henry worked on compiling his collection for most of his active career: from the early 1350s until shortly before his death.[20] Throughout this time he was on the lookout for whatever worthy prophetic texts he could find, gathering those that made their way to Bury and searching out others on his bibliographic travels to other monastic libraries in East Anglia.[21] Most often he did the work of recopying from his exemplars himself, but apparently when he was too busy he had another monk from Bury help him, and once when he acquired an old copy of a prophecy (by hook or by crook?) he simply bound it into his manuscript as he found it.[22] In addition to looking for new texts, he had his eye out for

allude *ex eventu* to the English Peasants' Revolt of 1381, viz.: "Et significat rebellionem et inobedienciam rusticorum et serviencium contra dominos suos."

20. Marjorie E. Reeves, "Some Popular Prophecies from the Fourteenth to the Seventeenth Centuries," *Studies in Church History,* 8 (1971), 107–134, appears to be correct in assuming that Henry copied the pope prophecies found on f. 41ʳ during the pontificate of Clement VI (1342–1352) because he names Clement but no succeeding popes (see further n. 28 below). He certainly copied a letter of John of Rupescissa's, f. 103ʳ⁻ᵛ, after 1356 because that was when the prophecy was first written. The entry pertaining to Urban VI described below had to have been written after that pope's accession in 1378.

21. A note in his hand added between fos. 6 and 7 indicates that he found Adso's treatise on Antichrist in Babwell, a Franciscan convent outside Bury. Further notes indicate that he found a passage about Joachim of Fiore from the chronicle of Ralph of Coggeshall in MSS from the Cistercian monasteries of Sibton (Suffolk) and Coggeshall (Essex) (f. 66ᵛ—see further n. 27 below), and a text concerning "rumors" about Antichrist in the Dominican convent of Norwich (f. 102ʳ⁻ᵛ): see my edition of the last text in the *American Historical Review,* 86 (1981), 552.

22. Evidence of another monk's help is in a copy of the *Pentacron*—Gebeno of Eberbach's anthology of the prophecies of Hildegard of Bingen—which appears in the second through fourth quires of the anthology (fos. 9ʳ–38ᵛ). The second quire is in Henry's hand, but the third and almost all of the fourth are in another. Since the text of the third quire links with the end of the second, it may be assumed that its copyist was another monk of Bury, working under Henry's supervision. A bound-in copy is on f. 39, an extra leaf containing the vision of "John the Hermit," written in a hand of "earlier type" (James, 273), that appears nowhere else in the MS. The vision in question is edited by Livarius Oliger, "Ein pseudoprophetischer Text aus Spanien über die Heiligen Franziskus und Dominikus," *Kirchengeschichtliche Studien P. Michael Bihl, O.F.M. als Ehrengabe dargeboten* (Colmar, 1941), 13–28, without knowledge of this

more complete versions of the ones he had already copied; for example, after copying the *Oracle of Cyril* from an exemplar that lacked a prologue, Henry found the prologue somewhere else and inserted a copy of it in the proper place, where sufficient blank space had fortunately been left.[23] Altogether Henry's persistent efforts resulted in the compilation of a remarkably rich collection: his manuscript contains the only known English examples of several texts.[24]

Henry did not just gather for gathering's sake but studied the materials he collected very closely, as can be seen from his own notes. Once, after copying a prophecy of the imminent coming of Antichrist and the end of the world, he wrote that this judgment agreed with that of Saint Methodius "in large part" but not with the views

---

copy. In addition to the hand that copied this vision and the hand of the third and fourth quires mentioned above, two other hands in the Bury MS are not Henry's. One executed a set of illustrated pope prophecies in the tenth quire (fos. 88^r–95^v): this could either have been acquired and bound in or done at Bury—the fact that it called for an accomplished artist may explain why Henry did not do it himself. The other is a hand that copied prophecies at the end of the MS (fos. 104^r–107^r). This was most likely the hand of a Bury scribe who worked when Henry was too infirm to write or shortly after Henry's death.

23. The prologue of "Gilbertus Anglicus" to the *Oraculum Cyrilli* appears in Henry's hand on f. 67^v, where there had been blank space at the end of the seventh quire of the MS. The main text of the *Oraculum*—also in Henry's hand, but from a different period—follows, filling up the eighth and ninth quires. It can be seen from Maier (see list of abbreviations), 55, and Konrad Burdach and Paul Piur, *Vom Mittelalter zur Reformation: II. Briefwechsel des Cola di Rienzo* (Berlin, 1912–1929), IV, 229, that some MSS of the *Oraculum Cyrilli* circulated in the Middle Ages that lacked the prologue of "Gilbertus"; Henry must have copied from one of these before he found another that contained the prologue. A similar addition in Henry's anthology is an introduction to the tract *De semine scripturarum* on f. 43^v, in space at the end of the fifth quire, coming before Henry's copy of the tract itself, which begins with the sixth quire.

24. Only surviving examples (known to me): *Quibus dies iudicii* (f. 7^r), edited by James, 270–271; the short texts *Exeunt equi nigri* and *Ioachim abbas in concordanciis suis* (f. 38^v); the introduction to *De semine scripturarum*, incipit: *Semen cecidit* (f. 43^r); *De Antichristo et fine mundi*, incipit: *Pro adventu Antichristi* (f. 65^{r-v}); the prophecy on the solar eclipse of 1371 (f. 97^v); the prophecy on kings of England, incipit: *Aquila Neustrie* (fos. 98^r–99^r); and "rumors," as above n. 21. The copy of the vision of "John the Hermit" is the only known English one, as is the *Visio fratris Johannis* (fos. 100^v–102^r), edited, without knowledge of this copy, by Donckel, "Visio."

expressed in the treatise *De semine scripturarum.*[25] In a subsequent note he added that the judgment also diverged from the views of the chronicler Henry of Huntingdon and then copied out the pertinent passage from that writer.[26] Still later, however, he found a chronicle passage concerning the views of Joachim of Fiore on the coming of Antichrist and added that passage as well. Since the last text spoke of the imminence of Antichrist's appearance, it seems clear that Henry was considering the problem extremely seriously and weighing all his authorities in the balance.[27]

By the time of the outbreak of the Great Schism, at the latest, Henry decided that Antichrist would indeed be coming soon and that earthly history was approaching its end. Being a close student of the prophecies in his collection, he saw that one group of them, a set of prophecies about popes, predicted that the fourth pope after Clement VI (1342–1352) would be the last pope of all—a terrible, cruel beast who would pull down the stars like the apocalyptic dragon (Rev. 12:4) and consume everything in his wake.[28] This prophecy was writ-

25. F. 65ᵛ. The text of this comment is given by James, 274. (Like other fourteenth-century Englishmen, Henry called the treatise *De seminibus litterarum* and falsely attributed it to Joachim of Fiore.)

26. Fos. 65ᵛ–66ʳ. Henry of Kirkestede was not the only fourteenth-century Englishman to cite Henry of Huntingdon's chronological reckonings: see also the reference to them by Henry of Harclay cited by Pelster, 49, 70. Apparently the two Henry's came across the passage independently.

27. F. 66ʳ⁻ᵛ. The passage copied by Henry from Ralph of Coggeshall is printed in Ralph of Coggeshall, *Chronicon Anglicanum*, ed. J. Stevenson (RS 66; London, 1875), 67–70. Since Henry reports that he used a MS from Coggeshall (as well as one from Sibton) his copy ought to be taken account of by future students of Ralph's work. It does, however, contain noteworthy omissions: it lacks mention of Joachim by name—probably because Henry, who mistakenly thought that Joachim was the author of *De semine scripturarum* had just attributed to him different views—and it omits the passage, *Chronicum Anglicanum*, ed. Stevenson, 68–69, wherein Joachim says that Antichrist was already born and that Innocent III would have no successor, perhaps because it was too obviously mistaken. Ralph of Coggeshall's account is treated by Reeves, *Influence of Prophecy*, 12–14, without knowledge of this copy: Henry's copy is important because it provides further evidence that the interview between Joachim and Adam of Perseigny took place according to Ralph of Coggeshall in 1195, a datum disputed by Reeves.

28. F. 41ʳ. If it is true, as Reeves and I believe (see n. 20 above) that Henry

ten well before 1378, and Henry certainly copied it before then, probably as early as the reign of Clement VI himself. But after 1378 he realized that the fourth pope after Clement VI was Urban VI, who had provoked the Schism, and that the prophecy of Urban VI as the last pope and a terrible beast seemed terribly fitting.[29] Accordingly, he related that prediction to another group of pope prophecies in his anthology, a set of fourteen illustrated texts pertaining to fourteen popes beginning with Nicholas III. At the top of each of these he added the name of the appropriate pope, thereby coming to the last, Gregory XI, whose death in 1378 he reported with his own hand. Then, on the next page (which had been blank), he wrote the name Urban VI in a hand that shows the quaver of age, and drew in (or had someone draw in for him) a picture of a bizarre black beast, a beaver-like animal with paws in front and webbed feet behind.[30]

Urban VI was Henry's *bête noire* for several reasons. Not only was it predicted that Urban would be a terrible beast, and not only did Urban provoke the Schism, but he was also responsible for a great

---

copied these prophecies before Clement VI's death (1352), that would provide a new *terminus ante quem* for their composition. Hitherto the earliest known reference to them was by Rupescissa in 1356, see Reeves, "Some Popular Prophecies" (n. 20 above), 118. At first Henry probably intended to copy all fifteen pope prophecies from this series because the five last ones appear on f. 41[r], but there is exactly enough room on the blank f. 40[r-v] (the beginning of the fifth quire) for the first ten.

29. The explicit identification of the cruel beast as Urban VI at the end of this group of pope prophecies is made in MSS UB Basel A V 39, f. 138[v], and UB Basel A VI 6, f. 18[va].

30. F. 95[r]. James, 276, calls this "a very good picture of a beaver," but I am unaware that beavers have webbed feet. Reeves, "Some Popular Prophecies" (see n. 20), 120, is mistaken in writing that the animal, which she calls "a mixture of a bear and a beaver, . . . must be a corrupt version of the horned animal over which the last pope should be holding his mitre": the illustration of the "last pope" holding a mitre already closes the group as Henry found it on f. 94[v]. Up until Henry's addition of Urban VI as the terrible beast, the Bury MS (fos. 88[r]–94[v]) contains prophecies for fourteen (instead of the usual fifteen) popes, herein running parallel to the set in the Bodl., Douce MS described by Reeves, "Some Popular Prophecies," 132–133 (the MS is Douce 88, not 58 as reported by Reeves). The Douce MS definitely antedates the Bury one, and was intended to be a set of fourteen and no more; for information on it I am most grateful to Miss Albinia de la Mare.

upheaval within the monastery of Bury.[31] Ever since 1302, abbatial vacancies had been filled by the election of the monks, but in 1379, when delegates from Bury arrived in Rome to seek confirmation of their most recent election, they found that Urban VI had already named a new abbot. Bitter controversies between the abbey and the pope and within the abbey itself ensued until 1383. To make matters worse, in 1381 some peasants during the great peasant revolt ransacked Bury and beheaded the prior (in lieu of an abbot) as well as a monk charged with collecting manorial dues.[32] Most likely Henry was still alive then; if so, he must have become more certain than ever that Last Things were at hand.

In all probability, Henry made his copy of the Tripoli prophecy before the outbreak of the Schism, but even then, as his whole anthology displays, he was very concerned about the eschatological future. The prophecy appears together with a number of other short vaticinations in the last two quires of his manuscript, most of which conclude with references to the advent of Antichrist.[33] Its position toward the end of the anthology is not conclusive for dating purposes: Henry could have written it any time between about 1350 and about 1380, although a dating after about 1365 and before about 1377 seems most probable.[34] The exemplar from which he worked definitely represented a stage many times removed from the original post-

31. See on this Thomas Arnold, ed., *Memorials of St. Edmund's Abbey* (RS 96, pt. 3; London, 1896), 113–125, 135–137, and Alfred H. Sweet, "The Apostolic See and the Heads of English Religious Houses," *Speculum*, 28 (1953), 468–484 (at 473).

32. *Memorials*, 125–135, and May McKisack, *The Fourteenth Century: 1307–1399* (Oxford, 1959), 415–416.

33. *Corruent nobiles* on f. 100[r]; Tripoli prophecy on f. 100[v]; Vision of "Friar John" on fos. 100[v]–102[r]; and rumors reported by William of Blofield on f. 102[r].

34. The Tripoli prophecy appears on f. 100[v]. My rough *termini* of 1365 and 1377 are based on evidence from the prophecies copied near it. The *Quando ego Thomas* prophecy on f. 99[v] has an appended note reporting that the text was discovered two hundred years after Thomas Becket's exile, i.e., ca. 1365, while the *Aquila Neustrie* prophecy on fos. 98[r]–99[r] has glosses in Henry's hand referring to English kings running up to Edward III but not Richard II, who became king in 1377 (but Richard is named by Henry in the table of contents of the MS).

Acre revision.[35] Enough can be deduced from the copy to know that Henry must have made his transcription with great care and fidelity: the only variants for which he may have been responsible were the addition of an *ibi*, a minor syntactic change, and a final injunction to pray.[36] The exemplar itself differed from others we have seen in one outstanding respect: namely, a report appended at the end to the effect that the abbot of the Cistercian monastery in Tripoli had sent two monks to the papal court with a written account of the prophetic miracle, and that the pope had then made the messengers take a solemn oath attesting to the truth of it.[37] Needless to say, this was just legendary embroidery, but it must have served to enhance the miracle story's credibility for subsequent readers.

Henry of Kirkestede, at any rate, manifested no doubts about the authenticity of the miracle or the reliability of the message. Indeed, he was not inclined to be skeptical about the truth of the prophecies he copied, a fact which can be seen even more clearly from his willingness to place faith in the prophecy of "Friar Columbinus."[38] Although "Columbinus" did correctly predict (*ex eventu*) that Acre would fall around 1291, he went on to predict many other things for specific subsequent years of the early fourteenth century that by no means ever happened. Yet Henry copied out this prophecy with as much

35. It is impossible to trace a direct line of descent for Henry's copy because there must have been several contaminations in its earlier transmission. It bears traits from both the German and Bloemhof transmissions as well as two peculiarities found earlier only in the partial version reported by Li Muisis (see n. 3 above). In addition, it contains readings found only in the Bardney MS and others found only in the version for 1347 discussed in the following chapter. See further Appendix III.

36. Viz.: *Quidam ibi monachus*, the naming of the Cistercian order in the second instead of the first sentence, and the addition of *et orate* to *Vigilate ergo* (cf. Matt. 26:41; Mark 14:38).

37. "Duo monachi missi ab abbate Cisterciensis civitate Tripolis retulerunt ista nova predicta coram summo pontifice in scriptis. Et summus pontifex fecit eos iurare super sacramentum suum si vera essent omnia que referebant." The following chapter shows that this story and variants also appear in a redated version of the prophecy.

38. It is true that on f. 102ʳ Henry wrote in the margin in reference to the rumors reported by William of Blofield the word *lie* (*mendacium*), but it is doubtful whether this evidence reflects any independent critical spirit because the text itself said that the prophecies in question were fictitious.

care as he copied the others, leaving blanks in places where he was uncertain of readings and warning in his margin that his text was defective.[39]

It seems reasonably clear that one aspect of the Tripoli prophecy that attracted Henry was its final prediction concerning Antichrist because he included it among a group of prophetic texts that had the coming of Antichrist as their ultimate concern. Insight into how Henry read eschatological prophecies in general is provided by his copy of the vision of "Friar John," which he entered into his anthology directly after the message from Tripoli.[40] Although Henry's exemplar reported that this vision transpired shortly before the accession of Pope Boniface VIII (1294), he concluded sometime after 1378 that it accurately foretold the Great Schism and the trials of his own day.[41] This he called attention to by drawing a pointing finger in the margin next to a passage that predicted a time of many excommunications, interdicts, and occupations of benefices by those who received them from excommunicates (he probably had the case of Bury above all in mind). In addition he marked the margin at a passage predicting the falling away of many Christian realms from the Roman obedience and wrote "take note" (*nota*) next to a passage that predicted the coming of a terrible Roman pope (no doubt in his eyes Urban VI). But Henry made no marks next to those parts of the prediction that were not so easily applicable to the Schism or to any other known events. Although the prophecy might have seemed accurate in predicting the coming of the terrible Urban VI, the passage immediately preceding described the two popes before the terrible Roman one in

39. Fos. 7v–8v, added in Henry's late hand at the end of the first quire. On the "Columbinus" prophecy, see further Chapter Three, n. 7. Henry's marginal comments *iste tractatus . . . est defectivus* and *deficit finis* are confirmed by the evidence of other MSS; nonetheless his text would be an important witness for a critical edition.

40. Fos. 100v–102 r. On the original vision, see above pp. 38–39.

41. The same conclusion was reached independently on the continent—see the remark in MS UB Basel A VI 6, f. 19rb: "Item visionem fratris Iohannis Romani . . . qui eciam satis aperte et manifeste prelocutus fuit de scismate paparum et ecclesie nunc currente. . . ." Sometime during the Schism, a German translation of the vision was made that thereafter circulated in Germany very widely: see provisionally the literature cited in n. 6 of the Introduction.

ways that could by no means have applied to Urban's actual predecessors, but Henry left that passage untouched. His approach, then, was selective: he fastened onto what seemed applicable to current events and left the rest without worrying about its veracity.

Henry's reading of "Friar John" strongly suggests that he also found some arcane applicability in the Tripoli prophecy in addition to its warning about the imminence of Antichrist—or at least that he could have done so if given sufficient time. Henry, who gathered prophetic texts for most of his mature life, must have studied them at intervals for whatever insights they provided, without becoming disquieted if certain passages seemed mistaken or impenetrably obscure: if he could not understand some things at some times, he might at others. Since the veracity of the miracle at Tripoli had been upheld on oath before the pope, since its message had already been proven true in part, and since the message led up to revelations about the coming of Antichrist, the Tripoli prophecy was certainly worth his attention.

As Henry of Kirkestede was on the alert for Antichrist, so a British prophetic anthologist a century later was on the alert for a coming political messiah. This compiler was a layman or cleric who copied the Tripoli prophecy in an anthology written around 1470 in the service of Henry Percy, fourth earl of Northumberland.[42] Henry Percy's family had supported the Lancastrians, and he himself had

---

42. The anthology in question is in MS BL Cotton Vesp. E. vii; the copy of the Tripoli prophecy therein is found on f. 90^{r-v} (old 87^{r-v}). The MS is described by J. Planta, *A Catalogue of the Manuscripts in the Cottonian Library* (London, 1802), 480, and Ward, I, 320–324 (both referring to an old foliation). Ward, 320, notes that the MS contains Henry Percy's coats of arms. It seems unlikely that it was copied before 1469 because Henry was in the Tower between 1461 and 1469, but it was probably not done much later than 1470 because many of the prophecies in the anthology relate to the 1460s. The entire collection bears more detailed study. For the text of the Tripoli prophecy from this MS, see Appendix III. An early-modern addition to it is discussed in Chapter Eight. After this book went to press, I learned that MS Cambridge, Gonville and Caius College 249, copied under the direction of the Cambridge doctor of medicine and vicar of Ashwell (Hertfordshire), John Harryson (or Herryson), in the years from 1464 to 1469 contains a section from fos. 181 to 183 that is closely related to BL Cotton Vesp. E. vii, fos. 86 to 90. (In the Harryson MS the Tripoli prophecy is at f. 183va.) Apparently a common exemplar made around 1464 lies behind both copies.

been confined to the Tower by the Yorkist Edward IV from 1461 to 1469. He was released by Edward in the latter year, however, and restored to his lands and honors in 1470 in order to provide a counterweight to the greater threat of "Warwick the Kingmaker."[43] This sudden reversal in fortunes understandably encouraged the ex-Lancastrian to flourish the white rose of York. The anthology done in his service includes texts that allude to the Percy family, others that trace Yorkist descent from Brutus, and others that treat of the death in 1405 of Archbishop Scrope, a martyred hero of both the Percy family and the Yorkists.[44]

Over fifty prophecies in the same collection were gathered to cast light on the coming of a messianic British king, the mysterious "sixth" invented in the twelfth century by Geoffrey of Monmouth.[45] According to Geoffrey's *Prophecies of Merlin*, the "sixth" would some day "destroy the walls of Ireland," unite "the diverse parts into one," "renew the seats of the saints throughout the lands," and "place the shepherds in suitable spots"; then he would be "raised in the favor of the Thunderer" and be "set among the blessed." Apparently the compiler hoped that by gathering enough prophecies that seemed in any way to relate to this hero he could show how they all interre-

43. For more details, see J. M. W. Bean, *The Estates of the Percy Family* (Oxford, 1958), 109-111; R. L. Storey, *The End of the House of Lancaster* (London, 1966), 194-195; and Charles Ross, *Edward IV* (Berkeley, Calif., 1974), 144-145.

44. Scrope was involved in a Percy conspiracy and later was revered by the Yorkists: see Scattergood (n. 16 above), 119-121. Henry Percy himself may have taken an active part in directing the compilation of the MS in question because it is known that he was sufficiently literate to write a complicated will—see K. B. McFarlane, *The Nobility of Later Medieval England* (Oxford, 1973), 240.

45. The best edition is by Acton Griscom, *The Historia Regum Britanniae of Geoffrey of Monmouth* (London, 1929), and the best translation by Lewis Thorpe, *Geoffrey of Monmouth, The History of the Kings of Britain* (Harmondsworth, 1966): see VII, 3. The Percy anthology contains a glossed version of this text at f. 120^{r-v}; further study might determine whether the anthologist wrote the glosses himself. Other students of prophecy also tried to identify the "sixth": a prophetic commentary in MS Wolfenbüttel 534 Helmstedt (ca. 1400) tried to demonstrate that the "sixth" was Edward II (see E. Herrmann, "Spätmittelalterliche englische Pseudoprophetien," AfK, 57 [1975], 107, n. 67); and a prophecy in MS BL Cotton Cleopatra C. iv (late 15th century) tried to demonstrate that he was Edward III (see Ward, I, 310-311).

lated and confirmed each other. Perhaps too he could demonstrate that the coming "sixth" would be a Yorkist.

Remarkably, the vision of the monk from Tripoli was one that he considered to fit into his plan. The anthologist's heading—"A Prognostication from the Holy Land on the Same Sixth"—explicitly states his belief that the Tripoli prophecy was relevant to his concerns.[46] Preoccupied by these concerns, he deleted large parts of the prophetic message that dealt with religious matters and coming disasters. The parts that were left told primarily of how the barbarians would be converted, peace brought to the earth, and the Holy Land won—predictions that could easily seem to correspond to Merlin's expectations for the "sixth." Above all, the anthologist saw applicability in the Tripoli prophecy's reference to a triumphant "beast of the West," calling special attention to this in his margin by adding the words "animal of the West" (*animal occidentalis*). This annotation was the only one he made and demonstrates, along with his heading, that he conceived the message from Tripoli to be a prediction of how a coming Western ruler would, like Merlin's "sixth," unite the world and "renew the seats of the saints."

The fact that the Percy anthologist ended his copy of the Tripoli prophecy with the prediction that the Holy Sepulchre would be visited by all and omitted reference to subsequent "news of Antichrist" shows most clearly how different his concerns were from those of Henry of Kirkestede. Henry hoped that the Tripoli prophecy would enable him to learn more about the present and future state of the Church and the time of Antichrist's coming, whereas the Percy anthologist wished to learn more about the political future of England and chances for a successful crusade. Yet, although one was searching for Antichrist and the other for a conquering hero, both thought the prophecy could illuminate their search, and neither was disturbed that so little of it had yet come to pass.

The same acceptance was displayed by an anonymous mid-four-

---

46. F. 90ʳ: *Prognosticacio Terre Sancte de eodem Sexto*. The rubrics of most of the neighboring prophecies in the anthology show how the collector understood many other texts to pertain to *eodem Sexto*: see Ward, I, 321–323. Further close study might show more clearly what he expected them to reveal.

teenth-century French author of a scientific treatise who thought the Tripoli prophecy might help him understand God's plan in the face of the numerous disasters of his day. These were dismaying enough: the humiliating French defeat at Crécy in 1346, the loss of Calais in 1347, and the terrible first visitation of the Black Death in 1348 and 1349. Seeking a way of learning what these events presaged, the observer in question put together around 1350 a "treatise," *On the Natural Causes of Certain Future Events and Tribulations and Other Changes in the World,* which is hardly a treatise at all but rather a compilation, with occasional commentary, of various texts he believed could help him fathom the recent disasters and foretell future ones.[47]

The "scientific" texts the French author chose for inclusion were astrological and prophetic because he believed that the science of understanding the present and future was most firmly based on astrology and three kinds of prophecy: biblical, Sibylline, and more recent divinely inspired visions. Accordingly, he opened his compilation with extracts from the treatise of a contemporary French astrologer on a planetary conjunction of Mars, Saturn, and Jupiter that occurred in March 1345, then presented extracts from Ptolemy, and then proceeded to prophecies from each of his three classifications: respectively Daniel, the Erythrean Sibyl, and Hildegard of Bingen. Toward the end of his work he added the vision seen by the Cistercian of Tripoli.

The full Tripoli prophecy would have been an appropriate text for anyone preoccupied with military reverses and plagues to con-

---

47. The only known copy is in MS Tours 520 (prov. Marmoutier), fos. 97ʳ–104ᵛ. (The Institut de Recherche et d'Histoire des Textes generously loaned me its microfilm copy of this MS.) On the Tours MS, see *Catalogue général des manuscrits des bibliothèques publiques de France: départements,* 37, pt. 1 (Paris, 1900), 428–433, and Alexander von Roes, *Schriften,* eds. Herbert Grundmann and H. Heimpel, in MGH, *Staatsschriften des späteren Mittelalters,* I, pt. 1, 87. On the treatise itself, the only previous notice is by Thorndike, III, 311–312. The work must be French because it appears in a French MS that contains materials of primarily French provenance and because it opens with extracts from an astrological treatise by a French astrologer. That astrological treatise is the best aid for dating since it refers to a conjunction of 1345 and shows knowledge of the Black Death (it predicts "imminent" corruption of the air and epidemics): 1348 is thus a *terminus post quem* and 1350 a rough *terminus ante quem* because the conjunction of 1345 would have lost interest after that time.

sider because it contained a line about coming battles, famines, and plagues that might have seemed genuinely prophetic. But the anonymous Frenchman could not have selected it for that reason because the version at his disposal came from the French family which had dropped that whole line.[48] In all probability, the prophecy attracted his attention instead because it alluded to Mars, Saturn, and Jupiter, the same planets in the conjunction of 1345 that had concerned him at the start.

This is just supposition, but what is certain from the author's own words is that he thought the prophecy was already partially confirmed and that it was to be taken earnestly as a warning of the coming of Antichrist. The events already confirmed were of course the losses of Tripoli and Acre: when the author came to the passage that predicted the fall of those cities, he added a gloss that the prediction had already transpired. That was his only infratextual gloss, a fact which suggests that he had no very clear notion of the rest of the prophecy's precise meaning. But he did introduce and conclude his copy with his own comments. By way of introduction, he stated that the prophecy was similar to one by Hildegard of Bingen that he had just treated and that both should inspire Christians to shun evil. By way of conclusion, he commented on the final words of the prophecy that read, "Therefore be vigilant." For him this meant that just as the "first parents" should not have been deceived by the serpent, so their descendants should beware of Antichrist's deceptions and adhere to the way of truth.[49]

Clearly, then, the French "scientist" of about 1350 was certain that the Tripoli prophecy rested on genuine inspiration. Like John of Paris he found it validated by its accurate "prediction" of the fall

48. On the French family, see Chapter Four, p. 70 above, and Appendix III.

49. MS Tours 520, f. 104ʳ: "Et post scripsit: *Ergo vigilate*, scilicet ne sicut primi parentes extiterunt decepti a serpente, caveat proles eorum ne per Antichristum sint decepti, sed adhereant veritati que est Christiana, fugientes errancium falsitates, sed eius qui est via veritas bonitate. Cum autem hec omnia hic prescripta fuerint ad finem ut mala fugiamus et bonis adhereamus, videtur expeditus recitare que secuntur:" (there follows the text of another prophetic vision). Aside from this ending and the statement that the fall of Tripoli and Acre had already transpired, the text of this copy bears no noteworthy variants from the main lines of the French family.

of the Holy Land without raising the possibility that that prophetic knowledge was gained *ex eventu*. As for the rest, it may not have yet predicted anything else with the same exactitude, and it may have been in large part very obscure, but that did not by any means invalidate it. On the contrary, its general purport as a message to beware the coming of Antichrist was clear, and that was important "scientific" news in France in the mid-fourteenth century.[50]

The last class of manuscripts in which the Tripoli prophecy appears is that in which the prophecy was not an obvious part of the context. The scribes of four identifiable manuscripts in this class were looking neither for historical facts, nor prophecies for anthologizing, nor scientific data. Instead, all added the text to their manuscripts where it might not first have been expected. But examination shows that all had reasons for copying it beyond merely filling up blank space.

Two English copies in question are directly related to each other, an extremely rare occurrence given the enormous number of copies of the Tripoli prophecy that have been lost. The first of these appears in a collection of devotional and ascetic texts copied in a northern English monastery around the middle of the fourteenth century.[51] Among the longer texts in the collection is an anonymous "Mirror for the Sinner" (*Speculum peccatoris*), which has been described as being

50. The whole text was also carefully read in the monastery of Marmoutier in the fifteenth century: sometime after 1422 (the date the treatise was copied in the Tours MS) a fifteenth-century marginaliast noted beside the prediction of the fall of Tripoli: "Anno 1288 [*sic*] fuit capta civitas Tripolis"; and beside that of the fall of Acre: "1291." Apparently he was struck by the accuracy of the predictions *ex eventu*. Another marginaliast repeated the words *bestia occidentalis*.

51. MS BL Harley 485; the Tripoli prophecy appears on f. 98ᵛ. This MS, once owned by Henry Savile of Banke (1568–1617)—see Cyril Ernest Wright, *Fontes Harleiani* (London, 1972), 380—almost certainly came from a northern monastery because Savile's collection consisted preponderantly of MSS from such sources: see Andrew G. Watson, *The Manuscripts of Henry Savile of Banke* (London, 1969), 9 (also 49, no. 162, for the MS in question). The dating of the part of the MS that contains the Tripoli prophecy can only be made on the basis of rough paleographical indices. I have not examined the Harley MS myself but have learned from the Keeper of Manuscripts of the British Library, to whom I wish to express my thanks, that the hand which copied the Tripoli prophecy is the principal one of the MS.

"severely ascetic . . . dwelling on the gloomy side of religion to the total exclusion of joy." [52] It is in such unlikely company, specifically between an extract from the monastic authority Cassian and a short text on contemplation,[53] that the Tripoli prophecy unexpectedly appears.

What relationship did the miraculous message have with such monastic and ascetic concerns? The textual state of the copy in question offers some hints. Like the earlier Bardney copy, the text the scribe copied omits the word *sect* in the line threatening the mendicant orders. The result is a general warning to the effect that "the mendicant orders and many others will be annihilated." Taken together with the fact that the copy neglects to state that the monk who saw the moving hand was a Cistercian, the message becomes more clearly a warning to all monks to beware of the future. Since it also contains an addition specifying that Tripoli fell because of the sins of its inhabitants, it implicitly offers the hope that monks who avoid sin might not be annihilated.[54] Considering that the major purpose of the northern English monastic compilation was to reprove license and encourage asceticism, the prophecy thus "fits." Whoever copied it must have taken the warning about the future very much to heart, despite the fact that it was almost a century old, and must have thought that it would help arouse vigilance among his monastic readers.

A direct copy made shortly afterwards put the text to a rather different use.[55] Around the end of the fourteenth century, someone

52. Hope E. Allen, *Writings Ascribed to Richard Rolle* (New York, 1927) 353–354.

53. Incipit: "Primus gradus contemplacionis est ut anima in se ipsa conversa." I have been unable to identify this text.

54. "Civitas Tripolis propter peccata inhabitancium in brevi destruetur." Another noteworthy change is that the MS has the papacy "becoming rich" instead of "dominating" in the last days (*ditabitur* for *dominabitur*). For the whole, see Appendix III.

55. MS Bodl., Bodley 158, f. 146ʳ. Miss Albinia de la Mare, who graciously answered several of my questions about this MS, has informed me that it probably belonged to one William Hanley in the mid-sixteenth century, about whom practically nothing is known, and that its whereabouts before then cannot be determined. Since the readings of this and the Harley copy are identical down to capitalization and since the two copies both came from the North, it is extremely unlikely that any copy intervened. My reason for believing that the

from the vicinity of Durham who had read the Tripoli prophecy in the monastic miscellany decided that it deserved to be copied again in a manuscript that contained William of Saint Amour's diatribe against the friars, *On the Perils of the Last Times*; a set of documents dating from around 1380 pertaining to a case of the Durham secular clergy against a Dominican; and a short thirteenth-century prophecy, pseudonymously ascribed to Hildegard of Bingen, which excoriated the friars in the same manner as the work of William of Saint Amour.[56] Since the manuscript still had a blank leaf remaining at the end, it had more space for additional antimendicant material and the Tripoli prophecy served the purpose because it contained an antimendicant line: the prediction that the mendicant orders would be annihilated.

Although we can see this connection now, it is nonetheless remarkable that the late fourteenth-century copyist made it. Certainly he could not have been combing through an ascetic and devotional miscellany looking for antimendicant ammunition. Rather, his linking came from a keen memory. Either he remembered the antimendicant line from the Tripoli prophecy while he was reading the antimendicant collection and resorted to the manuscript he had read earlier in order to recopy it, or else he remembered there was extra space in an antimendicant collection when he read the Tripoli prophecy in a completely different context. By either interpretation he had to have read the Tripoli prophecy with care because the antimendicant line appears in the middle. And by either interpretation he showed great respect for a prophecy that was about a century old.

Bodleian text is the copy are that it is the single loose one, that it is more abbreviated than the Harley text (especially at the end), and, most telling, that it seems to imitate some of the characteristics found in the Harley MS that are both in its copy of the Tripoli prophecy and other texts, such as the coloring of capitals and the abbreviation for *est*.

56. F. Madan and H. H. E. Craster, *A Summary Catalogue of Western Manuscripts in the Bodleian Library at Oxford* (Oxford, 1922–1953), II, pt. 1, 151. A dating of ca. 1380 for the documents in the case against the Dominican is confirmed by information pertaining to one of the authors, Henry Hedelham, in D. S. Boutflower, ed., *Fasti Dunelmenses*, Surtees Society, no. 139 (London, 1926), 58. On the pseudo-Hildegard prophecy *Insurgent gentes*, see M.-M. Dufeil, *Guillaume de Saint–Amour et la polémique universitaire parisienne, 1250–1259* (Paris, 1972), 317, 342 with n. 181 (but many more copies exist than Dufeil lists).

The remaining two copies in the last class of Tripoli prophecy manuscripts are both German. The earlier was copied around 1370 in the Dominican convent of Breslau in the blank space following a brief anonymous sermon on the Resurrection.[57] Although the prophecy was copied after the sermon to fill up some parchment on the bottom half of a verso page at the end of a quire, it was certainly not chosen at random, for the short sermon ended with reference to a passage about how Christ's disciples were going to have a *vision* of the Lord. That made the Dominican copyist think of the miraculous *vision* in the Cistercian cloister and thus he was moved to copy the text of the Tripoli prophecy in the space that followed. As in the case of the Durham scribe, the Tripoli prophecy must have made a great impression on the Breslau Dominican for him to have remembered it at the right moment.

But the Dominican's awe for the prophecy came from a different source, as can be seen from an additional statement he appended: "In the year of our Lord 1349 the flagellants came who were the people without a head."[58] In other words, as several different readers found the prophecy already confirmed by its prediction of the loss of the Holy Land, the Breslau Dominican found it confirmed by his identification of the "people without a head" with the flagellants. In this he

57. MS UB Breslau (Wrocław) IV F 6, f. 100ᵛ. Dr. B. Kuzak, director of the Breslau University Library, kindly responded to my query about possible copies of the Tripoli prophecy in the Breslau manuscripts by informing me about this specimen (according to my soundings the only one currently known in Poland). I have seen microfilms of f. 100ᵛ and 101ʳ but not the original MS. There is no published catalogue description; excerpts from an unpublished catalogue by Willi Göber kindly communicated to me by Dr. Kuzak indicate provenance from the former Dominican library at Breslau (I can add that the sermon beginning on f. 101ʳ refers to Aquinas as *doctor noster*) and cite f. 69ʳ: *Istum feci anno Domini MᵒCCCᵒLXXᵒ*. Since I do not know whether the hand that wrote in 1370 on f. 69ʳ is the same that copied the Tripoli prophecy on f. 100ᵛ, the dating of 1370 for the latter is only approximate. After my query to Dr. Kuzak, I learned from Professor Dr. Peter Dinzelbacher that the Breslau copy was edited by Joseph Klapper, *Exempla aus Handschriften des Mittelalters* (Heidelberg, 1911), 64. The text is clearly a pristine member of the German family, with the only significant variant being its mistaken date of 1277 for the original 1287: see further Appendix III.

58. "Anno Domini MᵒCCᵒxlixᵒ quando isti flagellatores fuerunt qui fuerunt gens sine capite."

was not at all as arbitrary as it might at first seem, for the flagellants were widely called a "people without a head" by contemporaries on the grounds that they had no known leader and also that they acted without brains or prudence.[59] Given that a new "people without a head" had appeared in the mid-fourteenth century, it is not surprising that the Tripoli prophecy was brought forth to apply to them; indeed, evidence suggests that the same application was made independently by others.[60]

The final copy of the Tripoli prophecy from the last class was written around 1460, somewhere in Bavaria.[61] Whoever copied it did

59. For example, Henry of Herford, *Liber de rebus memorabilioribus sive chronicon*, ed. A. Potthast (Göttingen, 1859), 280: "Eodem anno [1349] gens sine capite, ... ex omnibus subito Theutonice partibus exsurgunt. ... Dicebantur quasi prophetice sine capite, vel quia ad litteram caput non habebant, quo unirentur vel dirigentur, vel quia sine capite, id est cerebro, id est sine prudentia. . . ." See also independent designations of the flagellants as "headless people" in the Detmar chronicle of Lübeck cited by Stuart Jenks, "Die Prophezeiung von Ps.-Hildegard von Bingen: Eine vernachlässigte Quelle über die Geisslerzüge von 1348/49," *Mainfränkisches Jahrbuch*, 29 (1977), 36, n. 79, in versions of a satirical poem against the flagellants, ibid., 20, and in a theological *questio* about the flagellants, Martin Erbstösser, ed., *Sozialreligiöse Strömungen im späten Mittelalter* (Berlin, 1970), 27, n. 82.

60. I take Henry of Herford's remark *quasi prophetice* (as above) to be an allusion to the Tripoli prophecy and find another likely one in the fifteenth-century Dutch translation of the fourteenth-century chronicle of Johannes de Beka, as in Paul Fredericq, *Corpus documentorum inquisitionis haereticae pravitatis Neerlandicae* (Ghent, 1889–1906), I, 197: "Man seyde dat een Prophete propheteerde van desen volcke langhe te voren aldus: Veniet gens sine capite et flagellabit se pro peccatis suis." (This passage is not in the original Latin but must have its origins in an independent fourteenth-century tradition.)

61. MS Donaueschingen 793, fos. 62ᵛ–63ʳ. The MS is described by Karl A. Barack, *Die Handschriften der fürstlich Fürstenbergischen Hofbibliothek zu Donaueschingen* (Tübingen, 1865), and Gerhard Eis, "Nachricht über eine medizinische Sammelhandschrift der Donaueschinger Hofbibliothek," *Medizinische Monatsschrift*, 13, 2 (1959), 109–112. (Neither Barack nor Eis mentions the presence of the Tripoli prophecy.) A careful codicological study remains to be undertaken: suffice it to say that the MS consists primarily of medical and other "scientific" recipes and extracts written by different hands of the second half of the fifteenth century and the sixteenth century. The discrete unit of the MS of concern here consists of fos. 50–51, and 62–63, which originally followed each other before they were separated in the present binding (of uncertain date). I have learned from the librarian at Donaueschingen that the hand which appears on these folios differs from the hand of 1466 that copied fos. 30ʳ–33ᵛ, but I do

so in the space following a set of extracts from John of Rupescissa's mid-fourteenth-century prophetic treatise, *Vade mecum in tribulacione*, and extracts from an imperial chronicle and the chronicle of Martin of Poland on Charlemagne. After these texts, a bold new heading in the same hand announces: "Here are the determinations of the astrologers about future occurrences from the year 1461 to the year 1470," but no such determinations follow. Rather, without any further introduction the hand presents the Tripoli prophecy in a version differing only slightly from the text given almost two hundred years earlier by Eberhard of Regensburg.

Why the scribe did not copy the astrological "determinations" cannot be told. Maybe he misplaced them after he wrote his rubric, or maybe he decided after reading them that they were not as reliable or informative in their predictions for the 1460s as he hoped they would be. Certainly he was intent on gathering as much illuminating material on the 1460s as he could because the version of extracts from Rupescissa's *Vade mecum* that he copied was one that had Rupescissa's dire predictions for the 1360s altered for dates in the 1460s.[62] The Tripoli prophecy says nothing about the 1460s, but the Bavarian scribe still thought it relevant enough for inclusion in the space where he first thought he would copy the "determinations." Perhaps he read it in an old chronicle related to the annals of Eberhard of Regensburg. Wherever he found it, he knew that it was almost two centuries old, but in his mind it still in some way helped to illuminate the course of current and future events.

The Bavarian copy of ca. 1460 is the last of thirteen late-medieval copies of the Tripoli prophecy that are all related by their acceptance of the thirteenth-century text without demurrer. As we have seen, thirteen late-medieval readers of the old prophecy all found some truth in it despite its age. Three historians recopied the story of the moving hand primarily because it was a noteworthy past event, but they also accepted the truth of the message. For the others, the meaning of the message was paramount. Five anthologists and one "scien-

---

not know whether the prophecy hand appears elsewhere in the MS. Eis has convincingly established that the MS was assembled in Bavaria.

62. Similar versions are listed by Bignami-Odier, *Rupescissa*, 250–251, without knowledge of the Donaueschingen MS.

tist" gathered the revelations of Tripoli for inclusion in larger collections of prophetic truth, and four other copyists chose to transcribe the prophecy because of some special quality or truth it had to offer.

None of these men would have agreed that truth is relative, but their commitments bear out the adage that truth is the daughter of time. Clearly the old prophecy's credentials were established in the minds of many of its late-medieval readers by their confidence in its having already been partially confirmed. Li Muisis implicitly and Engelhus and the writer on *Natural Causes* explicitly called attention to the fact that Tripoli and Acre had fallen just as the moving hand had predicted. The Breslau Dominican found another confirmation: the accurate prediction of the coming of the flagellants as the "people without a head." If part of the prophecy was true, the remainder certainly had to be. But that was where prophetic truth in practice became the daughter of time, for readers preoccupied with their own concerns and faced with the crises of their own day were bound to read the obscure prophecy as a message concerning what they already knew and what they were looking for. Thus, Henry of Kirkestede placed the prophecy together with others concerning the advent of Antichrist while the Percy anthologist found confirmation in it of his hopes for a conquering British messianic hero. Similarly, one English monastic scribe considered it a spur to monastic asceticism, whereas another English copyist of exactly the same version was most impressed by its prediction of chastisement for the friars.

As time passed, the prophecy did not seem any less true or any less relevant to the readers we have considered, for the text contained just the right mixture of obscurity and clarity. It was obscure enough to be saved from the charge of having been proved flatly mistaken. How, for example, could anyone know whether one god and one faith had really come fifteen years after 1287 when it was uncertain what the coming of one god and one faith really meant? But the words of the prophecy were clear enough for readers to know that they alluded to disasters, wars, upheavals, a great crusade, and "news of Antichrist." Since every age worried most about its own disasters and upheavals, a German of around 1460 and an Italian of around 1470 could consider the prophecy to be as relevant to their own times as a Frenchman of around 1350 believed it was to his. The eschatological content of the prophecy in particular made it perennially "relevant" because observers for decade after decade thought that the last scenes of world history were beginning to be played out. In other words, late-medieval readers from different times and milieux could assume that the Tripoli prophecy spoke directly to them without suspecting that they were being chronologically self-centered since people from every decade saw themselves as being uniquely prominent in the eyes of God.

Chapter VI

THE MOVING HAND
WRITES AGAIN

This chapter will be about some new dates. "In 1239" or "in 1240," our miracle story first reported, "a Cistercian monk saw a vision. . . ." Then the account was improved to state that "in 1287 a Cistercian monk in Tripoli saw a vision. . . ." The improvement consisted in the localization of the miracle: although there was no Cistercian cloister in Tripoli, hardly any Europeans were aware of this, and those who read about the hand writing an awesome prophecy in a doomed city found the drama inspiring. But later the account took on alternate forms. "In 1347," it went, or "in 1367," or "in 1396 a Cistercian monk in Tripoli saw a vision. . . ." Or even still: "In 1387 a monk of a certain monastery of the Cistercian order . . . ," or: "In 1400 a Benedictine monk of Tripoli in the province of Calabria . . . ," or: "In 1487 a Cistercian monk in the city of Naples. . . ."

If the version for 1287 represented an improvement in setting the miracle in Tripoli, these later versions stated impossibilities. After 1289 no monk of any order could have seen a moving hand in Syrian Tripoli because there were no Christian monasteries there. The writers who devised the versions for 1400 and 1487 apparently recognized that fact, but their allusions to a Benedictine monastery in Tripoli in Calabria or to a Cistercian cloister in Naples were no improvements because there never was a Tripoli in Calabria or a Cistercian cloister in Naples. Only the version for 1387 avoided geographical impossibilities by leaving out the locale, but it still contained a chronological absurdity in "predicting" the fall of Acre, because that event had transpired a century before the "prediction" was made.

It might be asked whether there was such a paucity of good miracle stories in the later Middle Ages as to make these flawed creations necessary, but that would be a question poorly posed. The story of the moving hand was not continually updated in order to offer amusement but to provide edification. To some later readers, the moving hand's message was so urgent that they tried to increase its circulation by making it seem more current, even though getting all the details right was either beyond their inclination or their capacities. Prophetic *aggiornamento* was indeed a constantly recurring medieval phenomenon, and here we may examine the several redated versions of the Tripoli prophecy as a means for seeing under what circumstances and with what methods and effects this particular specimen of prophetic "truth" was continually readapted.

By far the most popular of the redated versions of the Tripoli prophecy was one for 1347, behind whose creation lay the unprecedented disaster of the Black Death. Exactly how the shock of this natural disaster compared with that of such man-made ones as the Mongol advance or the fall of the Holy Land is impossible to say, but certainly it was very great. To take one of numerous examples, we can apprehend the sense of horror experienced by surviving Europeans through the plague narrative in the contemporary chronicle of Mathias of Neuenburg. According to Mathias, there had not been such a disaster since the Flood. The epidemic struck so suddenly that ships on the Mediterranean lost their crews and floated aimlessly on the sea. On land many unfortunates died without the sacraments. Parents abandoned their children and children their parents. In Avignon, business at the curia came to a halt and the pope locked himself in his apartments next to a fire. "The sickness," Mathias concluded, "went through all countries, and although the philosophers said much, they could give no certain explanation for it except that it was God's will."[1]

---

1. Mathias von Neuenburg, *Chronica*, ed. A. Hofmeister, MGH, *Scriptores*

In 1348, while the plague was ravaging Europe, someone, most likely in France, reread the old Tripoli prophecy and decided to recirculate it as if it had just been revealed.[2] Undoubtedly he did this because the moving hand seemed to have foreseen the coming of plagues in different regions. Maybe he thought the date of 1287 given for the miracle in Tripoli that he read in his exemplar was a mistake; maybe he knew it was not. In either event, he certainly wanted others to take the prophecy to heart and accordingly recirculated it with a redated introduction stating that the miraculous message had appeared in Tripoli in 1347, the year before the plague had struck.[3]

Of course this redating created some glaring anachronisms, but the reviser of 1348 was untroubled by them. Although he had the miracle transpiring more than half a century after the Holy Land's fall, he made no attempt to alter any details to avoid the impossibility of having a Cistercian cloister existing in 1347 in Muslim Tripoli or the absurdity of predicting the capture of Tripoli and Acre long after those cities had really been lost. Not only that, but the reviser retained the most inappropriate element he found in his exemplar, namely, the report, already observed in Henry of Kirkestede's version, that the Cistercian abbot of Tripoli sent two monks with news of the prophetic vision to the pope. If the miracle were thought to have transpired in 1287, this story was as credible as the vision itself,

---

rerum Germanicarum, n.s., 4 (1924–1940), 263–264. I venture a broader survey of eschatological reactions to the Black Death than what follows here in my article, "The Black Death and Western European Eschatological Mentalities," *American Historical Review*, 86 (1981), 533–552.

2. I discuss below the ten surviving copies of this recirculated version known to me and edit them in Appendix III. The version must have originated in 1348 because it was inspired by the plague and reached Kilkenny, Ireland, by early 1349 (June 1349, at the latest). Internal textual evidence points to continental origins. France seems the most likely place of origin given the places where the prophecy is known to have been copied and the fact that during most of 1348 the plague raged worst in France.

3. The redating was definitely for 1347, even though one of the surviving manuscripts has 1346 and two have 1348, because the date 1347 appears in five of the other copies, and these come from very different lines of transmission found in areas as separate as England and Catalonia. (The two remaining copies give no date at all.)

but once the vision was redated to 1347 it reemphasized an obvious impossibility, for Christian monks could not have been sent from a Holy Land that had long since fallen.

Nor did the reviser attempt to alter the basic meaning of his text, with only one exception.[4] Like many others before and after him, he was disconcerted by the prediction that the mendicant orders and many other "sects" would be annihilated (*ordines mendicancium et alie secte quamplures adnichilabuntur*), so he changed this to read, "The mendicant orders certainly will oppose many" (*Ordines mendicancium certe quamplures adversabuntur*)! Although this alteration took away the antimendicant sting, its meaning was also much less clear than the original, and later scribes, not surprisingly, had trouble understanding it.

Otherwise the reviser's only changes came from attempts to make sense out of passages that must have seemed corrupt. One surviving copy allows the hypothesis that he turned the obscure "duke of the bees" (*ducem apum*) into the "white duke" (*ducem album*), but if so this offering did not satisfy others because none of the other known copies accepted it.[5] Worse, he definitely turned "woe to Christianity!" (*ve tunc clero et tibi Christianitati*) into the completely nonsensical warning, "Woe to sterility!" (*Ve tunc clero et sterilitati*). The result of his revision was thus not only to create an anachronistic story, but also to present a more incomprehensible message than most of those that had circulated with the original date of 1287.

Nevertheless, the revision for 1347 swept successfully throughout much of Western Europe. At least ten medieval copies survive, and

---

4. Although no single one of the surviving ten copies of the redated Tripoli prophecy presents a clearly uncorrupted version, it is possible to have a reasonably assured knowledge of what the pristine text must have looked like (aside from readings of a few individual words) by comparing the ten copies with the surviving text of the original Tripoli prophecy nearest to the reviser's model: the copy made between 1350 and 1380 by the Bury monk, Henry of Kirkestede (see the preceding chapter).

5. *Lo duch blanch* in the Catalan translation (on which see n. 11 below) points to a Latin *ducem album*. This seems confirmed by the reading in the best single MS—Clm 28229, f. 21ʳ—of *abim*. All the other copies have clear corruptions: *ab huic, adhuc, ab insulis, Albuch, ab m̄. v̄i, labym, Abmch* [Abimelech?].

the textual variants in these are so multifarious as to indicate that scores more must have been lost. Of the ten known examples, five are English,[6] one is Irish,[7] one is from Speyer on the Rhine,[8] one probably

6. Bodl., Bodley 761, f. 184ᵛ (=B) (Frau Waltraud Huber called my attention to this copy); Bodl., Digby 218, f. 107ʳ (=D); Bodl., Fairfax 27, f. 26ʳ (=F); Bodl., Hatton 56, f. 32ᵛ(=H); BN franç. 902, f. 96ᵛ (=P). MSS B, F, and H are described in F. Madan and H. H. E. Craster, *A Summary Catalogue of Western Manuscripts in the Bodleian Library at Oxford* (Oxford, 1922–1953), respectively II, pt. 1, 413–415; II, pt. 2, 785–786; II, pt. 2, 821–822. More on B can be found in Paul Meyer, "Notice du MS. Bodley 761 de la Bibliothèque Bodléienne," *Romania*, 37 (1908), 509–528. (In his article Meyer announced that he intended to publish a special study on the prophecies in Bodl., Bodley 761 and related ones, but he died in 1917 apparently without having gotten to this project.) There is no adequate published description of D, but I have learned from Miss Albinia de la Mare that f. 107 is a singleton sheet bound with other disparate materials in the seventeenth century. The English *Quando ego Thomas* appearing before the Tripoli prophecy and chronological notes referring to English events on the verso make English provenance certain; the chronological notes point to a dating of the Tripoli prophecy copy in D of ca. 1400. MS P is described in *Bibliothèque Impérial, Catalogue des manuscrits français* (Paris, 1868), 152–153, and dated by John E. Matzke, *Les Oeuvres de Simund de Freine* (Paris, 1909), xviii, and S. Harrison Thomson, *The Writings of Robert Grosseteste* (Cambridge, 1940), 154. Nothing is known about the exact provenance of P earlier than its presence in the Colbert collection, but English origins seem nearly certain because all the other texts in the MS are Anglo-Norman, and because the hand that copied the Tripoli prophecy uses a forked *r* going below the line, usually an English trait.

7. A copy included in annals written by the Franciscan, John Clyn of Kilkenny (=K). It is published in the edition of Clyn's annals by Richard Butler, *The Annals of Ireland by Friar John Clyn* (Dublin, 1849), 36, who used MS Trinity College Dublin E. 3, 20, collated with a later MS owned by Sir W. Betham, but not MS Bodl., Rawlinson B. 496. Knowledge of Clyn's copy was generously communicated to me by Mr. John R. Shinners of the University of Toronto. Unfortunately I learned of it too late to consult the original manuscripts.

8. I discovered the copy in Munich MS Clm 28229, f. 21ʳ (=M). The MS is a comparatively recent addition to the collection of the Bayerische Staatsbibliothek and therefore has not yet been described in a printed catalogue. For detailed information about it I am greatly endebted to Dr. Alexander Patschovsky, who noticed references to Speyer in astronomical reckonings on f. 54ʳ. In the sixteenth century the MS was acquired by Pfalzgraf Ottheinrich of Pfalz-Neuburg, who obtained some of his other Speyer MSS from the Cathedral chapter and the Carmelite monastery: see Karl Schottenloher, *Pfalzgraf Ottheinrich und das Buch* (Münster, 1927), 9–12, 27, and further p. 153 below.

from southern Germany,[9] one from Lilienfeld in Lower Austria,[10] and the last, a Catalan translation, from Catalonia.[11] Despite the numerical

9. Now Yale University, Marston 225, fos. 43ᵛ–44ᵛ (=Y). The MS, a prophetic anthology, is described by Jean Leclercq, "Textes et manuscrits cisterciens dans des bibliothèques des États-Unis," *Traditio*, 17 (1961), 166–169; Martha Hitchcock Fleming, "Sibylla: De Imperatore" (Ph.D. diss., Boston University, 1975); and Walter Cahn and James Marrow, "Medieval and Renaissance Manuscripts at Yale: A Selection," *Yale University Library Gazette*, 52 (1978), 173–283 (at 206–208) (kindly called to my attention by Martha Fleming). To the foregoing I can add that the MS appeared in *Ludwig Rosenthal's Antiquariat, Catalogue 120* (Munich, n.d. [ca. 1910]), no. 281. Although Leclercq posited southern French origins, southern German provenance appears more likely on the following grounds: (1) two independent witnesses (Rosenthal catalogue and an authority cited in Cahn and Marrow) view the miniatures in the MS as being most likely of south German style; (2) the MS was definitely in southern Germany in the sixteenth century; (3) a Sibylline text, f. 12ʳ, refers to a coming duke of Bavaria. Leclercq's analysis of the Tripoli prophecy itself is faulty because it is based on the assumption that the copy in Y is unique.

10. MS Stift Lilienfeld 49, f. 357ʳ (=L). The catalogue by Conrad Schimek, *Xenia Bernardina, pars II, I: Die Handschriften-Verzeichnisse der Cistercienser-Stifte* (Vienna, 1891), 498, omits reference to the copy of the Tripoli prophecy in this MS. I learned of it from the incipit list of the Hill Monastic Manuscript Library, Collegeville, Minnesota. (I wish to thank Dr. Julian G. Plante, Director of the Hill Library, for answering several questions about the Lilienfeld MS and obtaining permission for me to publish its text of the prophecy.) The sermons by Gilbert of Tournai that make up the bulk of the MS are copied in a fourteenth-century hand (not fifteenth-century, as Schimek indicated) different from the one that later wrote the prophecy, as is the German prayer on f. 356ᵛ (not 367, as Schimek).

11. Now Carpentras 336, fos. 75ᵛ–76ᵛ (=C), described in *Catalogue générale des manuscrits des bibliothèques publiques de France: départements*, 34 (Paris, 1901), 164–165, and Jordi Rubió, "Un text català de 'La Profecía de l'Ase' de Fra Anselm Turmeda," *Estudis Universitaris Catalans*, 7 (1913), 9–24 (at 13). The complete contents of the MS can be determined by reference to Pere Bohigas, "Profecies catalanes dels segles xiv i xv. Assaig bibliogràfia," *Butlletí de la Biblioteca de Catalunya*, VI, pt. 9 (Anys VII–IX; Anys 1920–1922) (Barcelona, 1925), 24–49: see 28, 29, 30, 27, 43, 44, 37 (later correctly identified by Bohigas as part of the *Vida d'Antecrist* of Francesc Eiximenis—see Bohigas title in n. 20 below, at 36, n. 48), 40. (Professor Teofilo Ruiz kindly located the Rubió and two Bohigas articles for me in the Biblioteca Nacional of Madrid and provided me with xerox copies.) The MS, which I have examined myself, is definitely from the second half of the fifteenth century (*terminus post quem*, 1449), but it bears no trace of provenance other than a watermark of two crossed hammers related to Briquet no. 11638: Perpignan 1463, Narbonne 1480 (but the Briquet example has a crown above the two hammers).

preponderance of the English copies, internal textual evidence reveals the Speyer copy to be the best, with traces of the earliest strata also appearing in the Lilienfeld and Catalan texts.[12] Thus we may posit a circulation pattern not unlike earlier ones we have seen: composition somewhere in central Europe—this time probably in France—and subsequent circulation in different directions, including over the Channel to England.[13]

As in earlier cases, the initial circulation was also very rapid. Of the ten surviving copies, seven appear to have been made during the time of the plague or only a few years afterward.[14] The earliest firmly datable copy was made early in 1349 in annals kept by the Irish Franciscan, John Clyn of Kilkenny. Clyn wrote while the Black Death was raging through Ireland: it had already decimated Dublin and, nearer to him, the Dominican cloister in his own town of Kilkenny. Looking for enlightenment about the place of this visitation within the divine plan wherever he could find it, Clyn stated explicitly that the plague had been foreseen in 1347, the year before it had struck, by a monk who saw a message written by a moving hand during mass in

12. The Speyer copy shows its superiority in having the proper original form of *bestia occidentalis* and *leo orientalis* (followed here by MSS C and L), in preserving the original *aquas congregatas* and *et vincent*, and in having a version of the final confirmation story (as does L). Although the Catalan translation, C, is in sum one of the two texts farthest away from the original revision (the other being H), it nonetheless contains a few readings which seem to be remnants of an early stratum: in addition to the proper form of beast and lion, the right date of 1347, and *lo duch blanch* (see n. 5 above), also the retention of the first reference to Saturn, which is missing in all eight Latin copies.

13. As in the case of the original Cistercian vision, the redating for 1347 appears to have reached England in only one copy and then been widely copied from the single exemplar: note that all five extant English versions have *marchiatus* [the margrave] *mundum superabit* in place of *Mars Saturnum superabit*, a trait found among the continental versions only in Y. The Irish copy, K, clearly descends from the English family.

14. C, D, and H were not contemporary with the plague, but B, F, K, L, M, P, and Y all definitely or almost certainly were: the much later dating of Y by Leclercq and Cahn and Marrow is mistaken, as can be seen from the shape of the *g*'s and some *a*'s in this copy. The fact that three of the English copies—B, D, and P—conjoin the 1347 Tripoli prophecy with *Corruent nobiles* (on which see Chapter Three, n. 39) redated for 1350 to 1365 provides additional evidence for English circulation before 1350.

the Cistercian cloister of Tripoli.[15] Then Clyn set down the entire revised Tripoli prophecy, adding in his own words that there had never
been such a disaster as the present pestilence since the beginning of
time. Not surprisingly in such circumstances, the Irish Franciscan
feared for his own life. In some of the most moving words surviving
from the entire plague period he wrote, "Waiting among the dead for
death to come . . . and lest the writing perish with the writer . . . , I
leave parchment to continue this work, if indeed the race of Adam
survives this pestilence and any man remain in the future." In fact
the annals break off one paragraph later and are followed by a note in
a different hand that says: "It seems the author died here."

Further evidence of how the prophecy circulated during the
time of the plague comes from the Lilienfeld copy. Although the
original 1347 text ended with a bogus report that the Cistercian abbot in Tripoli sent two monks to tell the pope of the miracle and that
the pope made them swear their account was true, the Lilienfeld copy
says nothing about the swearing but specifies that a report of the
vision was sent to Pope Clement [VI] at Avignon. Then it goes on to
state that there was then such a pestilence in Avignon that seventeen
hundred houses were deserted.[16] This last accretion was rooted in fact,
for an independent eyewitness of April 1348 referred to an enormous
number of houses in Avignon being shut up.[17] Apparently someone

15. Butler (n. 7 above): "De ista pestilencia facta est visio mirabilis, ut dicebatur, anno precedenti, scilicet 1347, in claustro Cisterciensium Tripolis, sub hac
forma: quidam monachus celebravit missam coram abbate suo. . . ."

16. Unfortunately, certain crucial words are illegible. As close as I can come
to deciphering it (with the aid of Dr. Plante), the report in L reads: "Hec visio
missa[?] est Pape Clementi Avinionis [de Ierusalem inde(?) super esiatis(?)]
quod talis pestilencia est in civitate Avinionis] quod mille et septingenti domus
sunt per minimis[?] pestilenciam deserte et desolate." (The passage in square
brackets was first omitted and then supplied in the margin, with a corresponding mark in the text to indicate where it belonged. There is also a heading at the
top of the page, but most of it was cut off in trimming and is now illegible.)

17. Letter of Louis Sanctus de Beeringen, included in the *Breve Chronicon
Clerici Anonymis*, ed. J.-J. de Smet, *Corpus Christianorum Flandriae*, III (Brussels, 1856), 16, which gives the figure of seven thousand houses. This is rejected
as an exaggeration by Bernard Guillemain, *La Cour pontificale d'Avignon (1309–
1376)* (Paris, 1962), 557, but the abandonment of seventeen hundred houses would
be quite possible.

who had been in Avignon during the time of the Black Death, or who had heard of the devastation wreaked there, added a comment about it to the transmission that reached Lilienfeld, in effect saying that the message which predicted coming mortalities was already coming true.

Although the pattern of rapid contemporary circulation over many far-flung parts of Europe is familiar enough, one difference between the mid-fourteenth-century circulation and earlier cases is that the mid-fourteenth-century version of the Tripoli prophecy began to make some real headway in lay as well as clerical circles. Of the seven known contemporary copies, three were written in monasteries or churches, but the four others were very likely of lay provenance, one almost certainly written for a member or retainer of the aristocratic Bohun family of England.[18] As for the Catalan translation, it was obviously made to reach a wider public than the clergy and perhaps was written in the late 1350s by a Franciscan who wished to spread prophetic truth to a concerned lay audience.[19]

18. MS L is from the Cistercian cloister of Lilienfeld and M probably from either the Speyer Cathedral or Carmelite cloister. On the connections of MS B with the Bohuns, see Edward Maunde Thompson, *Chronicon Galfridi le Baker de Swynebroke* (Oxford, 1889), xv; note too that an extensive and up-to-date prophetic anthology was presented by the Augustinian friar John Erghome to Earl Humphrey de Bohun around 1361: Reeves, *Influence of Prophecy*, 255, and P. Meyvaert in *Speculum*, 41 (1966), 657–658. I take P to be of lay provenance because of its nearly exclusive vernacular content. The provenance of F and Y is uncertain but F appears originally to have been a schoolbook (by F I refer here only to fos. 26 to 31 of MS Bodl., Fairfax 27, which Mr. Nigel Palmer kindly informed me was once a separate quire), and the contents and opulence of Y make aristocratic provenance a strong possibility.

19. Since the translation is found in C between other Catalan translations of Latin prophetic works first written in the mid-fourteenth century, I hypothesize that all the translations may have been done by the same translator shortly after the works appeared. The texts in question are John of Rupescissa's *Liber secretorum eventuum* (1349) and *Vade mecum* (1356) on fos. 1ʳ–75ᵛ, and the Joachite *Summula seu Breviloquium super concordia Novi et Veteris Testamenti*, on fos. 76ᵛ–116ᵛ. On the *Summula*, see Bohigas, "Profecies catalanes" (n. 11 above), 26–28, 34, and Reeves, *Influence of Prophecy*, 223; Reeves dates the work to ca. 1368–1370, but the fact that it contains an internal reference to Louis of Sicily as reigning king leads me to believe that it must have been written before 1355. (Mr. Harold Lee informs me that the problem of dating the *Summula* will be considered more fully in the forthcoming edition of the work he will be bringing out in collaboration with Marjorie Reeves.) I posit Franciscan origins because the entire contents of C are of preponderantly (perhaps exclusively) Fran-

Whenever the Catalan translation was done, it is worth noting before proceeding that it contains so many sweeping changes as to be in effect a full-scale revision of a revision. Although it is impossible to tell whether the alterations were made by the translator himself, or, more likely, by the creator of the missing Latin exemplar, the reviser was certainly a Catalan because his boldest liberty was to interpolate the entire "Spanish" section of the originally separate *Ve mundo* prophecy. Specifically, after the passage in the Tripoli prophecy that predicts coming battles and "mutations of kingdoms," the Catalan reviser built in the section of *Ve mundo* that tells of wars in Spain until a "bat" (in the reviser's view no doubt an Aragonese hero) comes to destroy the "gnats of Spain," conquer Africa, and "humiliate the inhabitants of the Nile in his posterity."[20] Clearly the reviser recognized an equivalence between the bat of the Tripoli prophecy and the bat of *Ve mundo* and saw to his own satisfaction how the two prophecies converged in predicting a triumph over the Muslims, alternatively expressed as the "humiliation of the inhabitants of the Nile" or the "conversion of the land of the barbarians." Since *Ve mundo* predicted events culminating one hundred years after the fall of the Holy Land, it was in fact reasonable to see it as complementing the Tripoli prophecy and filling out some details for Spain, because the version of the Tripoli prophecy with which the reviser worked alluded to events transpiring twenty-five years after 1347.

---

ciscan authorship, and because the translator of Rupescissa's *Vade mecum* appears to have been a friar (see the passage from his dedication in Bohigas, 29: *molt car frare meu*). See also the following note.

20. On the original *Ve mundo* and the bat as an Aragonese royal emblem, see above p. 40, with n. 6. The interpolation may offer some confirmation of my hypotheses concerning dating and provenance since the *Ve mundo* prophecy seems to have been particularly current in southern France and Catalonia in Franciscan circles between ca. 1350 and ca. 1380: see (1) the commentary on it by Rupescissa, O.F.M., of 1354–55 described by Bignami-Odier, *Rupescissa*, 130–139; (2) a pseudo-Rupescissa commentary seen by the southern French chronicler Aimeri de Peyrat in Cahors, and from his description done shortly after 1367, on which see Bignami-Odier, *Rupescissa*, 200, and MS BN lat. 4991 A, fos. 145^v–146^r; (3) its use in 1376 by the Aragonese Infante Peter, O.F.M., described below pp. 142–152; (4) its use in 1379 by the Aragonese Francesc Eiximenis, O.F.M., described by Pere Bohigas, "Prediccions i profecies en les obres de Fra Francesc Eiximenis," *Franciscalia* (Barcelona, 1928), 23–38 (at 28–29).

No other redated version of the prophecy circulated nearly as widely as the 1347 text, perhaps because there was no other disaster as frightening as the Black Death to propel later transmissions. The next redating is located at present in only one copy and cannot be associated with any identifiable disaster at all.[21] This version updates the miracle story to 1367 but does not otherwise contain any significant revisions, showing that its author, like the originator of the 1347 version, was unaware of, or indifferent to, the anachronisms he created. Although the sole surviving copy was probably made in Paris for a layman around 1379, it is impossible to say when and where the redating itself was done because the text of the prophecy most resembles those that circulated in eastern Germany.[22] It can be said, however, that the French copyist took it as a confirmation of *Ve mundo* because he added it to the blank space on a sheet where he had copied *Ve mundo* some time before. As with the Catalan version, the two texts must have appeared to him to have converged and confirmed each other in predicting dramatic eschatological events for the late fourteenth century.

A third reviser who altered the date of the Tripoli prophecy but otherwise made no substantial changes worked in the vicinity of Regensburg around 1400. His base text was a copy of the prophecy from the Eberhard of Regensburg version, the date of which he changed from 1286 to 1396.[23] Perhaps his motives for this updating arose from fears engendered by the Great Schism: as it was possible

21. In Paris, Bibliothèque Ste.-Geneviève MS 792, f. 12r, described by C. Kohler, *Catalogue des manuscrits de la Bibliothèque Sainte-Geneviève* (Paris, 1893–1896), I, 378–383. The MS is a miscellany done at different times by different hands and was owned in the fifteenth century by the layman Michel Nicholas. I date and localize the copy to ca. 1379, Paris, because of the colophon on f. 12v.

22. For the text, see Appendix III. The copy is faded at the edge, making parts illegible, but it is clearly related to the German family. Its only noteworthy variants are the new date; *esuries magna* for *strages magna*; and a few scribal errors, such as *sic sedetur* for *succidetur* and *fructuum per xii annos* for *per xv annos*.

23. The 1396 version was first noticed by Grauert (see list of abbreviations), 281–283. For the text, see Appendix III. The only divergences, other than the date, from Eberhard of Regensburg's copy are inadvertent or of a minor editorial nature: *communicacionem misse* for *communionem misse*; *consecrat* for *confecerat*; *per Christianos* for *per xv annos*; and *commune congregati ibunt ad terram sanctam* for *commune ultra aquas congregatas ad terram sanctam*.

to read the line about coming "plagues in many places" as an allusion to the Black Death, so it might have been possible to read the phrase about "the ship of Peter" tossing in the waves as a prediction of the Church's plight during the Schism. In that case the subsequent assurance that the ship would escape and dominate at the end of time offered some hope.

The new deception was successful enough to move at least two copyists from the Regensburg area to recopy the 1396 version. The identity of one is unknown, but the other was a well-known personage, Andreas of Regensburg, one of the leading historians of late-medieval Germany.[24] In order to preserve material for possible use in his histories, Andreas, canon of Sankt Mang's near Regensburg from 1401 until his death sometime after 1438, filled up notebooks with miscellaneous letters and reports that came his way. In one such autograph collection, the Tripoli prophecy for 1396 appears under the heading, "A Miraculous Prophecy on the Courses of the World" (*Prophecia mirabilis de cursibus mundi*), followed by two other eschatological messages—the Toledo Letter issued for 1395 and a fictive letter spuriously attributed to the Grandmaster of Rhodes about the birth of Antichrist in "Babylon" in 1385.[25] Andreas copied all

24. The unknown copyist's work is found in Eichstätt, Staatliche Bibliothek MS 698 (old 269), p. 380, a MS from Regensburg copied between ca. 1397 and ca. 1420 (see further the following two notes). On Andreas of Regensburg, see his *Sämtliche Werke*, ed. Georg Leidinger (Munich, 1903), and the sketch by H. Glaser, "Wissenschaft und Bildung im Spätmittelalter," in Max Spindler, ed., *Handbuch der Bayerischen Geschichte*, II (Munich, 1966), 720–766 (at 756–759), with citation of further literature.

25. Clm 903, fos. 22ᵛ–23ᵛ. The Toledo Letter for 1395 and the letter from the Grandmaster of Rhodes are found in the same order in very similar copies in Eichstätt 698, which then continues with eschatological texts that are not in Clm 903. Since the scribe of the Eichstätt MS made a mistake in his copy of the Tripoli prophecy—*quasi plures* for *quam plures*—that is not found in Andreas's copy and Andreas made some errors in copying the Toledo Letter that are not found in the Eichstätt text (see the edition by Grauert, 283–285), they must have both worked from a common source. To Grauert's list (283, n. 3) of three surviving copies of the Toledo Letter for 1395 (Eichstätt 698, Clm 903, Clm 17311), I can add a fourth: Chicago, Newberry Library MS Case 31.2, f. 23ᵛ. For Andreas's reconsideration of the Toledo Letter for 1395 when new copies of the same text with the altered date of 1422 came his way, see Grauert, 289–296. The spurious letter from the Grandmaster of Rhodes awaits scholarly treatment; see provisionally the references in Chapter Two, n. 11.

these texts from the same source around 1420.[26] Even though he surely knew that Tripoli had long since fallen in 1289, he entered the account of the miracle in the Cistercian cloister into his collection without objection.

Andreas's credulity might have been more understandable had it concerned a second southeastern German redating, one that placed the miracle in 1387, because that one was not just a redating but a clever revision. But Andreas could not have known this version because even though it gave the date of 1387 it was fabricated much later, well after Andreas's death. Although the versions for 1347, 1367, and 1396 were composed shortly after the dates they offered for the miracle, the one for 1387 had to have been made long after 1387 because it alludes implicitly to the fall of Constantinople in 1453 and survives only in two south German prophetic anthologies of the third quarter of the fifteenth century.[27] Clearly it was written between 1453 and 1467; the date 1387 was chosen not because it was a recent one, but because the reviser decided to alter only one digit in the figure 1287, and 1487 had not yet arrived.

26. The common source for Andreas and the Eichstätt MS must have been copied shortly after 1396 because it contained the Tripoli prophecy with that date and because the two other eschatological texts are dated to 1385 and 1395. Andreas probably made his copies in 1420 or shortly afterwards because they appear in his collection in the vicinity of another eschatological text (Vincent Ferrer's letter of 1412 on Antichrist) that Andreas copied, according to his colophon, on Easter of 1420 (f. 9^r). At the end of the MS is Andreas's copy of Gunther of Pairis's *Historia Constantinopolitana*, which he finished in June 1425, (f. 148^r).

27. The surviving copies are in MSS Wolfenbüttel 366 Helmstedt, fos. 60^v–61^r, and Schloss Pommersfelden 102, f. 67^v. On the Wolfenbüttel MS, see Otto von Heinemann, *Die Handschriften der herzöglichen Bibliothek zu Wolfenbüttel*, 1 (Wolfenbüttel, 1884), 294–295: the MS came from the Augustinian cloister of Regensburg and was copied in 1467. The Pommersfelden copy cannot be dated with the same precision, but a dating in the 1460s cannot be far wrong. The entire MS, which consists of many separate parts, is described in an unpublished catalogue located in the library of the MGH, Munich. All the parts were copied in Nürnberg in the fifteenth century; the one in question was definitely done after 1453 because it includes a vision of Dionysius the Carthusian alleged to have transpired in that year. A *terminus ante quem* is ca. 1500, the date of marginal comments in a later hand (f. 68^r, bottom). I suspect the anthology was made around the 1460s because it contains many texts that are also found in the Wolfenbüttel one without being directly related to it.

The German reviser in question was determined to tell a good story. Recognizing that there could not have been a Cistercian cloister in Tripoli in 1387, he avoided geographical problems by writing simply that the miraculous vision transpired "in a certain monastery of the Cistercian order." Then, to underscore the exceptional quality of the purported event, he stated that it was "exceedingly miraculous," that it was granted to a monk of "most holy life," and that the moving hand was "exceedingly dazzling." Moving to the text of the message, he provided several clever alterations. By the later Middle Ages, few German readers would have heard of the Syrian town of Tripoli, since it was no longer Christian, so the reviser changed a few letters and turned the place name into Ingolstadt (*Ariopolis* for *Tripolis*). In thus predicting that Ingolstadt would soon be destroyed, he introduced some local interest into the text, although whether he had any real reason to allude to Ingolstadt beyond the similarity of names is impossible to say.

The reviser left the original reference to Acre standing, either because that name would have been more familiar, or because he could not think of a German equivalent, but he then made one of his most radical changes by completely altering a number. Whereas the original prophecy foretold the coming of "one god and one faith" within fifteen years after 1287, his version has "one god and one faith" coming within sixty-six years after 1387, a replacement that could not have had anything to do with a misreading of numbers or words. Since sixty-six added to 1387 yields 1453 the reviser was clearly alluding *ex eventu* to the calamitous loss of Constantinople to the Turks. Within the context of the revised prophecy, the prediction of "one god and one faith" coming in 1453 was thus a prediction of the triumph of Islam.

Another trial that followed in the reviser's exemplar was the tossing of Peter's ship, but the reviser was not pleased with this forecast. Accordingly, he made a deft change, turning "the ship of Peter will be tossed in manifold waves" (*navicula Petri iactabitur in variis fluctibus*) into "the ship will be endangered by manifold waves" (*navicula periclitabitur variis fluctibus*)![28] Whatever ship was meant

---

28. The Pommersfelden text gives *variis fluctibus* instead of *validis fluctibus*. I assume that the original of the 1387 version had *validis* because that form is

was now up to the reader to decide. Although the reviser objected to the threat to the papacy, he had no sympathy for the mendicants. Thus where the original text predicted that "the mendicant orders will be annihilated," he added that "*all* the mendicant orders will be annihilated," and where the original referred to the annihilation of "other sects," he added "other sects of both sexes," probably intending to encompass in the threatened destruction female mendicants and beguines. The reviser also transformed the "beast of the West" into the "beasts of the West," most likely in recognition that there was more than one major western power in his day, especially at a time when Burgundy was rivalling France. Although he left the penultimate part of the prophecy more or less untouched, he gave way to his penchant for dramatizing in the conclusion by replacing "news will be heard of Antichrist" with "we will see evidence of Antichrist."

The oddest trait of the version for 1387 is that it achieves its extensive changes in meaning by the most economical changes in letters or words. Unlike earlier revisers who added or subtracted entire lines, the creator of the version for 1387 worked closely within the textual bounds of his exemplar while still managing to effect great alterations in sense. Apparently he felt some ambivalence about his work: he knew instinctively that the text of the prophecy was wrong in basic respects, but he did not feel at liberty to put most of it aside and start afresh on his own. In some way, the prophecy before him was exerting talismanic powers.

Another redating that was also a full-scale revision gave the date of 1400. This version, completed by 1403 somewhere in Italy, was unusual in being based on the original, pre-Acre, version of the Tripoli prophecy rather than on the post-Acre revision.[29] Acre ac-

---

found in its nearest relatives. Although *variis* appears in several early versions of the Tripoli prophecy, it is improbable that the Pommersfelden reading resulted from contamination with one of these since the Pommersfelden text shows no other signs of contamination. Apparently the reading arose independently; for evidence that *variis fluctibus* was a common literary phrase (although not biblical), see, in addition to the early Tripoli prophecy appearances, a fourteenth-century prophecy, incipit: *Post mortem presentis imperatoris Karoli quarti*, in Clm 14594, f. 50ᵛ (prov. Regensburg, St. Emmeram's): . . . *et precipue ytalia variis fluctibus et diversis naufragiis.* . . .

29. Vat. lat. 793 (old 204), f. 96ᵛ. The MS is described in August Pelzer,

cordingly plays no role in this text, but Tripoli very definitely does. Knowing that Tripoli was in Saracen hands in his own day, the reviser entitled his version, "A vision or prophecy made in Tripoli in the province of Calabria."[30] Then he copied the opening of the old text as he found it except for turning the original Cistercian monk into "a monk of the Benedictine order." An unsuspecting reader might have assumed that there really was a Benedictine monastery in Tripoli in Calabria, but actually there was not. The reviser's locale was just as bogus as the others provided before him.

A person who felt free enough to invent a Benedictine monastery in an unheard-of location would obviously have no qualms about taking other gross liberties with the prophetic text. Whatever displeased this reviser he simply cut out: in his version the triumph of the "bat" over the "lord of the bees," the triumph of "one god and one faith," the liberation of the "sons of Israel," and the coming of the "people without a head" are all missing. He did retain the prediction about Peter's ship tossing in the waves, but he deleted the appended assurance that it would escape and dominate at the end of days, probably because this seemed like an overly optimistic prediction after more than twenty years of aggravated Schism.

The Italian reviser also retained the warning of imminent chastisement for the clergy and for Christianity, but he reversed the meaning of the prophecy about the mendicants by replacing the original threat that "the mendicant orders and many other sects will be annihilated" with the prediction that "the order of Friars Minor will be

---

Codices Vaticani Latini, II, 1: Codices 679–1134 (Vatican City, 1931), 119–122, with an edition of the version of the Tripoli prophecy, 122. The Vatican MS is certainly Italian because it employs Italian orthography and refers to Calabria. Its readings are related to another witness of another pre-Acre version of the Tripoli prophecy in another Italian MS—BN lat. 16021—and very closely related to those in a preponderantly Italian family of John of Paris MSS, on which see Chapter Four, n. 17.

30. I assume that the heading and all the major revisions were made by one individual on the grounds that only the same person would have displayed so much confidence in adding, changing, and subtracting. For the text of the version for 1400, see Appendix II. Conceivably, some of the revisions in the 1400 version bear some relationship to the Florentine "Vision of the Holy Hermit of the Year 1400," described by Donald Weinstein, "The Myth of Florence," in Nicolai Rubinstein, ed., *Florentine Studies* (Evanston, 1968), 15–44 (at 38).

augmented and many sects will be annihilated." Perhaps he was a Franciscan himself. His version also attempts to convey new meaning in its setting of the lines about the "lion" and the "beast," but it does so with such obscure new imagery that its purport is now impossible to fathom. The "lion," who in the original version crossed the mountains and killed the "other lion," crosses the mountains in the version for 1400 to be destroyed by a "serpent." With the lion thus removed, the "beast of the West" alone subjugates the world. To this the revision adds a new prediction that "the bearers of the lily without the eagle will be supplied in abundance with their followers." This line may have had some meaning for its creator, but it is now impenetrable, especially because around 1400 the lily was an emblem of the French, the Florentines, and of rival Angevin dynasties claiming the kingdom of Naples.

The ending of the version for 1400 is clear enough. The reviser retained the prediction that there would be peace in the world and an abundance of things for fifteen years and also the prediction of a successful crusade and the "glorification of Jerusalem," but he deleted the reference to news being heard of Antichrist. With that menacing allusion gone, the prophecy ends on a hopeful note with the words, "Blessed is he who will then be alive, for he shall not suffer sudden death."[31] Obviously the creator of the version for 1400 had doubts about the truth of much that he found in the original prophecy. Still, he retained the text of at least half of it, preserving the basic messages of imminent chastisement and ultimate Christian triumph. Thus, in the most fundamental outlines, he still regarded the old text as true.

Since there are versions for 1287 and 1387, a fitting end to the history of the medieval redatings of the Tripoli prophecy comes with a version for 1487.[32] This last redating was made shortly after 1487,

31. The surviving copy adds in conclusion an assurance, probably added by the scribe, that "all the foregoing must be fulfilled from the current year 1403 and 1404, as has been determined by the astronomers," showing that the revision was made by 1403 at the latest. Later, when none of the predicted events actually transpired in 1403 and 1404, someone with unshakable faith in the prediction changed those dates into 1452 and 1453 by turning a roman *i* into a roman *l*.

32. The sole surviving copy is in Bodl., Lyell 35, fos. 16ᵛ–17ʳ. The MS is described by Albinia de la Mare, *Catalogue of the Collection of Medieval Manuscripts Bequeathed to the Bodleian Library, Oxford, by James P. R. Lyell* (Ox-

most likely in England, or perhaps in France.[33] The reviser's exemplar came from the French family, which had transformed the original considerably, but the late fifteenth-century reviser proceeded to transform it further. Aside from providing a new date, his major alteration was to set the miraculous vision in a Cistercian cloister in Naples. No doubt he recognized that Saracen Tripoli was not a suitable locale and hit upon Naples as a substitute because of its orthographic similarity: *Neapolis* for *Tripolis*. Although there was no Cistercian cloister in Naples any more than there was a Tripoli in Calabria, he may not have known that himself, and even if he did, most of his English or French readers would have been unlikely to have noticed the difficulty.

Recognizing that a vision for 1487 could not predict the fall of Tripoli and Acre, the reviser withdrew the reference to those two cities. But his substitute—at least in the surviving copy—is obscure: instead of the capture of Acre, his version predicts the capture of a place called "Agindubium." Whether he had a real locale in mind or invented a name at random is unclear. The surviving copy contains numerous other smaller changes, but these do not seriously affect meaning.[34] Apparently the reviser's purpose was only to make his updating seem credible, not to rewrite the prophecy to his taste.

The surviving English copy of the version for 1487 is in itself worthy of notice because it was definitely the work of a layman. The copyist in question was a southern English landowner named Reginald Andrew who was not a trained scribe but received some rudimentary education, apparently for business purposes. Equipped with some

---

ford, 1971), 87–92. I rely on her description for my comments on the MS and its compiler.

33. England seems the most likely place of origin since the English copyist, Reginald Andrew (on whom more below), would not normally have gained his texts from far off. But the exemplar of the 1487 version is from the French family. The dating to shortly after 1487 is established from the Lyell MS.

34. See the text in Appendix III. As against the best samples from the French family, the Lyell copy has *divino misterio presente* for *uno ministro presente*; *articuli manuscripti* for *articuli manus scribentis*; *ve clero et terror Christianis* for *ve clero et tibi Christianitas*; *vespertilio superabit ducum* [sic] *apum* for *vespertilio superabit dominum apum*; *filii ac filie Ierusalem liberabuntur a captivitate sua civitate Ierusalem* for *filii Ierusalem liberabuntur a captivitate* and *pax xx^tl annis* for *pax per xv annos*.

literacy, he kept a commonplace book from about 1478 to about 1491 wherein he made entries of legal proceedings, accounts, medical recipes, charms, and prayers. Although most of Reginald Andrew's interests were mundane, the opening of his collection, which consists of eschatological prophecies in Latin and English, shows that he hoped to learn more about the extramundane as well. Among the eschatological texts are descriptions of signs to come before the Last Judgment, an English vernacular prophecy about a king who will conquer the Holy Cross, and the vernacular prophecies "When Rome is Removed into England" and "The Cock in the North." In the midst of these texts stands the Tripoli prophecy for 1487, which Reginald took primarily as a warning about Antichrist, as can be seen from his own note at the end: "Here above on Antichrist." Despite his routine concerns, then, warnings about Antichrist were not forgotten.

Having now viewed six redated versions of the Tripoli prophecy, differences at first seem more plentiful than similarities. Two versions (for 1367 and 1396) were changed only by a date; one (for 1347) did make additional changes but aimed primarily to emend for clarity; and another (for 1487) also made changes but aimed primarily to emend for the sake of removing anachronisms. The remaining two (for 1387 and 1400) purposely altered the meaning of the prophecy, but one (for 1387) did so covertly by working within the linguistic framework of the old text, whereas the other made large-scale subtractions and additions at will.

Perhaps, however, a few generalizations may be salvaged. The most important is that all six of the revisers showed fundamental ambivalence about the authority of the texts they transmuted. All must have doubted that a monk in Tripoli saw a hand writing a message over the corporal cloth during mass in 1287, but none proceeded to dismiss the reported message as worthless. On the contrary, all found the message entirely or in part to be of such urgent importance that they took steps to recirculate it in ways that would gain it greater readership. To us their conduct seems irrational: either the entire account should have been accepted, or else it should have been dismissed as the fiction we know it to have been. But all six revisers did not react to the story of the moving hand in terms of such exclusive alternatives:

just because aspects of the account were mistaken did not mean that they should scoff at all of it.

The ambivalence of five of the six revisers can be seen most clearly in the new dates they chose for their resettings of the miracle. Excluding the author of the version for 1400, the other five revisers chose new digits that were very close to the old ones they found in their exemplars: 1347, 1367, 1387, and 1487 in place of 1287; and 1396 in place of 1286. As long as the revisers were inventing, they could have chosen any new dates at all, but these five felt bound to stay as close as they could to the figures they saw before them. Apparently they found something almost magical in the numbers they inherited.

Only the author of the version for 1400 made no attempt to come close to the digits in his exemplar (1287), and he too was the reviser who showed the least respect for the integrity of his text: instead of merely touching up or deftly tinkering with the prophecy he recirculated, he fully transformed it. But even he was ambivalent, for he did not invent a new story and prophecy from scratch but preserved about half of the old one. Most likely he told himself that he was not imagining anything about the future out of his own fancy but was reclaiming an old prophecy that was true in part.

Considering that the six versions varied widely in the extent and quality of their revisions, it is noteworthy that the most artful did not have the widest circulation. On the contrary, the most popular by far was the version for 1347, which was not especially well conceived. Surely the grounds for its popularity lay not in the quality of its revision but in the fact that it was put forth during the time of a frightful pandemic and offered some consolation to its distraught readers. Several readers seem to have noticed that the version of the prophecy for 1347 contained anachronisms,[35] but this did not prevent them from reading it with awe and finding solace in it. It was not their inclination to propose reasons for disbelieving what they wanted to believe. Nor were any of the other redatings, even the deftest of which contained some chronological or factual flaws, rejected as fakes, for late-medieval people, lay as well as clerical, took Last

---

35. See, e.g., MS F (n. 6 above), which omits reference to any date for the vision, and MS Y (n. 9 above), which tells of a vision in an unnamed Cistercian cloister.

Things seriously and were not too critical about the inspiration of prophecies that came their way.[36]

36. In addition to being frequently updated, the Tripoli prophecy was used as a source for plagiarism at least twice in the fourteenth century. One prophecy written in France shortly after 1315 (incipit: *Anno Domini MCCCXV, die decima quinta mensis marcii*—the only copy I know of is given at the opening of the chronicle of Jean de Venette) borrowed from the Tripoli prophecy for its setting and perhaps for its conclusion. Cf. H. Géraud, ed., *Chronique de Guillaume de Nangis et de ses continuateurs* [i.e., the chronicle of Jean de Venette] (Paris, 1843), II, 179–180: "Sacerdos quidam . . . celebrat missam suam in Bethleem ubi Dominus fuit natus, et dum esset in secretum misse sue . . . apparuerunt littere auree coram eo scriptum per hunc modum. . . . Ideo vos boni Christiani vigilate" with the fourteenth-century Chartres MS 322 copy of the Tripoli prophecy (from the French family): ". . . apparuerunt ei manus litteris aureis scribentes super corporale, inter elevacionem et oblacionem hostie salutaris hec verba. . . . Ergo vigilate." (N.B.: the secret of the Mass comes between the oblation and the elevation.) A translation of the Jean de Venette text is by J. Birdsall, *The Chronicle of Jean de Venette*, ed. R. A. Newhall (New York, 1953), 31.

The second plagiarism is a passage from the Tripoli prophecy—*tunc erit pax in toto orbe terrarum et copia fructuum*—embedded in the "lily" prophecy (incipit: *Lilium in meliori* [*nobiliori*] *parte*), originally composed around 1339, probably in England. The earliest copies of this text known to me are in MSS BL Royal 12 C XII, f. 16^r (ca. 1340); and Würzburg Mp. mi. f. 6, f. 37^r (ca. 1350), ed. Hermann Grauert, *Magister Heinrich der Poet* (Munich, 1912), 444. MS UB Basel A V 39, f. 137^r (early 15th century), dates the prophecy to 1339. There are scores of other copies and many editions, including PL 190, 394, and *Chronique de Guillaume de Nangis*, II, 180–181. Among insufficient scattered treatments of the "lily" prophecy, see Thorndike, III, 305–306, and Margaret E. Griffiths, *Early Vaticination in Welsh with English Parallels* (Cardiff, 1937), 170–171.

Chapter VII

THREE GLOSSES

Granted the perennial interest shown in the Tripoli prophecy throughout the later Middle Ages, exactly how did medieval readers interpret its details? We have not yet addressed this question directly because the evidence treated so far offers only the slightest aid in answering it. A few readers recognized that the fall of Tripoli and Acre were real historical events, but that was only acknowledging the obvious. Otherwise the sum of explicit interpretation set forth was minimal: the Percy anthologist considered the Tripoli prophecy to be "A Prognostication from the Holy Land on the Same Sixth"; the author of the treatise *On Natural Causes* emphasized that the last words were a warning to beware the deceptions of Antichrist; and the Breslau Dominican considered the "people without a head" to be the flagellants. None of the other copyists said any more.

The comparative silence of the scribes is not really surprising, for scribes were not expected to be glossators. They could gain their own private understanding of the prophecies they copied, but they did not have to offer commentaries. Yet in the later Middle Ages there were always a few self-elected experts who could be counted upon to explicate arcane predictions in detail, and the Tripoli prophecy did indeed have its close expositors—three independent commentators who all glossed the text closely with confidence. This chapter is dedicated to analyzing their findings and the principles of prophetic interpretation.

Two of the three expositors were fourteenth-century Franciscan visionaries who were among the more bizarre figures of their unsettled age. The first, John of Rupescissa (French: Rochetaillade; Provençal: Roquetaillade), was born near Aurillac shortly after 1300 and, from imprisonment in papal Avignon, played a role similar to that of John the Baptist in Herod's cistern.[1] Rupescissa had studied philosophy at the University of Toulouse from 1328 to 1332 and then entered the Franciscan order. As a Franciscan he became such an ardent exponent of absolute poverty that he fell into disfavor with his provincial minister, who in 1344 threw him into prison. From 1344 until his death shortly after 1365 Rupescissa spent almost all his time in captivity, first in a succession of Franciscan convents, where he suffered under appalling physical conditions, and then, after 1349, in papal imprisonment.

The comparison to John the Baptist and Herod is not as farfetched as it might at first sound. Like his namesake, Rupescissa believed he was a herald of the future and continually warned his captors that they would soon be chastised and succeeded by a new dispensation. Like the tetrarch of Galilee, the pope and cardinals at Avignon reacted with ambivalence. They tried Rupescissa for heresy but were forced to concede that he was no heretic, and they clearly did allow the possibility that he was an inspired prophet. Yet they were loath to grant him his liberty, no doubt because they did not wish to have him fulminating freely against them in public. So they just kept him in prison where he continued to prophesy their doom. From time to time they approached him with questions about the future that he answered with asperity and insolence, thus displaying an indifference to his own fate that must have made him seem all the more inspired.

---

1. I rely for biographical information on Bignami-Odier, *Rupescissa*, 15–50. E. F. Jacob, "John of Roquetaillade," *Bulletin of the John Rylands Library*, 39 (1956/57), 75–96, reprinted in Jacob, *Essays in Later Medieval History* (Manchester, 1968), 175–194, is derivative and directionless. On Rupescissa's alchemy, see Thorndike, III, 347–369. After this chapter went to press, articles on Rupescissa's prophecy and alchemy appeared in the *Histoire littéraire de la France*, 41 (Paris, 1981), 75–284, but neither presents any new information relevant to what follows.

Anxious to keep their oracle in inspirational trim, Rupescissa's captors supplied him with his prophetic needs: numerous books, news of current events, and writing materials. They also preserved and recopied his writings, with the probably unintended result that these quickly travelled beyond the limited circle of the curia. Thus Rupescissa's fame spread while his person was confined: copies of his prophetic treatises circulated throughout Western Europe and continued to be read, translated, and excerpted for centuries after his death.

Rupescissa's self-conception of his prophetic gifts was to some degree restricted. In his mind, he was not a prophet like Isaiah, Jeremiah, or Ezekiel, who received direct prophetic revelation from God, but was only gifted with "the intelligence of prophecies." By this he meant that he did have divine inspiration, but only inspiration to interpret preexisting prophetic texts that had been revealed directly. One of these was the Tripoli prophecy, which Rupescissa accepted as having been written by God or an angel in the city of Tripoli, and which he kept in his cell in more than one copy.[2]

Rupescissa knew the Tripoli prophecy so well that he cited it twice as if he had written it himself. In an introduction he wrote to his alchemical treatise, the *Liber lucis* (Book of Light), in 1354 (Rupescissa dabbled in alchemy as well as prophecy), he explained that it was time for him to reveal the secrets of the philosopher's stone because the Church was soon to be despoiled of all its temporal wealth: knowledge of alchemy would help the chosen people of God to relieve their wants. The historian of science Lynn Thorndike assumed that all of this passage was expressed in Rupescissa's own words, but in fact a sentence of it comes from the Tripoli prophecy, namely the line about the tossing of Peter's ship.[3] Similarly, a later source at-

2. Rupescissa wavered between having the prophecy written by God or an angel: see quotations in n. 9 below. His possession of more than one copy is indicated by the fact that he has Peter's ship "liberated" in three quotations that he gives from the prophecy in two different works (see nn. 3 and 9) but he has the ship "dominating at the end of days" in another (see n. 9). The former form is otherwise unique whereas the latter is canonical. None of the quotations from the Tripoli prophecy that Rupescissa gives in his *Liber ostensor* (see nn. 9, 10, and 12) fits into the French family, but the quotation attributed to him in n. 4 does in its use of *surget* instead of *veniet*.

3. Thorndike, III, 352, 365–369, and edition 737: "Sed licet iactetur in validis fluctibus Petri navicula est tamen liberanda in fine dierum domina generalis."

tributes to Rupescissa a prediction that the Franciscans will be chastised by a "people without a head," who will "annihilate the mendicant orders," clearly another citation from the message of the moving hand.[4]

Rupescissa's actual glossing of the Tripoli prophecy appears in his enormous *Liber ostensor* (Book of Revealings) of 1356.[5] This was a sprawling assemblage of commentaries on numerous prophetic texts based on the assumption that they all alluded to the present and immediate future and all concorded so fully that they could be used to interpret each other. Thus, arbitrary though it now may seem, Rupescissa argued in the *Liber ostensor* that several different prophecies referred to the devastation of Italy in the 1350s by contingents of freebooters known collectively as the Great Company. He was led to this idea by the text of a certain "Neapolitan prophecy," supposedly revealed by an angel in 1260 but which in his view alluded to events of his own age.[6] Since the Neapolitan prophecy spoke of "the coming of

Thorndike's qualms about attributing the *Liber lucis* to Rupescissa should be alleviated by the link between this quotation and the first one from Rupescissa's *Liber ostensor* cited in n. 9 below.

4. The source is an otherwise unknown treatise on Gen. 3:1 in MS Schloss Pommersfelden 102, fos. 95ʳ–102ᵛ. On this MS from Nürnberg, see Chapter Six, n. 27. This part of the MS must have been copied shortly after 1493 because it includes (fos. 103ʳ–104ʳ) a copy made from the printed *Versus reperti Jherosolimis* . . . which was published in that year. (A copy of the printed version is Munich, Bayerische Staatsbibliothek, Einblattdruck V, 54.) The citation from Rupescissa in question appears on f. 100ᵛ: "De fratribus minoribus dicit Rupecissa quod surget gens nova sine capite et ordines mendicancium anichilabunt et crudeliter devastabunt. . . ." I have been unable to identify the source for this quotation but there is good reason to believe that it is genuine because Rupescissa did otherwise predict the imminent devastation of the Franciscan order: see, e.g., Bignami-Odier, *Rupescissa*, 166. Many of Rupescissa's works have been lost (see Bignami-Odier, 186–190) and this quotation may be from one of them.

5. The *Liber ostensor* survives uniquely in MS Vat. Ross. lat. 753, where it runs to 149 octavo-sized folios. A summary of its contents and list of the prophecies it cites is provided by Bignami-Odier, *Rupescissa*, 140–156.

6. On this prophecy and Rupescissa's other references to it in the *Liber ostensor*, see Bignami-Odier, *Rupescissa*, 155. I have not seen any other trace of the Neapolitan prophecy in any other source. On the Great Company, see Emile G. Leonard, *Les Angevins de Naples* (Paris, 1954), 376–378, 536, and Peter Partner, "Florence and the Papacy, 1300–1375," in J. R. Hale et al., eds., *Europe in the Late Middle Ages* (Evanston, 1965), 102–103, both citing more specialized literature.

the wicked and of tyrants who would make conventicles without heads," Rupescissa concluded that these headless conventicles were bands of the terrible Great Company.[7] Another prophecy, that of the Erythrean Sibyl, confirmed this reading because it referred to the coming of a "congregation of many peoples living bestially"[8]—obviously the same Great Company—and the Tripoli prophecy's prediction of a coming "people without a head" further confirmed his interpretation.[9]

Once it was established that the freebooters of the Great Company were the Tripoli prophecy's "people without a head," other lines of the prophecy made immediate sense, for, even as Rupescissa was writing, the Great Company was threatening the security of the papal patrimony in Italy. In Rupescissa's view, the marauders would not soon be stopped because they were forerunners of Antichrist who were destined to bring great hardships to the Church and the papacy. Accordingly, the Tripoli prophecy's lines about "woe to the clergy and to all Christianity" and about the "tossing of Peter's ship" clearly alluded to their imminent chastisement.[10]

7. MS Vat. Ross. lat. 753, f. 10[r]: "*Surgent in partibus Ytalis tiranni et improbi absque capitibus conventicula facientes.*" Rupescissa explains that this is a reference to the Great Company on fos. 10[r] and 65[v]. Here and in the following quotations from the *Liber ostensor* my italicization follows the underlining found in the MS.

8. MS cit., f. 10[r]: "De qua gente scribit Erithea [*sic*] Sibilla . . . dicens: *Post hec . . . fiet congregacio multarum gencium bestialiter vivencium.*" The same passage is quoted to make the same argument on f. 65[v]. It comes from the original longer version of the "Erythrean Sibyl," in Holder-Egger, 15, 171.

9. MS cit., f. 10[r]: "Nam in prophecia que fuit in civitate Tripolitana scripta per angelum super corporalia dum missa diceretur, que incipit *alta cedrus Libani succidetur*, inter alia sic dicitur: *Gens veniet sine capite et tunc veh clero et toti Christianitati, quia navicula Petri iactabitur in validis fluctibus sed liberabitur in fine dierum.*" Cf. f. 38[r]: "Sexto appellatur Ionas [a future eschatological "reparator"] quia cum navicula Petri iactabitur nunc in proximo in validis fluctibus liberanda in fine dierum, salvabitur Ionas iste. . . ." Later in the same work, f. 65[v], Rupescissa makes the same argument concerning the people without a head: "Hec est gens sine capite de qua Deus in prophecia Tripolitana que incipit *alta cedrus Libani succidetur* sic ad literam prophetat, dicens: *Gens quedam veniet que vocabitur sine capite; veh tunc clero et omni Christianitati; navicula Petri iactabitur in validis fluctibus sed dominabitur in fine dierum.*"

10. MS cit., f. 10[r]: ". . . magna societas est signum et principium horrendorum malorum potissime futurorum contra ecclesiam Dei. . . . de qua gente dicit quod

As the "people without a head" were advance forces of Antichrist, so the "lion of the East" and "beast of the West" in the Tripoli prophecy were two heads of Antichrist himself. Rupescissa introduced this interpretation in the course of a close commentary on a vision revealed to a Franciscan friar of Aragon in 1345 that referred mysteriously to the casting down of two kings, one called vaguely "A. cedar" and the other simply "A."[11] Relying on arcane biblical exegesis, Rupescissa concluded that "A. cedar" was a coming Saracen ruler who would unite all the infidels against Christianity. That of course made this Saracen the "lion of the East," from which it followed that the other king was his counterpart, "the beast of the West." Since this beast bore the initial "A.," Rupescissa concluded that he must be either the king of England (*Anglia*) or the king of Aragon, both enemies in 1356 of Rupescissa's hero, the king of France.[12] As the Saracen king would unite the infidels, the Western king would soon succeed in wresting for himself the Holy Roman Empire. Then the two together would subjugate the world and act as Antichrist before being overthrown at the dawn of a new dispensation.[13]

---

elevabit Antichristum contra agnum et ad literam hanc gentem hodie prosperari videmus in regno Karoli [i.e., Naples]"; f. 65ᵛ: "Finem eorum post eorum profectum concludit ubi ait: *Super pennas ventorum ascendent in altum,* sicut est dies ista cum volaverunt super regem Ludovicum [Naples] et consequenter volatum superbie in altantes super legatum apostolice sedis [Cardinal Albornoz] in Romandiola, ut verificetur quod in Tripolitana dicetur *tunc veh clero et omni Christianitati,* . . . dicens quia *navicula Petri,* generalis ecclesia mater nostra Romana, *iactabitur* per eos *in validis fluctibus* tribulacionum, donec imperio Christi . . . cessent fluctus tempestuosi et infernales venti."

11. This is how Rupescissa understood the strange line "et iterum a cedar a rege cum altero prostruabitur." He gives the full text of the Aragonese prophecy of 1345 (which I have not seen elsewhere) in MS cit., f. 33ᵛ.

12. MS cit., f. 36ᵛ: "Secundum meam opinionem iste a. cedar erit unus rex potentissimus sarracenus qui veniet cum infinito populo infideli contra populum Christianum. Et estimo ipsum fore unum regem potentissimum orientis. . . . Et alterum a. regem estimo unum regem Christianum, sicut si dicerem regem Aragonie vel Anglie. . . . Nam et similiter opinor quod alter a. rex cum quo prostruabitur sit sibi contrarius rex Christianus futurus monarcha tocius occidentis, ac si esset rex Aragonie vel Anglorum. Et hos duos estimo fore illos de quibus in prophecia Tripolitana, que incipit *alta cedrus Libani succidetur,* dicitur sic: *leo orientalis,* quantum ad *a. cedar,* et *bestia occidentalis,* quantum ad alterum a. regem Christianum *universum orbem subiugabunt.*"

13. Ibid.: "Quapropter ego estimo quod angelus in hiis duobus regibus intro-

Needless to say, none of these predictions came true. We do not know how Rupescissa rationalized his mistakes, but of greater interest here is the fact that similar present-mindedness and similar faith in the concordance of prophecies yielded very different results when the same passages of the miraculous message from Tripoli were glossed by another Franciscan visionary only twenty-one years after Rupescissa wrote the *Liber ostensor*. The second Franciscan was no imprisoned prophet but the Infante Peter of Aragon—brother, uncle, and great-uncle of successive Aragonese kings.[14] Born in 1305, Peter led an active political life until 1358, governing his own counties of Ribagorza and Prades, twice serving as regent of Aragon, and participating in the Aragonese conquest of Majorca of 1344. But in 1358 the death of his wife, Joanna of Foix, moved him to forsake his worldly existence and become a Franciscan. Thereafter he exchanged the role of Aragonese magnate for that of religious visionary. In 1365 he proclaimed miraculous revelations to the effect that the popes should return to Rome (thus anticipating Catherine of Siena), and in 1379 he announced more revelations, this time communicating divine partisanship for the Urbanist cause in the Great Schism. From 1379 to 1381, Peter fought zealously for the lost cause of the Urbanists in Spain, dying in the latter year in Pisa on his way to a meeting with Urban VI. His remains were brought back to Valencia where they were subsequently venerated.

Peter's commentary on the Tripoli prophecy was written in Catalan in 1377 when he was an old man of seventy-two and is preserved in an enormous collection of documents gathered in the 1390s by the Spanish cardinal, Martin de Zalva.[15] Composed before the out-

---

ducit hos duos futuros monarchas, scilicet Antichristum orientalem et Antichristum occidentalem"; f. 37ʳ: "Et sine dubio ipse [the "beast of the West"] est rex qui Karolo inclito imperatori Romane succedet in imperio Romanorum in brevi."

14. For Peter's career I rely primarily on Pou y Martí, 308–396.

15. This collection, now housed in the Vatican Archivio Segreto, is described by Michael Seidlmayer. *Die Anfänge des grossen abendländischen Schismas* (Münster, 1940), 197–228; and more fully by Seidlmayer, "Die spanischen 'Libri de Schismate' des Vatikanischen Archivs," *Gesammelte Aufsätze zur Kulturgeschichte Spaniens*, Spanische Forschungen der Görresgesellschaft, ser. I, 8 (1940), 199–262. The original—the Tripoli prophecy in Latin and Peter's appended com-

break of the Schism, the conversion of the world and the advent of Antichrist, rather than papal politics, are its foremost concerns. That a seventy-two-year-old infante turned Franciscan should spend his time during a relatively uneventful year of the fourteenth century poring over an old prophecy he knew to have been written eighty years earlier in order to gain and promulgate hidden wisdom about the end of the world tells us much about the intensity of fourteenth-century eschatological preoccupations.

Peter prefaced his commentary with a copy of the Tripoli prophecy from a Latin transmission that is not otherwise represented in this study. In this version, the date of the vision is given as 1297 instead of 1287, and no location is specified for the Cistercian cloister in which it supposedly transpired. In order to understand Peter's commentary, it is also necessary to know that the version he used had the "bat" chasing away "Saturn" instead of the "lord of the bees" and had "one god and one faith" coming fifteen years after the bat chases Saturn.[16]

Try as one might to avoid patronizing the past, Peter's commentary itself appears bizarre, distorted, and at times touchingly naif. Although as far as Peter knew, the vision had transpired in 1297, he understood it to begin by predicting events that had happened before then. According to him, the high cedar of Lebanon was the "humility of holy mother Church," felled by pride in the time of Pope Nicholas III (1277–1280) when the cardinals and other prelates abandoned themselves to "disordered pomp."[17] Unable to refrain from

mentary in Catalan—is in Archivio Segreto, Armarium LIV, num. 17, fos. 126ra–127rb (modern 129ra–130rb). The whole is edited by Alfonso Maria de Barcelona, "El Infante Fray Pedro de Aragón," *Estudios Franciscanos*, 15 (1915), 58–65 (at 61–65). A better edition of most of the commentary is provided by Pou y Martí, 370–372. I am grateful to Professor William D. Paden for help in reading Peter's Catalan.

16. Peter's version has numerous smaller changes which do not affect meaning, except for one that has Peter's ship "enduring" instead of "dominating" at the end of days. At the end of the prophecy, without interruption, appear the words: "Joaquim: veniet dies in quibus gallici gallicos interficient." Apparently this is an incipit of a pseudo-Joachite text, but I am unable to identify it. For the full "Peter of Aragon" version of the Tripoli prophecy, see Appendix III.

17. The onset of venality during the pontificate of Nicholas III was a commonplace: see the "Vision of Friar John," in Donckel, "Visio," 372, 375: "A tempore infelicis Nicolai III pauci aut nulli facti sunt absque symoniaca pravitate"; the first of the oldest group of "Pope Prophecies"—*Genus nequam ursa*

displaying his erudition, Peter then explained that one could read about the corruption of the curia under Nicholas in a book about the popes and emperors called the *Martiniana* because it was written in the time of the Pope Martin [IV] who succeeded Nicholas III. In fact, while there was indeed a widely circulated chronicle about popes and emperors called the *Martiniana*, it took its name not from Martin IV but from its author, Martin of Troppau.[18]

Peter proceeded to comment that the destruction of Tripoli and the capture of Acre could be understood literally because Acre did indeed fall in the time of Pope Nicholas IV, who, he added proudly but irrelevantly, was a Franciscan. Of course the fall of Acre could hardly be interpreted as anything other than the fall of Acre, but Peter did not confront the difficulty that the city had already been lost by 1297, the year in which the prophecy, according to his version, was issued.

From there Peter took a great leap forward to his own age, and into what seems now like the purest caprice, by glossing Mars, Saturn, Jupiter, and the "bat" as, respectively, his nephew Peter IV of Aragon (1336–1387), Peter I (the Cruel) of Castile (1350–1369), Edward the Black Prince of England, and Henry II (of Trastámara) of Castile (1369–1379). All four figures played leading roles in the complicated struggles for the domination of Castile in the 1360s. Peter's commentary alludes to these struggles without mentioning that his son, Alfonso de Villena, count of Denia, was an active participant in them and that he himself occasionally played a part in the turbulent events.[19]

---

catulos pascens—as described by Herbert Grundmann, "Die Papstprophetien des Mittelalters," AfK, 19 (1928), 77–138 (at 91–92) (repr. Grundmann, *Ausgewählte Aufsätze*, II [Stuttgart, 1977], 1–57 [at 14]), or Reeves, *Influence of Prophecy*, 193, 523; and Dante, *Inferno*, XIX, 70–72.

18. The version of the *Martiniana* Peter referred to had to have been a continuation of the original chronicle of Martin of Troppau, which ended before the reign of Nicholas III: see the edition in MGH, *Scriptores*, 22, 377–475. There were numerous continuations of this extremely popular work, but I have been unable to find one that refers explicitly to corruption under Nicholas III.

19. A detailed account of the complicated Spanish politics of the 1360s can be found in P. E. Russell, *The English Intervention in Spain and Portugal in the Time of Edward III and Richard II* (Oxford, 1955), 13–148. Russell comments on Alfonso's and Peter's partisanship, 98, n. 2. A more general survey is J. N. Hillgarth, *The Spanish Kingdoms, 1250–1516, I: 1250–1410* (Oxford, 1976), 372–393.

According to Peter, Peter of Aragon was Mars because Mars was the god of battles and Aragon comes from the altar of battle (*ara agonis*) on which the heathens made sacrifice to Mars! Correspondingly, Peter the Cruel was Saturn because Saturn was the highest (i.e., farthest) of the planets and malevolent: before his fall, Peter had been the most powerful king in Spain and exceedingly cruel. These identifications established, it followed that the domination of Mars over Saturn alluded to the defeat and death of Peter the Cruel in 1369 because the king of Aragon had been one of the principal architects of Peter's downfall. (The same king of Aragon had been one of Rupescissa's candidates for the role of western Antichrist, but the infante knew nothing of that.)

Edward the Black Prince was Jupiter because Edward was as good and virtuous as the planet Jupiter. The Black Prince's entry into this forced exegesis arose from the fact that he was an important actor in Spanish politics of the 1360s. Although Edward had invaded Spain and won the battle of Nájera in 1367 as an ally of Peter the Cruel, he gained the infante's sympathy because afterwards he was allegedly cheated by Peter and forced to return north. For the infante, Peter's cheating of Edward was "Saturn's" ambush of Jupiter.

The royal commentator's real hero was Henry of Trastámara, the "bat." Henry, half brother of Peter the Cruel, had been raised as a pretender to the Castilian throne by the French and the Aragonese. It was his initial success that led to the intervention of the Black Prince against Henry at Nájera, where the infante's son Alfonso was one of the leading commanders of Henry's army. Defeated at Nájera, Henry of Trastámara escaped with his life and continued to oppose Peter the Cruel with French support. Important negotiations between Henry and the French took place in 1368 with the Infante Peter himself acting as intermediary.[20] In the following year, Henry, supported by the French commander Du Guesclin, surprised Peter the Cruel in camp at Montiel, and then, luring him out of a safe retreat, murdered him with his own hands.

The infante did not adduce any particular traits that made Henry seem like a bat, but he explained that the prediction of the bat chasing away Saturn alluded to the outcome at Montiel, where Henry not

20. Russell, 139, n. 3.

only put Peter the Cruel to flight but took his life. The infante here also introduced a prediction about a "bat" in another prophecy, the *Ve mundo in centum annis*, which said that "the bat will devour the gnats of Spain."[21] This he took as confirmation of his view that the bat applied to Henry of Trastámara. In fact, the line in the *Ve mundo* prophecy certainly gave Peter the idea that Henry was a "bat" in the first place because it appears within the context of a set of predictions specifically referring to Spain. Nothing in the Tripoli prophecy could have allowed Peter to believe that "Mars," "Saturn," "Jupiter," and the "bat" were figures from Spanish politics, but once *Ve mundo* led him to conclude that Henry of Trastámara was a bat, the rest followed, for all truly inspired prophecies were *ipso facto* harmonious. We will see later, moreover, that Peter relied on *Ve mundo* very heavily for his understanding of the future.

Peter set forth his belief in the harmony of prophecy again when he explained that the coming of "one god and one faith" and the disappearance of the "other god" pertained to the ultimate victory over the infidel to be gained by Henry of Trastámara. This he said was foretold by numerous prophets such as Merlin, the abbot Joachim, John of Rupescissa, the author of *Ve mundo*, the "hermit of the Lamposa," and others who had "the spirit of prophecy."[22] In particular, he believed that a prophecy of "Joachim's" concorded closely with the Tripoli prophecy.[23] According to Peter, this prophecy foretold

21. . . . *vespertilio scinifes Hyspanie devoret.* On the *Ve mundo* prophecy, see above pp. 40 and 123.

22. On the prophecies of "Merlin" and "Joachim" see, respectively, nn. 23 and 25 below. Most likely, Peter knew either Rupescissa's *Liber secretorum eventuum* or his *Vade mecum in tribulacione*: see n. 26 below. The prophecy of the "hermit of the Lamposa" [Lampedusa, island south of Sicily] was well known in late-medieval Spain: it was cited by the Catalan Francesc Eiximenis in his *Vida de Jesucrist* (shortly before 1404), on which see Pou y Martí, 413; by a certain Diego Ruiz, who influenced the wife of James, count of Urgel (around 1412), on which see José Tarré, "Las Profecías del Sabio Merlín y sus imitaciones," *Analecta Sacra Tarraconensia*, 16 (1943), 135–171 (at 161) (Mr. Harold Lee kindly called my attention to this article); and by Pedro Azamar (a Catalan who wrote in Castilian) in his *Derecho militar* (1476), on which see A. Morel-Fatio, "Souhaits de Bienvenue, addressés à Ferdinand le Catholique," *Romania*, 11 (1882), 333–356 (at 339–341). I have yet to locate a complete MS copy.

23. I cannot identify this text with certainty, but perhaps it is the prophecy *Leo surgit Yspanus*, which predicts the victory of a Spanish hero over the Sara-

that "the lion of Spain," namely Henry, would destroy the infidels in 1390. Since the Tripoli prophecy said that there would be "one god and one faith" within fifteen years after the triumph of the bat over Saturn, it came very close to predicting Henry's triumph over the infidel around the same time. (With a little forcing, Peter counted the fifteen years not from the battle of Montiel but from the year of composition, 1377, a reckoning that pointed to the ultimate victory in 1392; the difference between that figure and 1390, he explained, was accounted for by the fact that "Joachim" predicted the date for the beginning of the conquest of the infidels while the Tripoli prophecy predicted the date for the end of it!)

When the infidels were conquered, the Jews would be saved. This, according to Peter, was the meaning of the Tripoli prophecy's line about the "liberation of the sons of Israel from captivity." For him this prediction concorded with another prophecy by "Joachim," one that began, *Erit inicium leopardum.* In this prophecy, "Joachim" was mainly concerned with forecasting the triumphs of Henry of Trastámara (Peter credited the Calabrian abbot, who died in 1202, with remarkable foresight about a Spanish usurper of the later fourteenth century), but he also foretold that a "remnant" of the Jews would be converted.[24]

Up to this point, Peter had the Tripoli prophecy moving forward chronologically, but in glossing the following lines concerning the "people without a head" he moved backward. The "people without a head" were not some terrible race of the future but were contemporary Gascons and Germans, particularly Germans. The infante's explanation for this novel interpretation was first that both nations, and especially the Germans, possessed "little sense and little reason";

---

cens. This is cited in full by Rupescissa, *Liber ostensor*, in MS Vat. Ross. lat. 753, f. 58ᵛ, and appears in MS BN lat. 2599 (late 14th century), f. 266ʳ⁻ᵛ. Neither of these versions, however, attributes the prophecy to Joachim, and neither contains a clear prediction of Christian victory in 1390. (Professor Bernard McGinn kindly lent me his microfilm of BN lat. 2599.)

24. I am relying on the assumption—the best I can infer from the internal evidence—that Peter was working with two pseudo-Joachite texts: one which alluded to Henry of Trastámara as the "lion of Spain" (perhaps *Leo surgit Yspanus*), and another which calls Henry a leopard and which must be the *Erit inicium leopardum* that Peter cites in relation to the conversion of the Jews.

therefore, figuratively, they were headless! The Germans could also be recognized as the "people without a head" for two other reasons: they were "headless" insofar as their ruler, the Emperor, was weakened by the power of the princes and thus did not rule as strongly as other kings; moreover, the prophecy had the "people without a head" causing troubles for the clergy and all Christianity, and the Germans in their struggles with the papacy had brought great scandals to the Church.

As the "people without a head" were contemporary Gascons and Germans, so the tossing of "Peter's ship" in the waves had already begun in current events, above all in Italy, where "many cities and tyrannies" had risen up against the Church. Writing in 1377, Peter must have been thinking of the War of Eight Saints, then being waged against the papacy by Florence and several other cities, and perhaps also of the struggle between Milan and the papacy that had been concluded in 1375. The prophecy's lines about battles, famines, plagues, and "mutations of kingdoms" also referred to the present, a fact Peter deemed so obvious that it called for no further comment.

Although the prophecy referred to the present in large part, the prediction that "the land of the barbarians will be converted" alluded again to the future. Now violating chronological order completely, Peter explained that the conversion of the land of the barbarians was a rephrasing of what had earlier been said in the prophecy about the coming of "one god and one faith." In other words, he believed that the prophecy moved randomly back and forth in time and included repetitions. Orderly procedure was not a trait he expected from divine oracles.

Not surprisingly, the line that gave him the greatest trouble was the prediction that the mendicant orders and "other sects" would be annihilated. Since the Franciscan infante was himself a member of one of the mendicant orders, he could not have been expected to have been pleased with this prediction. But to his credit he did not try to alter or suppress it. Instead he took the sting out of equating the mendicants with "sects" by glossing "sects" as "forms of life" (presumably such as tertiaries and beguines). Then he said that there was no purpose in interpreting the whole passage because "what would come of it, the Lord only knew."

That hurdle obviated, Peter was at ease in expatiating on the meaning of "the beast of the West and the lion of the East," the two creatures who would subjugate the world. The "beast of the West" was again Henry of Trastámara, the king of Castile, who, according to Peter, had elsewhere been called a beast by "Merlin" and by "Joachim."[25] Henry could also be identified as "bestial" because he was sensual and was "the beast of the West" because Castile is located at the western extremity of the world. As for the "lion of the East," that creature was Antichrist, an eastern lion in his diabolical nature and cruelty. The "eastern lion," furthermore, had to be Antichrist because modern prophecies predicted that Antichrist would come out of the East.

Whereas the apparent meaning of the line about the beast and the lion was that they would subjugate the world jointly, Peter interpreted it to mean that they would rule the world by turns. It is doubtful that he would have reached this conclusion from reading the Tripoli prophecy alone, but his understanding of it was once again aided by the *Ve mundo* prophecy, which he at this point glossed within his gloss. Where *Ve mundo* referred to a culmination of war in Spain during the time of a "young beast of burden," Peter glossed it to refer to the troubles during the time of Peter the Cruel. Where it talked of the "devouring of the gnats of Spain by the bat," he took it to refer to the triumph of Henry of Trastámara. He then took the subsequent lines of *Ve mundo*, which predicted that the "bat" would subjugate Africa, "receive the monarchy," and "humiliate the inhabitants of the Nile in his posterity," to refer to the future triumphs of Henry and his successors. In conquering Africa and the Nile, the house of Trastámara would rule the world, but thereafter, according to *Ve mundo*, Antichrist would appear suddenly to separate "the sons of Jerusalem" from "the sons of Babylon." That, for Peter, was the same prediction as the reference in the Tripoli prophecy to the subjugation of the world by the "eastern lion."

Since Peter believed that there would be two successive conquests of the world, one by Henry of Trastámara and the other by Antichrist, he was free to choose which of these conquests the Tripoli

25. The pro-Trastámara Spanish Merlin prophecy that refers to Henry as a lion is described by Tarré (n. 22 above), 157.

prophecy's prediction of peace and abundance of fruit for fifteen years applied to. Remarkably, he took the pessimistic alternative and interpreted the coming peace and abundance to refer to the temptations or deceptions of Antichrist. The prediction of a coming successful crusade, however, alluded again to the glorious deeds of King Henry. The prophecy had already said in several ways that Henry would destroy the infidel, and here it said so again. In conclusion it predicted that during the time of Christian triumph and great tranquillity under Henry "news would be heard of Antichrist," and that one therefore should be vigilant. Peter himself closed with the declaration that all he had said was subject to the correction of the holy mother Church.

From the foregoing, it may be seen that three major influences were dominant in determining the lines of Peter's interpretation—the text of *Ve mundo*, Peter's partisanship for Henry of Trastámara, and his conviction that history was reaching a climax. Peter's reading of the *Ve mundo* prophecy alone was not too forced. That text did refer explicitly to troubles in Spain, to the emergence of a "bat" or hero who would triumph in Spain and Africa, and to the reign of Antichrist thereafter. Even in choosing Henry of Trastámara for the role of the "bat" Peter was not being entirely arbitrary. In fact, this interpretation might have been pointed out to him by John of Rupescissa, for in several works written between 1349 and 1356—at least one of which the infante knew—Rupescissa wrote that the "beast of burden" in *Ve mundo* who would precede the "bat" was Peter the Cruel.[26] Since Rupescissa did not yet know of Henry of Trastámara's emergence, he could not possibly have placed Henry in the role of the "bat," but Peter could easily make that identification given Henry's victory over Peter the Cruel at Monteil. Aside from that, some con-

26. The infante's knowledge of one of Rupescissa's works is indicated by his reference to Rupescissa in his commentary. Rupescissa makes Peter the Cruel the beast of burden in his *Liber secretorum eventuum* of 1349, his commentary on *Ve mundo* of 1354/55, his *Liber ostensor* of 1356, and his *Vade mecum* of 1356: see, respectively, Bignami-Odier, *Rupescissa*, 121, 136–137, 144–145, 160. The infante was most likely to have known either the *Liber secretorum eventuum* or the *Vade mecum*, both of which circulated widely. It is virtually certain that he did not know the other two works because copies of them were rare and because his readings of *Ve mundo* and the Tripoli prophecy otherwise show no trace of their influence.

temporary Spanish ruler simply had to play the role of the "bat" because *Ve mundo* predicted events that would happen within one hundred years after the fall of the Holy Land, and those hundred years were about to be completed around the time the Infante Peter wrote.

It was in forcing a correspondence between *Ve mundo* and the Tripoli prophecy that Peter became capricious. Nothing in the latter text, with the possible exception of the single reference to the "beast of the West," hints at Spain. Nor does anything in the prophecy suggest that the "bat" at the beginning is the same as the "beast" at the end or refer clearly to Antichrist except the last words. Peter probably only became inspired to gloss the Tripoli prophecy once he recognized the possibility of identifying its bat with the Spanish bat (Henry of Trastámara) of *Ve mundo*, and once he started there was no stopping him.

Although Peter's partisanship for Henry of Trastámara explains his conviction that Henry was the messianic hero of both texts, in 1377 such conviction was quixotic. After murdering Peter the Cruel at Montiel in 1369, Henry of Trastámara was hardly able to consolidate his rule in Castile, let alone move on to foreign conquests, for until his death in 1379 Henry was constantly beset by internal and external enemies (including the Englishman John of Gaunt, who had married Peter the Cruel's heiress and become intent on building "castles in Spain").[27] But throughout these vicissitudes, the Infante Peter and his son Alfonso remained Henry's loyal supporters, and Peter was clearly willing to believe that miracles might happen.[28]

Behind that willingness lay the infante's ultimate preoccupation: his view that the drama of earthly history would soon be reaching its end. For him, current events and God-granted prophecies pointed to the same conclusion. By 1377 Peter had lived through the Black Death, the prolonged retreat of the papacy in Avignon, and unceasing

---

27. On the diplomatic and military history of Henry's troubled reign, see Russell, 149–282. On the security of Granada in this period, see C. J. Bishko, "The Spanish and Portuguese Reconquest, 1095–1492," in Kenneth M. Setton, ed., *A History of the Crusades*, III (Madison, Wisc., 1975), 443.

28. Peter's son Alfonso remained loyal to the Trastámara line in the succeeding reign at least until 1385: see Russell, 394.

bitter warfare in Spain and all of Europe. As we have seen, he thought that the troubles of the papacy in Italy were part of the final trials of the Church, and he thought that the Tripoli prophecy had already been proven accurate in its prediction of wars, famines, plagues, and "mutations of kingdoms." Such multiple afflictions must have been signs of the End, a view that prophecy confirmed. *Ve mundo* told him of apocalyptic events that would occur before the end of the four-teenth century, a prophecy by "Joachim" told him that the whole world would begin to be converted in 1390, and the Tripoli prophecy told him that this conversion would be completed three years later. Once the world was converted, Antichrist would soon come and the Last Judgment would not be far off. In this light, there was every reason to be vigilant.

In Peter's case, vigilance included studying all available prophe-cies to see how they corresponded, interrelated, and charted the fu-ture. But those very concerns encouraged forced readings. The in-fante let his reading of *Ve mundo* affect his reading of the Tripoli prophecy whenever it was in any way applicable, and when *Ve mundo* failed to guide him he looked for concordances in other obscure pro-phetic texts. When he could find no concordances at all, he inter-preted details of the Tripoli prophecy in the most idiosyncratic ways, as in making Mars the king of Aragon on the grounds of the supposed derivation from *ara agonis*, or in making the "people without a head" Gascons and Germans.

The fact that John of Rupescissa saw in the same "people without a head" the Great Company of the 1350s makes it clear that lines of the Tripoli prophecy could be read in remarkably different ways by near contemporaries. In fact, almost all of Rupescissa's interpretations were different from Peter's. For Rupescissa the tossing of Saint Peter's ship was the imminent chastisement to be dispensed by the Great Company, but for Peter it was the harrowing of the papacy by Florence and other Italian states. For Rupescissa the "beast of the West and the lion of the East" would reign concurrently, but for Peter they would reign by turns. For Rupescissa the "beast of the West" was a villainous king of England or Aragon, who would be a western Antichrist, but for Peter he was a heroic Henry of Castile, who would be a western messiah. Only in making the "lion of the East" an evil

Antichrist did the two agree, but even there one conceived of him as being less of a general Antichrist than the other.

The comparison between the readings of Rupescissa and Peter of Aragon is particularly telling because both were Franciscans who worked only a score of years apart and because Peter had even read some of Rupescissa's work. Moreover, both shared basic assumptions and methods. Both believed that earthly history was facing an imminent crisis, both believed that the Tripoli prophecy was a guide to understanding it, and both believed that the prophecy could best be understood in the light of current events and of other prophecies. Even though the two Franciscans shared these assumptions and methods, their interpretations differed because times had changed and because the prophecies they used to establish their concordances were different. Someone who looked for the reign of Antichrist around the 1390s was bound to find different portents than another who looked for it in the 1360s, and someone who read the Tripoli prophecy in the light of *Ve mundo* was bound to interpret it differently than another who read it in the light of the Neapolitan prophecy, the Erythrean Sibyl, and the vision of an Aragonese friar of 1345.

John and Peter, therefore, could virtually have been reading a different prophecy when it came to their explanation of details. Nonetheless, they did agree that the Tripoli prophecy pointed to an imminent crisis in history. Insofar as they both believed that details of the prophecy were reflected and confirmed by current events and the words of other prophecies, such a belief strengthened their certainty of the imminence of Last Things. The Tripoli prophecy, in other words, provided validation and encouragement for their belief that the trials they were experiencing were signs of even more dramatic events—evil and beneficent—still to come. The message written by the moving hand helped them come to grips with contemporary troubles by charting a path from the troubled present to the dreadful and wonderful future.

The third surviving commentary on the Tripoli prophecy was written in a completely different time and place, yet it still fits into the same pattern. This was an exposition written about 1527 in Speyer on the Rhine in the form of scattered interlinear glosses added in a tiny script to a much older copy.[29] The copy in question, made in Speyer in the middle of the fourteenth century, was one that had the miracle transpiring in 1348. It is certain that it remained in Speyer until around 1548 because in that year or a year or two earlier the manuscript containing it was acquired by the Wittelsbach prince and book collector, Ottheinrich of Pfalz-Neuburg, who was residing and gathering manuscripts in the vicinity.[30]

Whoever made the interlinear glosses around 1527 knew that the Tripoli prophecy was centuries old but nonetheless read it confidently as a message pertaining to contemporary and imminent events. In his view, the opening alluded not to the fall of Christian bastions in the Holy Land in the late thirteenth century (which would have been a highly improbable interpretation given the fact that his copy dated the miracle to 1348), but to events he expected in the near future. The Turks had recently won the Holy Land from the Mamlukes (1516) and they would soon lose it. More specifically, the high cedar to be felled was the Turk; the destruction of Tripoli was the expected destruction of Jerusalem; and the capture of Acre was the capture of the Turkish Sultan.

But after this, in the commentator's view, the prophecy went on to foretell events that had recently transpired. The ambushing of Jupiter by Saturn was the attack on "all literate men" (presumably wise, like Jupiter) by "Saturnians and rustic peasants" (Saturn with

29. MS Clm 28229, f. 21ʳ, treated above pp. 118–120. For the text of the glosses see Appendix III. (Dr. Alexander Patschovsky aided me greatly in helping to decipher some of the glossator's nearly illegible script.)

30. The binding of the MS identifies it as Ottheinrich's, an identification called to my attention by Dr. Patschovsky, who learned of it from Dr. Günter Glauche, Munich. In fact, the MS can be identified as one listed in an inventory of Ottheinrich's Kammerbibliothek made in 1566: for this see Karl Schottenloher, *Pfalzgraf Ottheinrich und das Buch* (Münster, 1927), 27. Since the binding bears the date 1548, the MS must have been acquired in that year or shortly before. It must have come from Speyer because of entries on f. 54ʳ (see Chapter Six, n. 8); Schottenloher, 9–12, shows that Ottheinrich acquired other MSS from Speyer (from the Cathedral chapter and the Carmelite monastery) in the years around 1548, when he was residing in nearby Weinheim. After the MS was acquired by Ottheinrich it travelled from Weinheim to Neuburg, where over the course of centuries it was transferred from a princely collection, to the Jesuit library, to a public library, to make its way in the twentieth century to Munich!

his scythe and sinister characteristics could stand for peasants),[31] no doubt an allusion to the Peasants' War of 1525. Similarly, the "bat's" chasing of the "Duke Abim" (the corruption in this manuscript for the "lord of the bees") was the Muslims chasing the king of Bohemia, an allusion to the defeat of Louis II of Bohemia and Hungary by the Turks at the battle of Mohács in 1526.

Thereafter the Rhenish commentator continued to read the prophecy as alluding by turns to the future and to the present. The prediction that within fifteen years the "other god would vanish" was for him an assurance of the vanishing of the faith of the Lutherans. As that was yet to come, also in the future was the onslaught of the "people without a head," for him a leaderless tribe of "Agarenes" (from Hagar, Abraham's maidservant) or "Ishmaelites" (descendants of Ishmael, Hagar's outcast son).[32] But when the commentator came to the warning of woe for the clergy he wrote "already the time threatened," probably thinking again of the Peasants' War or perhaps of Luther. Similarly, the "tossing of Peter's ship" applied to "all priests," no doubt because he was thinking of the troubles priests had been experiencing in his own days.

So far most of this commentary was sombre, but the last glosses reveal that the commentator had an unshakable faith in the beneficence of Providence. The "land of the barbarians" to be converted was the land of the Saracens, and the "beast of the West" and "lion of the East" were two contemporary heros destined to accomplish the conversion and conquer the world. Specifically, the beast and the lion were Charles V, "the king of the Romans from Spain," and his brother Ferdinand. Charles's designation as "king of the Romans" reveals that the glosses were written before February 1530, when Charles was crowned Emperor, and shows that in the dark years between 1526 (Mohács) and 1530, when the Turks seemed on the verge of taking Vienna, a steadfast Christian could nonetheless hope that the Habs-

31. On Saturn standing for poor peasants and dressed as a rustic, see Erwin Panofsky, *Studies in Iconology* (New York, 1939; repr. 1962), 77.

32. On Saracens as "Agarenes" or Ishmaelites, see Norman Daniel, *Islam and the West* (Edinburgh, 1960), 79, and R. W. Southern, *Western Views of Islam in the Middle Ages* (Cambridge, Mass., 1962), 16–17; on Mongols as Ishmaelites, see Chapter One, n. 26.

burgs would snatch victory from defeat: not only would the Turks
be driven out of Europe but also out of the Holy Land. The glosses
about the beast and the lion were, with one minor exception,[33] the
last given because the rest of the prophecy could be understood
clearly and congruently enough as describing a final wondrous time
of peace and the glorification of Jerusalem.

The Rhenish commentator's designation of Charles V as the
"beast of the West" is a good example of how different his glosses
were from those of his fourteenth-century predecessors, for the same
figure was understood by Rupescissa to have been a coming evil king
of England and by the Infante Peter to have been a triumphant Henry
of Trastámara. In making the "lion of the East" stand for Ferdinand
of Habsburg instead of Antichrist, the commentator similarly diverged widely from his predecessors, as he did again in making the
"people without a head" Agarenes instead of the Great Company, or
Gascons and Germans. (If by "Agarenes" he meant Tartars, he stum-
bled here unwittingly onto the meaning of the original prophet of
ca. 1240!) All these examples reflect the passage of centuries: a sixteenth-century commentator, convinced that the Tripoli prophecy
applied to current events, was *ipso facto* bound to interpret most of
its specific allusions differently from commentators of an earlier age.

But if times had changed, they also to a remarkable degree had
stayed the same. The very fact that a reader of about 1527 sought
illumination and consolation from a prophecy he thought had been
revealed in 1348 shows how relevant the old document still seemed
and how much the glossator thought like men of earlier times. Like
his fourteenth-century Franciscan predecessors, he was upset by the
state of his own world: the Black Death or Babylonian Captivity were
not his concern, but now Lutheranism was spreading, the peasants
had just given their German lords a fright, and the Turks were advancing westward. Like his predecessors, the sixteenth-century glossator was sure that these dreadful events were signs of worse evils to

33. A final gloss is the name "Waradach" given for the phrase "and they [the
Crusaders] will triumph." Waradach was a fictional, prototypic name assigned
in the West to the "Sultan of Babylon"—see, e.g., Joachim Vennebusch, ed., *Die
Theologischen Handschriften des Stadtarchivs Köln: Teil 2. Die Quart-Hand-
schriften der Gymnasialbibliothek* (Cologne, 1980), 182. Presumably the glossator
meant to say that the Crusaders would triumph over the supreme ruler of Islam.

come, and like them he had ultimate faith in the eschatological conversion of the world. The Tripoli prophecy confirmed his fears and
hopes, as it had done two centuries before, because it seemed to have
predicted some things he knew about and showed how they were
linked to others he feared or hoped for. Thus did the prophecy speak
in similar ways over the ages.

Assuming that the three cases discussed were typical—and their
similarity seems to allow this assumption—readers from the late thirteenth century to the sixteenth could not have found the Tripoli
prophecy easy reading. The affairs of the "bat" and the "lord of the
bees" probably made no more obvious sense immediately after the
lines were written than they do today, and the "people without a
head" and the "beast of the West" could not have been identified
without some artifice. But the prophecy was not therefore dismissed.
On the contrary, its overall purport was clear: imminent trials followed by Christian triumph before the coming of Antichrist. Moreover, the very obscurity of the prophecy's more difficult lines allowed
readers to make of them what they would. Since readers always
thought their own age was at the center of divine attention, they
found allusions to current events where none could have been intended, and once they concluded that parts of the prophecy had
recently been fulfilled, they could then have no doubts that the remainder was soon to follow. Thus the interpretation of "bats" and
"beasts" might differ, but the understanding of how they fitted into
God's plan remained constant.

Chapter VIII

EARLY-MODERN ALARUMS

Germany. December, 1520. The Empire is in turmoil. Several months earlier Martin Luther had proclaimed open warfare against the papacy in his incendiary letter, *To the Christian Nobility of the German Nation.* The first run of four thousand copies had sold out within eighteen days and numerous reprintings had followed. Readers were galvanized by the letter's call for thoroughgoing reform of the Church. Many expressed their approval, and even Luther's opponent, Duke George of Saxony, wrote to Rome that the criticism had been necessary, for "if no one ventures to speak of the evils in the Church . . . the very stones will eventually cry out."[1] In October Luther followed his first success with the publication of *On the Babylonian Captivity of the Church,* which presented theoretical support for his antipapal campaign by attacking the sacramental system. Most observers now recognized that the friar of Wittenberg was not just attacking abuses but calling for a thorough reconception of the faith. One reader of the new pamphlet wrote that the whole world had seemed blind before then, and another that he felt "as if he were being lashed from head to foot."[2] As December approached, Germans were

1. Quoted by Heinrich Boehmer, *Martin Luther: Road to Reformation,* trans. J. W. Doberstein and T. G. Tappert (Philadelphia, 1946), 321.

2. Ibid., 325.

waiting to see how the fiery Augustinian would respond to Pope Leo X's bull *Exsurge Domine,* which gave him until the tenth of the month to recant or be excommunicated. On the tenth they gained their answer: early that morning Luther presided over the lighting of a bonfire outside the gates of Wittenberg and then cast into it copies of the papal bull and all of Church law.

The bonfire outside Wittenberg helped end the Middle Ages insofar as the flames helped burn apart the unity of the medieval Western Church. But characteristically medieval ways of interpreting events persisted then and afterwards. Awed by the drama of Luther's defiance, many contemporaries interpreted it in apocalyptic terms. Some saw Luther as an evil eschatological apparition and others saw him as a messianic hero. To take an example from each side, the bishop of Chiemsee, Berthold Purstinger, thought that Luther and his followers were apocalyptic locusts whose appearance presaged a new age of Antichristian persecution to occur before the final glorious sabbath of the Church, whereas Albrecht Dürer prayed that Luther or someone in his footsteps would unite Christianity, convert the Turks and other heathens, and bring the heavenly Jerusalem down to earth.[3]

Such reactions were just as "medieval" as apocalyptic reactions to the onslaught of the Mongols, the fall of the Holy Land, or the spread of the Black Death. Quite appropriately, then, the drama of Wittenberg also called forth resurrections of the Cedar of Lebanon text in the same manner as the earlier dramas had inspired the prophecy's medieval creation and resurrections. As in the thirteenth and fourteenth centuries, so in the sixteenth, people tried to comprehend disturbing upheavals by relating them to a plan of future events, and some resorted once more to the Tripoli prophecy for help in compassing the future.

One Lutheran partisan who drew on the prophecy for inspira-

---

3. On Purstinger's *Onus ecclesie*, published anonymously in 1524, see Reeves, *Influence of Prophecy*, 467–468, and Heinrich Werner, *Die Flugschrift "Onus ecclesiae" (1519)* (Giessen, 1901). Dürer's famous prayer on hearing a rumor of Luther's death in 1521 is in Albrecht Dürer, *Schriftlicher Nachlass*, ed. H. Rupprich, I (Berlin, 1956), 171.

tion during the 1520s was an anonymous Frenchman who built parts of the old prophecy into a new one of his own devising. His Lutheran proclivities can be seen in his predictions that "Martin" would be burned but that Luther's enemies would then be destroyed, that "the law of Paul will be increased," and that "wives will be given to priests."[4] These lines were original, but most of his text was taken from the old Tripoli prophecy. How he interpreted the doings of the "bat" and the "lord of the bees" is anyone's guess, but it seems fairly clear that his borrowing of the line that "all the mendicant orders will be annihilated"[5] was another way of expressing his fervently Protestant hopes. His prediction, in language taken directly from the Tripoli prophecy, that there would be a great crusade to the Holy Land and that the city of Jerusalem would be "glorified" must also have expressed his hopes for what would transpire in the wondrous Lutheran future. The prophecy, in short, helped him grapple with turmoil and strengthened him in his newfound faith.

Closer to the scene, a German writer around 1521 was similarly convinced that the uproar created by Luther marked the beginning of an eschatological drama. Consulting numerous old Latin prophecies to see what the future offered, he found them pointing so clearly to the same imminent events that he decided to publish selections from all of them in German. But instead of presenting them as an anthology of diverse prophecies that he selected himself, he promulgated them

4. The prophecy beginning *Casleti* [?] *paludum vermiculi leone captivat.* . . . is written on a flyleaf of MS Tours 520, f. i[v]. This is the only copy I know: unfortunately it is often extremely difficult to decipher. It must have been French because its borrowings from the Tripoli prophecy come from the French family and also because it appears in the Tours MS which originally came from the monastery of Marmoutier. It must have been composed in the 1520s because of its reference to priests marrying (Luther married in 1525) and because the fear that Luther would be burned receded by about 1530. For the text of the prophecy, see Appendix III.

5. To the sentence "Omnes ordines mendicancium adnichilabuntur," the prophecy adds another: "Beguini cum begardi prohibentur." Whether this was the work of the French prophet of the sixteenth century or was already present in his exemplar is impossible to say. At any rate, beguines and beghards were often associated with the mendicants: on this see my *Heresy of the Free Spirit in the Later Middle Ages* (Berkeley, 1972), 35–60, and passim.

as if they were all part of one prediction, or *Practica*, made earlier, in 1500, by an astronomer named Jacob Pflaum of Ulm.[6] This Pflaum had been a real person. In 1477 he had published a calendar of astronomical data for the years up to 1552 that went into three editions. Later, in 1499, he published with Johannes Stöffler, a noted astronomer from the University of Tübingen, an astronomical almanac for the years from 1499 to 1531 that gained great notoriety and was frequently reprinted in the early sixteenth century because it predicted that a planetary conjunction would bring a great flood in 1524.[7] Most likely it was the fame of Pflaum's collaboration with Stöffler that led the anonymous author of ca. 1521 to consider him an appropriate authority on whom to father a prophetic pastiche. Since Pflaum must have been dead by 1521, he was probably in no position to object.[8]

The *Practica* allegedly written in 1500 begins by predicting events for 1520 with unfailing accuracy. In that year, says the "prophet," someone will rise up who will publish books in German and Latin against the pope, the cardinals, and priesthood that will create an uproar against the clergy. Around the same time a new king and future Emperor will be elected in Germany. Short of actually

6. *Practica das kunfftig ist und geschehen soll, das hat gepracticiert und gemacht Jacob pflawm von Ulm. Im iar 1500. Und der anfang dieser Practica sol anheben Anno Christi 1520* (n.p., n.d. [ca. 1521]). I use a copy from the Bayerische Staatsbibliothek, Munich: 4° Astr. P. 510 (9). A second edition of 1527 [Nürnberg?] follows the first closely but gives *ai* for *ei* spellings and changes the last part of the title to: *Und der anfang diser Practica hat angehebt Im jar. 1520. Und wirt noch etliche jar weren*; a copy is in the British Library: C. 71. h. 14 (16); the title page is reproduced as the frontispiece of this book. On two Wittenberg editions of 1532, see below pp. 166–167 with nn. 20 and 22. Brief summaries are in J. Rohr, "Die Prophetie im letzten Jahrhundert vor der Reformation als Geschichtsquelle und Geschichtsfaktor," *Historisches Jahrbuch*, 19 (1898), 29–56, 447–466 (at 50–52), and Douglas D. Overmyer, "The Concept of Christian Militancy in the First Decade of the German Reformation" (Ph.D. diss., Princeton University, 1972), 93–94 (Charles Radding kindly called my attention to the latter).

7. On the conjunction of 1524 and the vast literature it provoked, see Thorndike, V, 178–233, and Overmyer, 105–118.

8. If Pflaum was still alive in 1521, he would most likely have been over seventy. The *Practica* of ca. 1521 was entirely different in content and manner from Pflaum's real work, and it is clear that the pseudonymous author was only reaching for a prestigious name.

naming Martin Luther and Charles V—who was elected king in 1519 and crowned at Aachen in 1520—the author here could just as well have been writing history.[9]

The rest of the *Practica* was genuinely devoted to the future but was not based on independent inspiration. Instead, it presented a pastiche of plagiarisms from numerous medieval prophecies, translated or paraphrased into German and presented in such a helter-skelter fashion that no clear chronological order can be discerned.[10] To the reader's bewilderment, the heathen are recurrently conquered and reconquered, and Antichrist appears and reappears. The Tripoli prophecy was just one of numerous texts on which the author drew, but along with the others it confirmed him in his belief that Luther's coming had brought world history to its last precipice. Thus he predicted that "Tripoli will be destroyed and Acre will be captured,"[11] most likely meaning that these cities would fall to the Christians in a last crusade. Then he went on to declare in language also drawn from the Tripoli prophecy that there would soon be

9. Friedrich von Bezold, "Zur deutschen Kaisersage," SbM, 1884, 574, followed by Rohr, 52, already doubted that "Pflaum's" prophecy could have been written before 1520 because the author knew of Charles V's election and the appearance of Luther. Since the prophecy clearly alludes to the uproar caused by the appearance of Luther's pamphlets in the autumn of 1520, it had to have been written after that time. It was probably not written later than 1521 because the author probably would have "predicted" subsequent dramatic events had he known about them. The pamphlet certainly was written before 1524 because it ends with erroneous predictions for that year.

10. Unacknowledged borrowings from the prophecies of Gamaleon, Pseudo-Methodius, Joachim of Fiore, Telesphorus, and Vincent Ferrer (presumably the *Mirabile opusculum de fine mundi* spuriously attributed to Ferrer) were already noticed by von Bezold, 574-575, n. 1, and Rohr, 50-51. Still more borrowings are from "Master Samuel" (incipit: *Audite verbum Domini principes Sodomorum* as in Bayerische Staatsbibliothek, Einblattdrucke V, 54, and V, 56): in *Practica*, f. 4ᵛ (foliation is the same in the first two editions); *Gallorum levitas* (as in Holder-Egger, 33, 125-126): in *Practica*, f. 3ʳ; and *Ve mundo* (on which see Chapter Three, n. 6): in *Practica*, f. 4ᵛ. The only borrowing the author explicitly acknowledges is from *sant Pirgitta* (f. 5ʳ), actually from an assemblage of extracts from the work of St. Bridget made in the fifteenth century by Johannes Tortsch: see the edition by Ulrich Montag, *Das Werk der heiligen Birgitta von Schweden in oberdeutscher Ueberlieferung* (Munich, 1968), 267, for the "seven plagues" referred to in the *Practica*.

11. F. 4ᵛ: "Trippolis wirt zerprochen Acharon wirt gefangen."

"great plagues" and "mutations of kingdoms" but that subsequently there would be an abundance of fruit and wondrous peace throughout the world for fifteen years.[12] In other words, coming times would be dreadful, but the vigilant and upright would still have some rewards before the Last Judgment. Countless medieval observers of earlier crises had thought the same.

The two reappropriations of the Tripoli prophecy of the 1520s were only a preview of its early-modern afterlife. In fact, far more people must have read the prophecy in the sixteenth and seventeenth centuries than ever read it in the Middle Ages because much of the text became available for the first time after 1532 through the media of printing and vernacular translation. "Pflaum" only translated a few snippets of the prophecy, and his entire *Practica* was ephemeral, but an unknown Protestant contemporary, who was associated with the circle of Luther at Wittenberg, offered a fuller version that was to prove far more enduring in its printed life.

Late in 1531 or very early in 1532, the unknown Lutheran in question happened across a prophecy concerning a royal Charles in a fifteenth-century manuscript in Magdeburg. Even though this text was embedded in Alexander of Roes's thirteenth-century *Memoriale* and was minted around 1280 to support the imperial pretensions of Charles of Anjou, the sixteenth-century reader took it as an allusion to the reigning Emperor Charles V because it applied to the latter Charles remarkably well.[13] Just a few lines long, it stated that an

12. Ibid.: "Werden grosssterben und gross endrung in allen reich," standing for the original "hominum mortalitas per loca et regnorum mutaciones." Then, f. 5r: "In der zeit wirt auch wein und korn und ander frucht uber al massen wol wachsen und vast wolfeil funftzchen iar und frid gantz gut in allen landen." This is a paraphrase rather than an exact translation of "tunc pax erit in toto orbe terrarum et copia fructuum per 15 annos." See also f. 5r: "Die iuden werden erlost von irer gefencknuss" for "filii Israel a captivitate liberabuntur."

13. The fullest description of the source for the beginning of what, as the following account explains, became known as the Magdeburg prophecy appears in Johann Carion, *Chronica* (Augsburg, 1533), f. 144v: "Zů Magdeburg ist ein Chronica vor hundert jarn geschriben darinn dise wort Lateinisch am end stehen." The "Chronica" can be identified with certainty as Alexander of Roes's *Memoriale* which was called *Chronica* in many late-medieval MSS and which indeed has toward the end the source for the opening portion of the Magdeburg prophecy: "Quod de Karlingis, id est de stirpe regis Karoli et de domo regum Francie, imperator suscitabitur Karolus nomine, qui erit princeps et monarcha

Emperor named Charles, from Carolingian and French royal lineage, would arise to become ruler of all Europe and reform the Church and the Empire. Since Charles V's Habsburg family claimed descent from the Carolingians, since Charles, through his Burgundian heritage, unquestionably descended from the French kings (and through them also from the Carolingians), and since Charles already ruled much of Europe, the prophecy seemed in large part fulfilled. It only remained for Charles V to conquer the rest of Europe from the Turks and begin his work of reformation.

Clearly a trustworthy prophecy which not only foresaw that Charles V would conquer the Turks but that he would preside over the Reformation would have pleased any Lutheran. This one indeed was so pleased that he wanted others to know about it. But before recirculating it, he decided to flesh it out with more medieval prophetic material that expanded on the themes of reformation and Turkish conquest. And this he found in none other than the last two-thirds of the old message supposedly delivered from on high in Tripoli.

The part of the Tripoli prophecy the Lutheran borrowed for his new creation seemed appropriate because it began with a threat of imminent "woe to the priests" and went on to predict the "tossing of Peter's ship," the "annihilation of the mendicant orders and many other sects," and the conversion of "the land of Barbary." To be sure, there were other forecasts in the prophecy that were either less clearly apposite or totally at odds with Lutheran hopes—particularly the ultimate triumph of "Peter's ship." But committed readers of prophecies were always able to filter out from their minds lines they did not like, and there was more than enough in the last two-thirds of the Tripoli prophecy to have suited any Protestant. In fact, had anyone striven to unite the two most popular prophetic themes of the

---

totius Europe et reformabit ecclesiam et imperium, sed post illum nunquam alius imperabit." I quote from the edition by Grundmann and Heimpel (as cited in Chapter Three, n. 33), 136. Grundmann and Heimpel, 43–54, describe 18 MSS of a "B" family, most of which were copied in fifteenth-century German-speaking territories and call the text a *Chronica*, and all of which are curtailed so that very little would follow the passage with the prophecy. (The Magdeburg MS of the *Memoriale* itself, however, does not appear to have survived.) For final proof that the *Memoriale* was the source for the beginning of the Magdeburg prophecy, see n. 19 below.

day, messianic imperial triumph and Church reform, in suitably ancient and gnomic language, he could hardly have done better than to merge the old Charles prophecy with the last two-thirds of the Tripoli prophecy. It is not clear whether the Lutheran enthusiast who did this found the Tripoli prophecy in Magdeburg or elsewhere, but, wherever he found it, his hybrid quickly took on a life of its own and became known as the Magdeburg prophecy for generations of readers.[14]

Perhaps, though, it might better have been known as the Wittenberg prophecy because Wittenberg was both the source of its inspiration and the center of its dissemination. More even than that, its first known commentator was the most famous person ever to comment on any passage of the Tripoli prophecy, Martin Luther himself. Early in 1532 the confector of the hybrid brought it to Wittenberg, where it appeared as a topic for discussion at Luther's dinner table in March.

Although Luther passed on the prophetic passages he heard approvingly, he was certainly not an uncritical believer in whatever portentous prophecies came his way. Quite to the contrary, he reacted to prophecies differently according to their alleged sources of inspiration, their content, and his mood. Thus his attitude even toward one and the same prophetic text could change: in 1527 he endorsed the publication of Johannes Lichtenberger's *Prognosticatio* by writing a cautious preface which explained that, even though Lichtenberger's astrological forecasts were far from infallible, they were very frequently on the mark; but in "table-talk" of 1532 he rejected Lichtenberger's and similar prophecies by saying they were "all from the devil."[15] If one can generalize, Luther's attitude toward non-Scriptural prophecy was usually critical and often dismissive, but he nonetheless allowed that some prophecies could be accurate and might be aids for understanding God's will.

Quite clearly, Luther was bound to react more favorably to a

14. For the earliest forms of the Magdeburg prophecy, see Appendix III. The source for the Tripoli prophecy borrowing seems to have been a copy from the German family. It should be noted that in the earliest printings of the Magdeburg prophecy, the Tripoli prophecy part is set off from the Charles part by paragraph indentations.

15. Dietrich Kurze, *Johannes Lichtenberger* (Lübeck, 1960), 59–61, who gives further evidence of Luther's ambivalence concerning Lichtenberger.

prophecy if it confirmed his preconceived hopes or expectations. Thus in 1532, when he was still hoping that Charles V might be converted to his cause and was concerned about the Turkish threat, he responded more favorably to the Magdeburg prophecy than to the "diabolical" prophecies of Lichtenberger and others.[16] While at table in March, Luther heard from an interlocutor that a prophecy had been found in an "old book" which foretold that the Emperor Charles would subjugate all of Europe, reform the Church, and annihilate the mendicants and "many other sects."[17] Certainly this selection from the Magdeburg text was made to highlight its most Protestant points. So far as the "table-talk" record stands, Luther let it pass without comment, but when the speaker went on to report the predictions that "the beast of the west and the lion of the east will subjugate the whole world for fifteen years, and then the land of the barbarians will be converted," the master of the dinner table indicated his credence in the whole prophecy by stating that the "beast" was Charles and the "lion" the Turk. Then he added: "Something will soon happen; they will come up against each other, for one hears the Emperor is now in Passau, which is not more than sixty miles from the Turkish camp."[18] The topic then changed, as table-talk topics will do, but the snatch of conversation makes it clear that Luther took the portentousness of the

16. On Luther's hopes for Charles in the early 1530s, see Karl Brandi, *The Emperor Charles V*, trans. C. V. Wedgewood (New York, 1939), 326. Also *Tischreden* (Weimarer Ausgabe), II, 1687 (June or July 1532): "Caesar est probus. Wir haben einen frommen kayser. . . ."

17. The discussion of the Magdeburg prophecy at Luther's table can be pieced together from three independent accounts: *Tischreden*, II, 2509a, 2509b, 1687. Closest to the source here is 2509b: "P[rophetia] ex antiquo codice de Carolo: Carolus imperator subiget totam Europam, reformabit ecclesiam, et annihilabitur ordo mendicantium et pleraeque aliae sectae."

18. Ibid., 2509b: "Item in eodem: Bestia orientalis et leo occidentalis [cf. 2509a (correctly): bestia occidentalis et leo orientalis; 1687: Die Bestia gegen Abend und der Löwe gegen Morgen] subiugabunt totum orbem terrarum, et erit annis 15. [2509a: Quod intelligo de Turca et Carolo.] Deinde terra barbarorum convertetur.—Respondit Lutherus: Es wirdt etwas werden; sie werden an einander kommen. Aiunt caesarem esse in Passau, quod non est ultra 60 miliaria, ubi exercitus Turcae est." Cf. 1687: "Da sprach D. Martinus Luther: 'Es wird etwas werden; sie werden an einander kommen! Denn man sagt, der Kaiser sey zu Passau, welches uber 40 Meil Weges von hinnen nicht ist. Nicht weit davon soll der Türk liegen.'"

Magdeburg prophecy as confirmation of his own certainty of imminent dramatic change.

The same sense in Wittenberg that "something will soon happen" inspired the publication in 1532 of a German translation of the Magdeburg prophecy that was to become the point of departure for the prophecy's subsequent extremely wide circulation. Luther learned of the prophecy in the original Latin, directly or indirectly, by word of mouth from the prophecy's fabricator.[19] Latin, however, was not an appropriate medium for mass communication, so the fabricator translated or had it translated into a vigorous German, which, among other things, changed the "mendicant orders" to be annihilated into simply "the monks." Then he conveyed it, directly or indirectly, to a Lutheran printer of Wittenberg, Nickel Schirlenz, who brought it out sometime in 1532 as an appendix to a reprinting of pseudo-Pflaum's *Practica*.[20]

In a preface to this edition, Schirlenz revealed an attitude toward the Magdeburg prophecy quite similar to that of Luther. Specifically, he did not insist that all or any non-Scriptural prophecies were infallible, but he did find that many were currently speaking urgent truth to the present troubled age, just as God had once spoken through Balaam's ass. Thus he decided to print some himself on the grounds that "although no one should believe certainly in such prophecies, they do sometimes hit the mark. For the world's evil and God's anger are so enormous that things cannot stay as they are. That much

19. No Latin edition of the Magdeburg prophecy of 1531 or 1532 is known. It should also be noted that the *Tischreden* record indicates that Luther went on to consider a theory on the origin of the name "German" that must have stemmed from a verbal report of another passage from Alexander of Roes (cf. 2509b with Alexander, c. 16, Grundmann and Heimpel, 111).

20. *Ettlich weissagung durch den hochgelarten Astronomum Jacob Pflawmen zu Ulm zusamen getragen Anno M. CCCCC*, f. 8ᵛ. I use a copy from the British Library: 8610 aaa 58 (2). Following the Magdeburg prophecy is: "Ware und gewisse Prophecey Abbatis Joachim: Ein grosser Addler wird komen. Der wird alle potentet uberwinden auf einen. Der wird aber bald hernach selb von seinem anhange verlassen werden." To my knowledge this is the earliest appearance of the prophetic extract more familiar in the Latin version as *Veniet Aquila grandis quae vincet omnes. . .*, on which see Reeves, *Influence of Prophecy*, 368–369, n. 4. and 532.

is certain."[21] Schirlenz must have decided to reprint "Pflaum's" *Practica* in particular because it had hit the mark in foreseeing Luther and also spoke of an imminent imperial victory against the Turks. As for the prophecy "found at Magdeburg," it had hit the mark in foreseeing the advent of Charles V and concorded with "Pflaum" in foreseeing a successful march East. Since both in addition foresaw numerous dreadful upheavals—in the words of the Magdeburg prophecy, "Schreckliche verenderung aller Reich"—knowledge of their contents would not only instill hope but also prompt sinners to repent. Schirlenz probably did not notice that the *Practica* and the Magdeburg prophecy used the same words in parts and certainly did not know that some of these words had been written three hundred years earlier when the Mongols rather than the Turks were the looming menace.

Schirlenz's prophetic collection sold well enough to warrant a second, anonymous, printing in Wittenberg in 1532,[22] but had the Magdeburg prophecy appeared only at the back of two editions of pseudo-Pflaum, it would not have had much of a future. What gave it its independent longevity was its appropriation in 1532 by an acquaintance of Luther's, an obese polymath named Johann Carion.[23]

21. "Die weil sich zu dieser zeit mancherley weissagung finden und ettliche fast zutreffen, das es scheinet wie Gott der Herr solche verenderung der welt auch hie durch Balaams esel verkundiget hat, haben wirs für gut angesehen auch diese weissagung Jacobs Pflawm, so vor hin auch gedrückt und ausgangen ist im 1500 jar, widderumb aus zulassen, damit vernünfftigen leuten ursach nach zudencken gegeben, und die bosen, ob es helffen wolt, gewarnet werden. Denn wie wol solche weissagung niemand gewiss glauben kan, ist doch zubesorgen sie möchtens zu weilen treffen. Denn der welt bosheit und Gottes verachtung so gros ist, das es so nicht bleiben stehen kan. Das ist ja gewiss."

22. *Etlich Weyssagung durch den hochgelerten Astronomum Jacob Pflawmen zu Ulm zusamen getragen.* I use Bayerische Staatsbibliothek: Astr. P. 511 (34). I conclude that this postdates the printing by Schirlenz because its anonymity suggests it was pirated and because it corrects some of Schirlenz's eccentric spellings and mistakes. Note too that in Schirlenz's edition the two supplementary prophecies appear on a final verso side to fill what would otherwise be wasted space, whereas in the anonymous edition they come on the final recto.

23. A thorough biographical study of Carion is lacking; no one has even yet gone to the trouble of listing his numerous writings with all their even more numerous editions. For the high points of Carion's career, see Aby Warburg,

The latter earned his living primarily as court astrologer, advisor, and factotum to the elector of Brandenburg but gained his greatest fame as the author of a *Chronica*, or short German world history. Carion had some help in writing this from his old Tübingen University classmate, Philipp Melanchthon, but the conception and most of the execution were his own and showed that he could sense very well what the public wanted. Readers newly accustomed to buying books in the initial swell of Lutheran enthusiasm for controversial religious pamphlets and bibles were ready for a short vernacular outline of history, and Carion, whose "telling judgments and at times astonishingly good selections of materials" have been praised by the modern authority, Joachimsen, was the first to provide such an outline in 1532, thereby initiating a tradition that continued through H. G. Wells and Hendrik Willem Van Loon.[24]

Carion's knowledge of the Magdeburg prophecy certainly came from a copy of Schirlenz's prophetic pamphlet,[25] probably one he had bought for his own use as court astrologer and occasional writer of his own eclectic "Prognostications." His purchase must have been made in Wittenberg in the spring of 1532, because he was definitely there in April to confer with Luther and Melanchthon on a religious problem posed by his Brandenburg employer.[26] Almost certainly on

---

"Heidnisch-Antike Weissagung in Wort und Bild zu Luthers Zeiten," in Warburg, *Gesammelte Schriften*, II (Leipzig, 1932; repr. Nendeln, 1969), 487–558 (at 532–533), and Gotthard Münch, "Das Chronicon Carionis Philippicum. Ein Beitrag zur Würdigung Melanchthons als Historiker," *Sachsen und Anhalt*, 1 (1925), 199–283, both of which list older literature. I have not seen Otto Tschirch, "Johannes Carion, Kurbrandenburgischer Hofastrolog," *Jahresbericht des historischen Vereins zu Brandenburg*, 36/37 (1906), 54–62.

24. Joachimsen, cited by Münch, 201, n. 8.

25. This can be concluded without doubt from the omission of a clause in Carion's version owing to homoiotheleuton. In the Schirlenz printing, the words *welt, und* appear twice at about the same place on two successive lines, causing Carion inadvertently to have missed a whole line.

26. Carion's arrival in Wittenberg a day or two before 23 April 1532 is attested to by letters from Luther and Melanchthon to Kurprinz Joachim of Brandenburg: see Luther's *Briefwechsel*, Weimarer Ausgabe VI, 302–304, and *Melanchthons Briefwechsel*, ed. Heinz Scheible, II (Stuttgart, 1978), no. 1234. *Melanchthons Briefwechsel*, II, no. 1248, suggests but does not conclusively prove that Carion returned to Brandenburg sometime in May.

this same occasion he brought his *Chronica* to the Wittenberg printer, Georg Rhau, for its first edition, and since a second edition was published in 1532 by none other than Nickel Schirlenz it seems quite likely that Carion had dealings with Schirlenz, too, while he was still in Wittenberg. At the same time, he must have learned from someone in Luther's circle, possibly Melanchthon, of circumstances concerning this discovery of the Magdeburg prophecy which had not appeared in print.[27]

The first two or three editions of Carion's *Chronica* ended by describing events of early 1532,[28] but back in Berlin by the late summer, Carion was moved to append to his work a coda that included the text of his new prophetic acquisition. The grounds for this revision were dramatic events concerning the Turkish menace.[29] At the Diet of Regensburg in April, Charles V had tried to raise a large German army to face Suleiman the Magnificent but was stymied by the resistance of Protestant princes who were holding out for religious concessions. Fear, however, soon proved an excellent recruiter. On the twenty-fifth of April, a large Turkish force left Constantinople and began to advance steadily up the Danube; by the summer, Suleiman's forces had made their way to Güns, within easy reach of

27. Schirlenz's edition of the *Chronica*, which I have neither seen nor located, is referred to by Werner Goez, *Translatio imperii* (Tübingen, 1958), 258. The differences between Carion's introduction to the Magdeburg prophecy and Schirlenz's, which can be seen in the edition in Appendix III, indicate that, unlike Schirlenz, Carion knew that the MS in Magdeburg had been copied in the fifteenth century, that the Charles prophecy therein came from a "Chronica," and that it appeared in the Chronica toward the end. Circumstantial evidence not only points to Melanchthon as Carion's informant (the two were close friends and Melanchthon was likely to have been at Luther's dinner table) but also raises the possibility that Melanchthon himself may have been the confector of the Magdeburg prophecy.

28. I refer to the Rhau edition and to an edition of 1532 published at Augsburg by H. Steyner (in Newberry Library: Case/F/09/.144). I do not know whether the same is true of the Schirlenz edition referred to above.

29. See the narrative in Stephen A. Fischer-Galati, "Ottoman Imperialism and the Religious Peace of Nürnberg (1532)," *Archiv für Reformationsgeschichte*, 47 (1956), 160–180. My source for the elector of Brandenburg's departure is the revised version of Carion's *Chronica*. Reeves, *Influence of Prophecy*, 368, places Carion's revised conclusion together with other similar expressions of great expectations for 1532 but mistakenly states that these had to do with a campaign of Charles V against the infidel in North Africa.

Vienna. In the face of this danger the Protestants patched up a religious peace with Charles at Nürnberg in July, and by August the Emperor had gathered the army he sought, including Protestant as well as Catholic German troops and contingents from the Low Countries and Italy. Carion's employer, the elector of Brandenburg, marched away from Berlin with his own troops to fight the Turks on the tenth of August. From Carion's point of view, it thus seemed as if a prelude to Armageddon was in the offing. In a *Prognosticatio* of 1521 he had already predicted that 1532 would be a momentous year for the Empire and for Christianity:[30] now he was inspired to append to the end of his chronicle an addendum referring to Charles V's imminent march against the Turks and citing prophecies which foresaw Charles's victory and the approaching culmination of world history. Among these was the prophecy about Charles "found at the end of a chronicle written a hundred years earlier in Magdeburg."

In the event, the Turks, held up by unforeseen delays, withdrew in September before a decisive battle could ensue, but by then Carion had rewritten his text.[31] The new version of his chronicle appeared in 1533 and became one of the great publishing successes of the sixteenth century, going into no less than fifteen German editions between 1533 and 1564. In 1534 it was also published in *Plattdeutsch* and was later reprinted once in that language. Nor did its printing history end there. In 1537 it was translated into Latin in a version which became so popular that it was reprinted more than thirty times, not just in Germany but also in Paris and Venice. From the Latin, Carion's chronicle was translated into Italian, Spanish, Czech, Dutch, English, and French—the French translation itself becoming so successful that it was printed at least ten times. The major explanation for this great

---

30. *Prognosticatio und Erklerung der grossen Wesserung.* I use the edition of Leipzig, 1522 (Bayerische Staatsbibliothek: Astr. P. 510 (43), where the passage in question is at sig. Aiiii[r]. I have not seen Carion's *Bedeutnus und Offenbarung warer Influxion* of 1526 that went into numerous later editions.

31. See the Augsburg, 1533 edition (Bayerische Staatsbibliothek: 4° Chron. 10), f. 144[v], and all following editions and translations. The treatments of Carion's version of the Magdeburg prophecy in Katherine R. Firth, *The Apocalyptic Tradition in Reformation Britain* (Oxford, 1979), 21, and Martin Haeusler, *Das Ende der Geschichte in der mittelalterlichen Weltchronistik* (Cologne, 1980), 162, are unreliable.

popularity was that Carion's text was short and simple: sometimes it was published in duodecimo format so that it could be sold as cheaply as possible to the widest audience, and it was often used as a history primer in the schools.[32] Few readers would have bought Carion's chronicle in order to read the prophecies it contained, but the enormous success of the book ensured that Carion's report of the Tripoli prophecy became available to more readers than had seen it in the three prior centuries.

To say "Carion's report" without qualification is not strictly accurate because the Latin translation done by Hermann Bonus, a schoolmaster of Lübeck, did change some details, and the Latin translation was the exemplar for all the non-German vernacular ones. Some of Bonus's changes were merely rhetorical flourishes: for example, he made the imperial hero reform "the collapsed state of the Church" instead of merely the Church and made him "restore the old glory of the Empire" instead of merely reforming the Empire. Such amplifications did not seriously affect meaning, but one of Bonus's other changes did just that. Whereas Carion's German text offered the prediction that "the monks will perish," Bonus's translation turned this into "the estimation of monks will perish":[33] people would no longer value monks, but the monks would still be there. This alteration is an excellent example of how the language of prophecy continued to be taken very seriously in the sixteenth century. Just as numerous medieval scribes were unwilling to accept the original prediction that the mendicant orders would be annihilated and rewrote the line more to their liking, so Bonus changed Carion's line either because he himself found it too radical or because he thought potential Catholic readers of his Latin translation might prefer his milder version.

In fact Bonus's translation served as the basis for an Italian trans-

32. On the printing history and uses made of Carion's chronicle, see Goez, 258–259, and Münch, 253–254, 279–281. These accounts omit mention of a Czech version of 1541, reprinted in 1584, listed in the *National Union Catalogue*, XCV, 352; and a Dutch one of 1586 listed in the *British Museum Catalogue*, XXXIII, 1047.

33. *Monachorum aestimatio peribit* for *die Münch werden undergeen*. I use the edition of Paris, 1544, fos. 258ᵛ–259ʳ (Newberry Library: Wing ZP/539/.F823).

lation of 1548 that was published with papal authorization. This, not surprisingly, altered the once radical line even further: now the reputation of monks would not "perish" but would simply "become less."[34] In 1550 in Protestant England, on the other hand, the English translator saw no need to alter Bonus's line, and neither did the French translator, who worked before the aggravated tensions of the French wars of religion.[35]

To locate all the extant reactions to the Magdeburg prophecy as transmitted by Carion in all its different forms would be a nearly impossible project, but enough examples may be displayed here to show that it continued to be singled out and used diversely for over a century. A clear example of the Latin version's acceptability to Catholics is provided by its appearance in the work of Wolfgang Lazius of Vienna.[36] This author was a Catholic professor of medicine and court historian who included Carion's text among an enormous number of prophecies he published in 1547 to show that the Emperor Charles V was on the verge of reforming the Church and uniting the world. Lazius had ample ulterior motives for heralding Charles as a messianic hero, for he was the private physician of Charles's brother, King

34. *Chronica di Giovanni Carione. . .* , trans. Pietro Lauro Modonese ("Con privilegio del sommo Pontefice Paolo III") (Venice, 1548—Newberry Library: Case/F/09/.152), f. 158ᵛ: "La reputatione di Monachi verra meno." An appendix to this edition contains a catalogue of all the popes down to Paul III. The Italian translation also leaves out, probably from oversight, the number of years Christians were supposed to move freely in Asia. Other evidence of acceptability to Catholics is that copies of Latin and French printings of Carion's *Chronica* were in the library of the Avignon Dominicans; see Avignon, Bibliothèque Calvet: sig. 8° 11491 and sig. 8° 11496.

35. *The Thre bokes of Chronicles whyche John Carion . . . Gathered wyth great diligence . . .* [with an introduction by Walter Lynne, an ardent Protestant, and dedicated to King Edward VI] (London, 1550—STC 4626), f. 191ʳ: "The settyng store by monkes shall peryshe"; *Les Chroniques de Jean Carion Philosophe . . .* , trans. Jean le Blond (Paris, 1560) (I am uncertain whether this is the first edition), 261: "L'estimation des moines sera à néant." (I have not seen the other translations.)

36. A biography is by A. Horowitz, *Allgemeine Deutsche Biographie*, XVIII (Leipzig, 1883), 89–93. On Lazius's historical work, see Michael Mayr, *Wolfgang Lazius als Geschichtsschreiber Oesterreichs* (Innsbruck, 1893), and the summary by A. Lhotsky, *Oesterreichische Historiographie* (Munich, 1962), 85–86 (neither Mayr nor Lhotsky deals with Lazius's study of prophecy).

Ferdinand, who paid him a generous yearly salary for writing history that would reflect the glory of the Habsburg house. But Lazius most likely believed what he wrote, for in 1547 Charles had seemingly reached the zenith of his power by soundly defeating the German Protestants at Mühlberg and appeared to be on the verge of pressuring the Council of Trent to promulgate substantial religious reforms.

Current events and prophecy thus seemed to be converging. Since Charles could be viewed as the heir to numerous earlier German and French prophecies of triumphant eagles and lilies through his combined German and French lineage, Lazius quite likely believed that all sound prophecy pointed to the Emperor's imminent messianic triumph. Certainly the Magdeburg prophecy printed by Carion and now reprinted approvingly by Lazius pointed in that direction.[37] Since it originally had been shaped to fit Charles V, there was nothing farfetched about Lazius's reading. The only difference was that the Protestant fabricator had conceived of Charles as a hero who would bring about reforms congenial to Lutherans, while Lazius conceived of him as a Catholic reformer working in league with the Council of Trent. Though a Catholic, the layman Lazius did not doubt that the clergy needed to be reformed sternly, so the Magdeburg prophecy was congenial to him on that score. Had he known the original, most "Lutheran," line about the destruction of monks, he might not have approved of it, but Bonus's translation obviated that difficulty. Above all, the Magdeburg prophecy, which Lazius accepted as having been found in a manuscript copied a century earlier, seemed miraculously inspired in pointing to the present and future triumphs of the reigning Charles. Together with other similar texts, it must have convinced Lazius that the culmination of history was really at hand.

We, of course, know that Charles V was further away from uniting the world in 1547 than he had been in 1532. After he died in 1556

---

37. Wolfgang Lazius, *Fragmentum vaticinii cuiusdam . . . Methodii. . . .* (Vienna, 1547), sig. Kiiii^v. In the copy I used (Bayerische Staatsbibliotek: L. impr. c.n.m. 1040), a penned-in gloss has *Papa* for *bestia occidentis* and *Turca* for *leo orientis*. This shows that a later reader was still struggling with the meaning of those two obscure allusions. Reeves, *Influence of Prophecy*, 369–372, summarizes Lazius's appropriation of numerous earlier prophecies without recognizing that he borrowed the Magdeburg prophecy (and several others) from Carion.

there was no imperial "Charles of the race of Charles" to inherit the expectations vested in Carion's text.[38] But the prophecy did not fall into oblivion. In 1600 the German Protestant scholar, Johann Wolf, included part of it in his *Lectiones memorabiles*, a vast two-volume collection of historical excerpts, selected to display the truth of the Protestant religion. For Wolf's purposes, the opening references to Charles were immaterial and he therefore simply omitted them. He also omitted the next part of the text running through the reference to "Peter's ship," no doubt because he did not like the prediction that the ship would ultimately obtain victory. Having thus stripped away so much that he found inappropriate, Wolf began to quote Carion's prophecy—saying it was found in a book over two hundred years old —at the point where it alluded to coming "mutations of kingdoms" and the "perishing of the estimation of monks."[39] Obviously it was the latter prediction, even in Bonus's mild version, that caught the Protestant Wolf's eye and prompted him to add the second half of Carion's prophecy to his tendentious anthology.

If Lazius was primarily interested in the Magdeburg prophecy for its dynastic application and Wolf for the sake of its religious propaganda, a third reader of Bonus's Latin version found both dynastic and religious uses for it. This was the Scotsman James Maxwell, hack poet, panegyrist, religious pamphleteer, and antiquarian, who worked in London during the reign of James I.[40] One of Maxwell's chief occupations was publishing celebrations of the English royal family, and another was arguing in favor of Anglicanism. To both ends he resourcefully resurrected the old Magdeburg prophecy, applying it to the royal heir, Prince Charles, and introducing it as a

38. I have searched in vain for applications of Carion's prophecy to the French King Charles IX (reigned 1560–1574).

39. Johann Wolf, *Lectiones memorabiles. . .* , 2 vols. (Lauingen, 1600), II, 296, under the entry for the year 1528, headed "Joan. Carion, Astronomus": "Idem ex libro vaticiniorum vetusto, reperto Madgeburgi ante annos ducentos, inter alia, imminebunt, inquit, horribiles mutationes omnium regnorum et Monachorum aestimatio peribit: Bestia Occidentis et Leo Orientis dominabuntur in toto mundo, et perambulabunt Christiani in servitute [*sic*: for Bonus's securitate] multa annos N. [*sic*: for Bonus's quindecim] Asiam. Posta [*sic*] horribilia de Antichristo audientur."

40. See on him the entry in the *Dictionary of National Biography* (hereafter DNB), XIII (Oxford, 1894), 115–117.

witness in favor of the Reformation. Maxwell no doubt did this above all to make a living, but that does not mean he thought himself dishonest.

Maxwell's first published flattery of young Charles—the future Charles I—appeared late in 1612 in a collection of poems issued primarily to lament "the deplorable death" of Charles's elder brother, "our late peerlesse Prince Henry." Now that Henry was dead, Maxwell included a poem about the new heir, then all of twelve years, entitled "Prince Charles his happie Entrie into the World." Among other conceits, he likened the young prince to the fifteenth-century Albanian hero George Castriota, alias "Scanderbeg," because Charles, titular duke of Albany, was ruler of "Albany in the north" as Scanderbeg had been ruler of "Albany [i.e., Albania] in the south"! As Scanderbeg was earlier a glorious foe of the Turk, so would Charles, the new Albanian, be so again; or, in Maxwell's none too inspired verse:

> O happy sight to see Prince Charles one day
> With Castriote once chief of chivalrie
> Against the Turks his Banner to display,
> That as hee's named the Duke of Albanie:
>> So men may him a Scanderbeg enstile
>> Th'horror of Turks, the Hector of this Ile.[41]

Maxwell did not introduce Carion's Magdeburg prophecy in this panegyric, but he brought it forth in his next collection of flatteries, a volume published in 1613 to honor the magnificent wedding in Heidelberg of Charles's sister Elizabeth and Frederick of the Palatinate. The marriage of Elizabeth, namesake of the great English queen, to the seemingly mighty elector palatine represented a high point of Jacobean optimism and self-congratulation,[42] and it was therefore natural for Maxwell to turn from his celebration of that alliance to a contemplation of the future triumphs to be expected from the might of Elizabeth's brother, the heir apparent.

41. James Maxwell, *The Laudable Life, and Deplorable Death of our late peerlesse Prince Henry* (London, 1612—STC 17701), sig. F1ʳ.

42. On this, Frances Yates, *The Rosicrucian Enlightenment* (London, 1972), 1–14. Of course Elizabeth and Frederick were later to become tragic victims of the Thirty Years' War—the pathetic "Queen and King of Hearts."

According to Maxwell, "the most glorious prophecy" that had ever been made about any prince was the one that Johann Carion had applied in his *Chronicle* to the Emperor Charles V. Carion's application, however, could not have been accurate, as a comparison of Charles's real deeds with the "tenure of the prediction" would show. Therefore the Emperor must have "left the accomplishment thereof to some other Charles than himself," and Maxwell made bold to hope that the true heir to the prophecy would be his own Prince Charles. He did not raise the difficulty that the Charles of Carion's prophecy was to be an Emperor who descended from the Carolingians and the kings of France; instead he repeated his comparison of Prince Charles to Scanderbeg and his hope that Charles, like the latter, would become "Christ's champion and the terror of the Turks."[43]

Two years later Maxwell withdrew his appointment of Prince Charles as surrogate for Charles V. Now his publication was dedicated to the archbishop of Canterbury and was mainly concerned with religion, specifically with showing how prophecies issued earlier by "24 famous Romain Catholickes" pointed to the "defection, tribulation, and reformation" of the Roman Church. In the course of this learned exposition, Maxwell returned to the prediction "touching the reformation of the Church" found by Carion in the "Chronicles of Magdeburg."[44] This time he quoted the prophecy in full in his own English translation, one which adhered very closely to Bonus's Latin. Then he went on to explain that although Carion had applied the prophecy to Charles V, it really had to be applied to some other Charles "either now living or that shall be hereafter." But instead of raising the possible candidacy of the English heir, Maxwell delicately stated that "as for any personal application, I for mine own part will not presume to

43. James Maxwell, *A Monument of Remembrance Erected in Albion, In Honor of the Magnificent Departure From Brittanie and Honorable Receiving in Germany, Namely at Heidelberge, of the two most noble Princes Fredericke and Elizabeth* . . . (London, 1613—STC 17703), sig. D4ᵛ.

44. James Maxwell, *Admirable and notable Prophesies uttered in former times by 24 famous Romain Catholickes, concerning the Church of Romes defection, Tribulation, and reformation* (London, 1615—STC 17698), 32–36. On this work, see further Reeves, *Influence of Prophecy*, 391, 499–500, and M. E. Reeves, "History and Eschatology: Medieval and Early Protestant Thought in some English and Scottish Writings," *Medievalia et Humanistica*, n.s. 4 (1973), 99–123 (at 113–114).

make any, for I love not to be censured, neither for a false prophet, if mine application should fail, nor for a flatterer." Here one wonders whether Maxwell had recently been just so censured for his flattering application of the prophecy to Prince Charles. At any rate, events would show that Charles as king was to find his crown weighing sufficiently heavily on his head without having to bear up under the weight of messianic prophecies first devised four centuries before.[45]

After Charles I lost both his crown and his head in 1649, Carion's Magdeburg prophecy was published one more time in England in relation to its possible application to current events. Although Charles had been executed by Parliament, his son Charles was still alive and recognized as Charles II in Scotland. While a battle was shaping up between Charles junior and Oliver Cromwell, a battle of prophecies was already being waged by Royalist and Parliamentary forces.[46] In both cases the Parliamentarians were most fortunate in their leaders: as Cromwell was the unsurpassed military leader of his day, so the Parliamentarian astrologer, William Lilly, was the unsurpassed prophet and propagandist whose words were "worth more than half a dozen regiments."[47]

William Lilly's major prophetic effort against the young Charles was his *Monarchy or No Monarchy*, which he completed on 23 July

45. In his *Carolanna* (London, ca. 1619—STC 17699), sig. D2r, lines 435–444 (the date of 1614 given in the DNB must be in error because the book was inspired by the death of Queen Anne in 1619), Maxwell continues to predict that Prince Charles would be another Scanderbeg but makes no allusion to the Carion text. A contemporary of Maxwell's who studied Carion's Magdeburg prophecy independently was the Welsh antiquarian John Jones of Gelli Lyvdy: for evidence that Jones copied the text between 1606 and 1623 from the English Carion translation of 1550, see MS Aberystwyth Mostyn 133, pp. 388–389, described by J. Gwenogvryn Evans, *Report on Manuscripts in the Welsh Language* (London, 1898–1910), I, pt. 1, 100–115. Exactly what Jones made of the prophecy cannot be told, but in some way John Carion of Brandenburg still spoke to John Jones of Wales over the breach of a century.

46. This was the last stage in a war of prophecies that had been raging throughout the 1640s: see Harry Rusche, "*Merlini Anglici*: Astrology and Propaganda from 1644 to 1651," *English Historical Review*, 80 (1965), 322–333, and especially Rusche, "Prophecies and Propaganda, 1641 to 1651," *English Historical Review*, 84 (1969), 752–770.

47. Keith Thomas, *Religion and the Decline of Magic* (New York, 1971), 343, quoting a contemporary source.

1651.[48] In this work, Lilly was primarily concerned to expose the falsity of a pro-Royalist rendering of a sixteenth-century prophecy by one Paul Grebner, a German who had originally offered his prophecy to Queen Elizabeth. Shortly before Charles I's execution, and again a year afterwards, English Royalists had published versions of Grebner's prophecy with spurious interpolations designed to show that "Charles, descended from Charles . . . shall overthrow His Adversaries, and shall govern His Kingdom wonderfull happily, and shall bear Rule far and near; and shall be greater then [*sic*] Charles the Great." Lilly's achievement was to demonstrate that the Royalist versions of Grebner diverged tendentiously from the original text, and that the original could by no means be interpreted to predict that Charles II would soon defeat Parliament.

Having accomplished that end, Lilly went on to treat a large number of other prophecies in order to forestall any future Royalist applications of them. Among these was the Charles prophecy from "the Chronicles of Magdeburg, testified by Carion in his third Booke." As Lilly's quotations reveal, he did not discover this by poring over Carion but learned of it from Maxwell's collection of prophecies by "Romain Catholickes." Lilly stated that the author of this Charles prophecy was "indued with Prophetick-spirit" yet quoted the text in its entirety to show that it "in no wayes points out the King of *Scotland*, though his name is Charles."[49] The prophecy was "authenticall," but it had to be applied in some other way.

The cases of Maxwell and Lilly are only two of numerous examples of how intently Englishmen continued to study "ancient prophecies" in the seventeenth century.[50] Aside from resort to Ca-

48. William Lilly, *Monarchy or No Monarchy in England* (London, 1651— Wing Catalogue L2228). The best treatment is by Rusche, "Prophecies," 765–768. See also Thomas, 411–412. Marjorie Reeves, *Joachim of Fiore and the Prophetic Future* (London, 1976), 159–160, uses a defective copy of Lilly's work which prevents her from recognizing his authorship. I have been unable to locate a copy of *The Lord Merlins Prophecy* (London, 1651), which Thomas, 412, describes as an anthology "mostly culled out of *Monarchy or No Monarchy*."

49. *Monarchy or No Monarchy*, 59–60. Lilly follows Maxwell (n. 44 above), 32–33, almost verbatim, except for omitting two sentences.

50. By far the best general treatment of this subject is Thomas, 389–432. Peter Burke, *Popular Culture in Early Modern Europe* (London, 1978), 274, is simply incorrect in saying that after 1600 "only the prophecies of the Bible continued to

rion's Magdeburg text, such continued interest led others back to the original Tripoli prophecy in different medieval manuscript versions. One anonymous seventeenth-century British antiquary was moved to complete an abbreviated copy of the Tripoli prophecy in a manuscript at his disposal. This was the copy in the fifteenth-century Yorkist anthology where about half of the Tripoli prophecy was deleted in order to make it appear more political.[51] The seventeenth-century antiquarian knew his prophecies well enough to recognize the text when he came across it. Impelled by a desire to restore completeness, he found another full copy of the prophecy and used it to supply the missing parts in the appropriate margins of the Yorkist anthology. Since both the fifteenth-century scribe and the early-modern supplementer worked carefully from good copies, between them they provided one of the best surviving English texts.

Another similar seventeenth-century Englishman who displayed interest in the Tripoli prophecy was Charles Fairfax, a mid-century Yorkshire antiquarian and uncle of Thomas Fairfax, the Parliamentary general.[52] Having found the 1347 version of the prophecy in a

---

be taken seriously by the learned" and that the prophecies of Joachim and Merlin sunk into "oblivion": on the contrary, the prophecies of Merlin were probably more widely circulated and studied in seventeenth-century England than ever before owing to their proliferation in print, see, e.g., Rusche's articles cited in n. 46 above. Bryan W. Ball, *A Great Expectation: Eschatological Thought in English Puritanism to 1660* (Leiden, 1975), is useful but overlooks continuity with medieval ideas. See also Christopher Hill, *Antichrist in Seventeenth-Century England* (London, 1971); Hill, *The World Turned Upside Down* (London, 1972), 70–78; and Herschel Baker, *The Race of Time* (Toronto, 1967), 58–59.

51. See Chapter Five, pp. 101–103. The MS in question, BL Cotton Vesp. E. vii, comes from the collection of Sir Robert Cotton (1571–1631), but I have learned from the Keeper of Manuscripts of the British Library that the hand which completed the Tripoli prophecy is not Cotton's. It should also be noted that the same hand made other marginal additions of prophetic material in Vesp. E. vii, as for example at the bottom of f. 87^r. See Appendix III for a composite edition of the Tripoli prophecy from this MS. After this book went to press, I learned from information kindly provided by Professor Michael J. Curley that MS BL Harley 6148 contains prophecies copied in the early seventeenth century by Cotton's associate, the antiquarian Richard St. George (d. 1635), from Cotton Vesp. E. vii. It may well be, then, that the person who completed the abbreviated Tripoli prophecy in Vesp. E. vii was Richard St. George.

52. DNB, VI (1888), 994–995.

fourteenth-century manuscript, Fairfax became so intrigued by it that he recopied it twice. One of these transcriptions survives and shows by comparison with the original that he worked with care and ability.[53] Not only is Fairfax's transcription almost flawless, but whereas the exemplar had only erratic punctuation, his copy consistently provides commas and periods in ways which show that he read the text with the fullest attention to sense.

Charles Fairfax's nephew Bryan reported that his uncle was "an excellent scholar" who delighted most in antiquities.[54] While this evaluation is beyond argument, Fairfax clearly preferred some "antiquities" to others. Assuredly he did not copy every old text that he found, let alone habitually recopy old texts twice. He and the seventeenth-century British antiquarian who supplied the missing parts of the Tripoli prophecy in the Yorkist anthology must have retained some sense of wonder before the old miraculous message. The two seventeenth-century students of the old message from Tripoli must surely have agreed with another dabbler in prophecy, Isaac Newton, who argued that "if God was so angry with the Jews for not searching more diligently into the Prophesies which he had given them to know Christ by, why should we think he will excuse us for not searching into the Prophesies which he hath given us to know Antichrist by?"[55]

53. Fairfax's fourteenth-century exemplar was Bodl., Fairfax 27, f. 26ʳ, on which see above p. 118 with n. 6. A note in Fairfax's hand on the bottom of this leaf refers to his having made two transcriptions. I have been unable to locate the first, in a "M.s. F [Fairfax] B in fine," without going through all the surviving Fairfax MSS in the Bodleian. The second appears in Bodl., Fairfax 28, f. iiiᵛ, a MS described in F. Madan and H. H. E. Craster, *A Summary Catalogue of Western Manuscripts in the Bodleian Library at Oxford* (Oxford, 1922–1953), II, pt. 2, 787.

54. Cited in the DNB article given in n. 52 above.

55. Isaac Newton, fragments from an unpublished and undated treatise on Revelation, in Frank E. Manuel, ed., *The Religion of Isaac Newton* (Oxford, 1974), 109. Manuel, *Religion*, 85–104, revises his earlier position, taken in his *Isaac Newton Historian* (Cambridge, 1963), 144, that Newton only allowed true prophetic insight to derive from Scripture; in this as in other areas of Newtonian research, there is need for attention to the chronological development of Newton's thought and for studying his unpublished work: the young Newton in Cambridge thought very differently about prophecy than the older man who wrote the *Observations upon the Prophecies of Holy Writ*. See also Margaret

Only around 1700 did learned antiquarians stop gathering and poring over "ancient prophecies" to gain occult wisdom. This abandonment of prophecy was part of a general demystification of the world and "emancipation from the past" that scholars are only now beginning to appreciate in full measure.[56] Though far more study remains to be done concerning the causes of this epoch-making break with old habits of thought, it appears that the triumph of "mechanistic" assumptions among men of learning made miracles seem less and less credible. Concurrently, a new sense of historical perspective made it clear that old documents had to be read as products of their times: details in old prophecies no longer could be applied anachronistically to current situations. Finally, a new faith in progress replaced the medieval conviction that the world was in its old age, with the result that upheavals and disasters were no longer viewed as preludes to the End.

Not just the Tripoli prophecy, but medieval prophetic texts as a class ceased to be recirculated and studied seriously around the turn of the seventeenth century.[57] Whereas historians and antiquarians

---

C. Jacob, *The Newtonians and the English Revolution, 1689–1720* (Ithaca, N.Y., 1976), 134–135.

56. The quotation is from Thomas, *Religion and the Decline of Magic* (n. 47 above), 431. Thomas's analysis, 427–432, of the reasons for the declining popularity of "ancient prophecies" in the late seventeenth century is outstanding. Also see Jacob, 139–142, whose argument—limited to England—emphasizes the growth of political stability. For a parallel decline in belief in eternal torment in hell, see D. P. Walker, *The Decline of Hell* (London, 1964). Peter Gay, *The Enlightenment: An Interpretation. I. The Rise of Modern Paganism* (New York, 1966), 327–328, dates the emergence of a new religious rationalism in England "with spectacular precision" to the years shortly before 1700.

57. See Thomas, and Reeves, *Influence of Prophecy*, viii: "Only reluctantly in the seventeenth century was prophecy as an attitude towards the future acknowledged to be outmoded." W. Frijhoff, "Prophétie et société," in M.-S. Dupont-Bouchat et al., *Prophètes et sorciers dans les Pays-Bas, XVIe–XVIIIe siècles* (Paris, 1978), 273, roughly estimates that prophetic texts comprised between 3 and 6 percent of all books and pamphlets printed in the Low Countries in the sixteenth century, between 1 and 3 percent in the seventeenth century, and only 0.5 percent in the eighteenth century (Professor E. W. Monter kindly called my attention to the Frijhoff study). The sixteenth-century percentages for the Netherlands were probably higher than the European average because of the heightened interest in prophecy during the Wars of Religion. Frijhoff, 275, remarks that tracts on the prophetic significance of comets ceased being published

like Carion, Lazius, Wolf, Maxwell, Lilly, and Fairfax cited medieval prophecies with alacrity, their eighteenth-century successors laughed at the same old texts. In 1746 the German Church historian Mosheim came across a medieval prophetic anthology from a collection in Helmstedt that included a copy of the Tripoli prophecy. But instead of recirculating the prophetic material he found, as a Lutheran before him had recirculated the prophecies he had found in nearby Magdeburg, Mosheim disdainfully offered some examples to exhibit "the sort of fictions that deceived people in medieval times." Then, wearying of the game, he concluded by saying that "readers will probably be as tired of reading such silliness as I am of recounting it."[58] Luther's bonfire may have ended the Middle Ages in one respect, but the medieval history of prophecy ended about two centuries later.

---

entirely in the Netherlands around 1680. Scholars such as Frijhoff and Burke (n. 50 above) tend to assume that prophecy continued to be taken seriously in lower-class or popular culture during the eighteenth century, but this assumption remains to be tested.

58. Johann Lorenz Mosheim, *Versuch einer unpartheiischen und gründlichen Ketzergeschichte* (Helmstedt, 1746), 353: "Ich rükke hier dieses Prophetenverzeichniss ein, damit man daraus sehen möge, durch was für Gedichte man in den mitlern Zeit sich habe verführen lassen. . . ."; 356: "Ich . . . lege darauf den Bruder Theoloforus auf die Seite. Die Leser werden vermutlich eben so müde seyn, seine Thorheiten zu lesen, als ich bin, sie zu erzählen." The prophetic anthology Mosheim used is today MS Wolfenbüttel 366 Helmstedt, which contains the Tripoli prophecy on fos. 60^v–61^r: see Chapter Six, n. 27.

CONCLUSIONS:
A MODERN LOOK
AT MEDIEVAL PROPHECY

Although we all still wish that we could look into the seeds of time to say which grain will grow and which will not, modern attitudes toward prophecy and eschatology vary considerably from those described in this account. Molly Bloom spoke for most of us when she mused about the woman who "had too much old chat in her about politics and earthquakes and the end of the world let us have a bit of fun first God help the world if all the women were her sort down on bathingsuits and lownecks of course nobody wanted her to wear...." But this does not quite sum it all up. Having pursued the Cedar of Lebanon vision over the centuries, it now appears worthwhile to consider the differences between medieval and modern prophetic practices and mentalities.

Starting with the composition of prophecy, an immediately obvious contrast lies in the habitual medieval resort to pseudonymity, for the prophets now among us most often speak in their own voices. The contemporary seeress Jeane Dixon, for example, has had no reason to avoid publicity: a book about her predictions, *A Gift of Prophecy* (1965), sold more than 260,000 hardbound copies and 2,800,000 more in paperback. But medieval observers would probably have been skeptical about Jeane Dixon's alleged clairvoyance. Millions of modern Americans believe in the random appearance of extrasensory perception and are therefore willing to accept the possibility that a Jeane Dixon has a "gift of prophecy," but in the Middle Ages it was assumed that such a gift came from God alone and was exceedingly rare. Mere prophetic "conjecture" was scorned. Only extraordinary individuals who radiated an aura of sainthood, like Hildegard of Bingen or Catherine of Siena, were ever thought to have been granted supernatural prophetic vision—and not everyone agreed that even such holy women could really see into the future.[1]

Assuming that one did not behave like a saint and still wished to predict, three paths remained open. The first two, however, were open to only a few. One might predict the future on the grounds of astrological prognostications, but for this it was necessary to display some credentials—usually an advanced university education, or at least familiarity with the technical writings of a Ptolemy or an Albumasar. Otherwise one might offer prophetic exegesis, that is, interpretation of texts that all acknowledged to be prophetic but were patently obscure, such as books of the Bible, Sibylline oracles, or recognized visions. The most highly regarded of medieval male prophets who spoke in their own voices—Joachim of Fiore, John of Rupescissa, and Vincent Ferrer—all maintained that they were not really prophets themselves but were only inspired interpreters of genuinely revealed prophecies.[2] Even they, however, needed reputations for sanctity (they were all heroic ascetics) and of course they also needed much learning. Moreover, writers like Joachim or Rupescissa could not have been at all certain when they began to work that they would gain favorable hearings.

Faced with these obstacles, most medieval prophets took the

---

1. On contemporary incredulity of St. Catharine's visionary powers, see Raymond of Capua, *The Life of St. Catherine of Siena*, trans. George Lamb (New York, 1960), 259–260 (I owe this reference to Richard Kieckhefer). On scorn for conjecture, see the references given in my "Medieval Prophecy and Religious Dissent," *Past & Present*, 72 (August, 1976), 3–24 (at 8, n. 14).

2. On Joachim's self-estimate, see Reeves, *Influence of Prophecy*, 13, 16; on Rupescissa's very similar one, Bignami-Odier, *Rupescissa*, 126–127, 159, 174. Ferrer's major eschatological writing, his letter "de tempore Antichristi et fine mundi" to Benedict XIII of 1412, fits into the same pattern: see ed. by H. Fages, *Notes et documents de l'histoire de Saint Vincent Ferrier* (Louvain and Paris, 1905), 213–224, and also S. Brettle, *San Vicente Ferrer und sein literarischer Nachlass* (Münster, 1924), 194–195.

course of least resistance and wrapped themselves up in pseudonymity. Instead of speaking in their own voices, they spoke in the voices of
saints like Hildegard or Francis, or of acknowledged prophetic experts like Joachim, or of reputedly inspired twilight figures like
Merlin and the Sibyls. Another form of pseudonymity was to claim
a miraculous vision for a fictitious recipient and thereby father one's
own prophecy implicitly on God. Though the introduction of a
fictitious miracle story like the appearance of a moving hand during
mass in "Snusnyacum" or doomed Tripoli doubled the deception,
such a marvelous story was bound to attract attention and was not
likely to be doubted. In an age when belief in God's frequent intervention in human affairs was universal, people were seldom skeptical
of miracles, and the prophet who spoke as if he were God or an
angel could hope to be listened to more attentively than if he spoke
as if he were any human.[3]

Pseudonymity was one kind of typically medieval prophetic
deceit, and the device of *ex eventu* prediction was another. Modern
prophets cannot predict what has already happened as long as they
speak in public. Obviously a prophecy that appears in a newspaper
or a magazine can hardly predict what happened the year before.
But medieval prophecies that were supposed to have been discovered
or brought from "overseas" could easily be backdated and could
then "predict" events that had already transpired. Pseudonymous
medieval prophets almost always predicted some events after the fact
and probably could not help themselves for two reasons. First, the
device was such an excellent way to gain credence that it must have
seemed irresistible; second, the most urgent concerns of the prophets
themselves were to link the problems of the present to the outcomes

3. Impressive recent research distilled by Charles Radding, "Superstition to
Science: Nature, Fortune, and the Passing of the Medieval Ordeal," *American
Historical Review*, 84 (1979), 945–969, and in a review article by Elizabeth A. R.
Brown, *History and Theory*, 19 (1980), 319–338, demonstrates that there was
a turning point in the history of mentalities during the twelfth century in favor
of greater resistance toward the notion of God's frequent intervention in human
affairs. But this was still a matter of degree even among the most "advanced"
thinkers, and anyone who has a nodding familiarity with late-medieval sources
knows that they all but invariably take for granted an activist God who continually makes His will felt on earth.

of the future. The authors of the Cistercian vision and the Tripoli prophecy could scarcely have omitted reference to the coming of the Mongols or the fall of the Holy Land because these events were what led them to prophesy in the first place.

A third characteristic medieval prophetic fraud was obscure allusiveness. At first it might be objected that obscurity is not so "characteristically medieval" a trait because modern prophecies are also often obscure. But there does seem to be a difference, for modern prophetic obscurity is simply the obscurity of hedging. Writers of newspaper horoscopes shroud their predictions in obscurity or forked-tongued ambiguity in order to make them seem true no matter what really happens afterwards; if they did not do this they would quickly lose their audiences. But medieval prophets like the authors of the Cistercian vision and the Tripoli prophecy were not journeymen working for pay. They did not intend to write new predictions every day, and they really thought they knew what was going to happen. Accordingly, the broad outlines of medieval prophetic texts are usually clear. Perhaps some prophets interspersed some obscurities throughout their texts because they were unsure about certain details of the future course of events, but it seems far more likely that most provided obscurities because patches of dark allusiveness were meant to be authenticating.

More specifically, medieval prophecies were expected to be full of emblems, and they were also expected to be difficult, for it was assumed that God preferred to communicate with humans by means of images and preferred to spur thought by difficulty. Not all emblems were difficult: surely all readers knew more or less what the "ship of Peter" stood for. But most emblems had to be puzzled over, and some may not even have been understood by those who first employed them, for difficulty in and of itself was authenticating. A prophet who wrote lines that he did not understand may have consoled himself with the thought that even the Old Testament prophets did not always themselves understand the messages they communicated from on high. A proponent of the prophecies of Saint Hildegard identified the degree of difficulty as a mark of authentication explicitly when he argued that the deep obscurity of Hildegard's texts was a sign of their inspiration.[4] If this attitude seems perverse, we must remember that every age has its own conventions. Today poets instead of prophets are expected to be inaccessible and not always certain of their own meaning: André Gide once wrote, "Before I explain my book, I want to wait for others to explain it to me," and Gérard de Nerval maintained that his sonnets "would lose some of their charm if they were explained—supposing that were possible."[5] Just as a serious contemporary poet would hardly eschew broken syntax and puzzling allusiveness, so medieval prophets had to adhere to similar conventions. To violate these would have been as self-defeating as issuing prophecy in their own voices.

But was it necessary to plagiarize—to moderns perhaps the unkindest fraud of all? As we have seen, the Tripoli prophecy was built from extensive plagiarism and provided material from which others plagiarized in their turn. The Tripoli prophet's borrowing might seem particularly cynical because it shows that he did not write spontaneously but worked designedly, picking and choosing his plagiarisms from different sources. Yet the plagiarizing prophet was again working within his culture's norms. Modern freshmen who feel insecure about their own abilities do not always take naturally to the injunction to "say it in your own words," but most of them gradually absorb our culture's repugnance for literary theft. "Say it in your own words," however, was not one of the medieval writer's first principles: quite to the contrary, he might have had a sign over his desk which read "don't say it in your own words if you don't have to."[6] What was once said well was there to be said again, espe-

---

4. Gebeno of Eberbach, cited by R. W. Southern, "Aspects of the European Tradition of Historical Writing: 3. History as Prophecy," *Transactions of the Royal Historical Society*, 5th ser., 22 (1972), 159–180 (at 161), from J. B. Pitra, *Analecta sacra*, 8 (1882), 483. On the role of imagery in the medieval theory of the prophetic imagination, Morton W. Bloomfield in *Speculum*, 54 (1979), 865–867, reviewing J.-P. Torell, *Théorie de la prophétie et philosophie de la connaissance aux environs de 1230* (Louvain, 1977).

5. Both examples cited by Henri Peyre, *The Failures of Criticism* (Ithaca, N.Y., 1967), 223–224.

6. Cf. John of Salisbury, Prologue to *Policraticus*, ed. C. C. J. Webb (Oxford, 1909), 16: "Quicquid ubique bene dictum est, facio meum."

cially if the borrower thought the saying had become more applicable than ever. So borrowed words became the stock-in-trade of the medieval prophet as much as of the medieval writer of any other sort of prose.

Admitting that the assumption of false identity, the prediction of events that had already happened, the introduction of meaninglessness, and the resort to plagiarism were various species of fraud, there can be no doubt that all these frauds were pious. The fabricators of medieval prophecy worked with no hope of petty gain or personal fame; they had urgent messages to communicate and wished only to communicate them in the best and most convincing ways possible. P. B. Medawar has well described the kind of people who will stop at nothing to spread their convictions when these seem to them "so *right*, so obviously in keeping with their sense of the fitness of things that people who do not share their beliefs must somehow be persuaded in their own best interests to do so."[7] Medawar said this not about medieval forgers but about modern biologists intent on showing the influence of heredity on intelligence, yet the self-righteous assumption of serving the highest cause of truth is undoubtedly the same.

As the motivations of the prophets were pious, so also were the motivations of the medieval revisers of prophecy. These revisers do not seem to have a modern equivalent. Possibly sometime or other someone has plagiarized parts of a prophecy of fifty years ago, but in general plagiarism today is too difficult and risky to make such a practice worthwhile. Moreover, if a prophecy of Jeane Dixon's about the imminent marriage of a celebrity or the outcome of a presidential election failed, no one would think to revive it by merely switching names. Jehovah's Witnesses, it is true, may be saying more or less the same thing over the decades, but the syntax of *The Watchtower* differs from issue to issue. The Cedar of Lebanon vision, on the other hand, like many other medieval texts, was revised and rewritten for centuries because people found in it a bedrock of truth that was inseparable from the words themselves.

Most of the words of the original vision in "Snusnyacum" reappeared in the Tripoli prophecy, and revision of the Tripoli prophecy

7. *New York Review of Books*, Feb. 3, 1977, 17.

ran the gamut from tinkering with passages that made no obvious sense, to taking out offensive parts, to redating the prophecy, to completely rewriting it. The self-justifications on this spectrum must have shaded into each other as do colors in a rainbow. At one end, a scribe correcting an obscure line could have thought that he was merely correcting a copying error in his exemplar. Once bolder copyists began to think this, they could have rationalized to themselves that lines they understood but did not like were excrescences that needed to be fixed. Some revisers, however, clearly decided that the setting or whole passages of the prophecy were simply wrong and had to be eliminated or reconceived. They differed from moderns in not throwing away the whole text as trash but salvaging the words they believed because these still had for them some sort of numinous power.

The persistent medieval faith in the words of prophecy can also be seen in the pattern of a prophecy's appearances. When the Cistercian vision, and then the Tripoli prophecy, and then some of the Tripoli prophecy's redated avatars were first promulgated, they were most often reported in chronicles or added to flyleaves or blank spaces of manuscript books. The prophecies in their first appearances were "news" and thus were included in the nearest medieval equivalents of newspapers or bulletin boards. But when the Tripoli prophecy was no longer news, it was still copied, now in anthologies, treatises, or occasionally still in blank spaces of books. Although the prophecy should have seemed out-of-date, if not in some respects simply mistaken, different readers continued to find enough inspiration in it to make it seem worth preserving.

That, of course, raises the central question of exactly what meaning generations of readers found in the various forms of the Cedar of Lebanon text. One result of the preceding analysis has been to show that readers by no means always read the details of the Tripoli prophecy—to concentrate on that major form of the text—in the same way. Scribal confusion itself reveals that from the start certain lines of the prophecy were unclear, and the survival of glosses proves that various readers interpreted most of the allusive lines differently. Certain readers, too, were particularly attracted to certain passages. The antimendicant lines, for example, were particularly attractive to some, and the prediction of coming great rulers of greater interest to others. To a considerable degree, then, readers of the Tripoli prophecy over the centuries could make of much of it what they would.

But certainly there was an irreducible minimum that had to be accepted by all. No matter how one read the details, the Tripoli prophecy stated clearly that contemporary troubles would be followed by more dreadful future ones, that all these trials would be followed by a wondrous time of peace and Christian triumph, and that news would then be heard of Antichrist. (Only the Percy anthologist suppressed this last component.) While the number of years mentioned in different versions of the prophecy varied, the implication in all was that the predicted events would happen soon and in quick succession, that within the lifetimes of contemporaries, or at the latest of their immediate descendants, history was going to be played out.

This irreducible minimum comprised a message that most people expected and presumably wanted to hear. I would argue that this can be seen not just from the perennial circulation of the Tripoli prophecy and its variants, but also from the appearance of the same basic message in other popular eschatological prophecies. Without pretending in any way to be exhaustive, a brief look at a few of these should serve to demonstrate that the foregoing devotion to the career of one has not been a self-indulgent exercise in nursing an intriguing but unrepresentative case.[8]

Probably the most popular short medieval prose prophecy was the Toledo Letter. This first circulated in the later twelfth century, was continually redated, and by the later Middle Ages had been translated into at least one French, two Italian, and five different German vernacular versions.[9] The letter underwent ceaseless revision, but its

8. I am planning a book-length study that will investigate the themes of a variety of medieval prophecies in more detail and pay more attention to differences as well as similarities.

9. On the Toledo Letter, see the Introduction, n. 8. Grauert treats two German versions, 288–289, 297–298, but not a fourteenth-century French one found in MSS Bodl., Bodley 761, fos. 184^v–185^v, and Bodl., Rawlinson G. 127, f. 3^r; nor two Italian versions in, respectively, Pietro di Mattiolo, *Cronaca Bolognese*, ed. C. Ricci (Bologna, 1885), 11–12 (for 1411), and MS London, Wellcome Institute 506, f. 112^v (for 1472); nor German versions in MSS Vat. Pal. lat. 1438, f. 104^r

basic message was usually the same: very soon the world would be buffeted by great winds and by practically every other imaginable natural disaster. The earth would heave so much that mountains and valleys would be levelled. But afterwards all those who survived would grow rich and the Saracens would accept Christianity.[10]

Typical of eschatological prophecies with a more explicitly political orientation were three texts usually bearing the incipits *Aere corrupto, Veniet aquila,* and *Gallorum levitas.* These all originated in the thirteenth century and circulated widely with considerable variants in the later Middle Ages. All began with references to current and imminent political trials instead of to winds and natural disasters, but they all also saw trial ultimately giving way to peace and worldwide Christian triumph.[11]

Neither the Toledo Letter nor the three political prophecies referred to the coming of Antichrist, no doubt because they preferred to emphasize the advent of an earthly messianic kingdom, a preference which they shared with the original Cistercian vision. Moreover, their authors knew that Antichrist was bound to come after the time of peace. But most high- and late-medieval prophecies were similar to the message from Tripoli in referring explicitly to Antichrist and thus in presenting a three-stage division: current and impending trials, peace, and Antichrist's advent. Some popular texts that have

---

(for 1432), Clm 18881, fos. 109ᵛ–110ᵛ (for 1461), and Cgm 216, fos. 159ᵛ–160ʳ (for 1479). No doubt this is still not a complete listing of all surviving vernacular versions.

10. I have not yet undertaken an exhaustive survey of all the numerous Toledo Letter variants, but as of now I find a final optimistic part missing only in certain fifteenth-century copies usually appearing under the name of Jerome of Erfurt.

11. On *Aere corrupto,* see Töpfer, 182–184, who refers to the older literature; a hitherto unnoticed MS copy is in Wolfenbüttel 42.3 Aug. 2°, fos. 304ᵛ–305ʳ. The thirteenth-century form of *Veniet aquila* is the prophecy *Regnabit Menfridus,* on which see Chapter Three, n. 38. On the later *Veniet aquila,* see Töpfer, 172–173; Reeves, *Influence of Prophecy,* 333–334, 361; R. Kestenberg-Gladstein, "A Joachimite Prophecy Concerning Bohemia," *Slavonic and East European Review,* 34 (1955), 40; and my "Medieval Prophecy" (n. 1 above), 21, n. 53; hitherto unnoticed fifteenth-century MS copies of *Veniet aquila* are legion. On *Gallorum levitas,* see Töpfer, 185–186, and Reeves, *Influence of Prophecy,* 312; unpublished MS copies of this text, which underwent numerous alterations, are so numerous as to be virtually beyond surveying.

already been referred to in this study illustrate this quite clearly. The short *Corruent nobiles* prophecy that was drawn on for a line by the Tripoli prophet saw present Christian defeats and trials getting worse year by year but foretold a complete healing of the Eastern Schism before news of Antichrist's preaching would be heard. The longer *Ve mundo in centum annis* also linked up present trials, such as the fall of the Holy Land, with even worse future ones but then told of ultimate Christian triumph before the coming of Antichrist, "the son of perdition." Similar was the vision of "Friar John." This went into great detail about present and future trials; among other things, coming chastisements would be so great that "hardly any cleric would dare show his tonsure." But again trials were to be followed by defeat of the infidels and good times before the coming of Antichrist.[12]

One apparent exception to the pattern just discussed is presented by the prophecy of "Brother Columbinus." This work falls into a different category from the others insofar as it foresaw present trials extending without interruption into the reign of Antichrist. But according to "Columbinus," Antichrist's terrible reign was to end after three and a half years and be followed by two hundred twenty years of good times on earth before the end of the world. The prophecy stops there, but since everyone knew that the Last Judgment would be fiery, the pattern was ultimately the same: terrible trials, good times, final trials—in this case the trials attending Armageddon.[13]

In addition to the basic pattern of trials—respite—end, medieval eschatological prophecies worked within the same basic time frame— a short one. All focused on the immediate future and all posited the certainty that present evils would get worse tomorrow. To this end the device of *ex eventu* prophecy was particularly effective because it made present evils look like the merest foothills in comparison to the Alps soon to come. But although the imminent trials were to be terrible beyond imagination, they would be relatively short. In Friar

12. For literature on *Corruent nobiles*, see Chapter Three, n. 39, and Chapter Six, n. 14; on *Ve mundo*, see Chapter Three, n. 6; on the prophecy of Friar John, see the Introduction, n. 6.

13. On the "Columbinus" prophecy, see Chapter Three, n. 7. I study the alternate prophetic tradition of good times coming after Antichrist in my "Refreshment of the Saints."

John's vision they last vaguely for "a while" (*per tempora*); in *Ve mundo* the internal logic of the predictions forces the conclusion that they can only last for well under a hundred years; and in the political prophecies a messianic ruler clearly comes very soon. The other prophecies are the most precise: the Toledo Letter assures its readers that some will live through the coming trials and *Corruent nobiles* and the "Columbinus" prophecy explicitly limit the duration of coming trials to fifteen years.

Clearly, then, medieval people had a basic formula for linking up the present to the certain End. The defeats, hardships, or depravities they saw around them were not random but part of a foreordained divine plan. Sufferings were bound to get worse, but they would cease within the life expectancies of most readers. As Christendom had been sullied and humbled, so would it be purified and exalted before the ultimate scenes of the great eschatological drama would be played out. No matter how much or how often details might be changed, this pattern constituted what might be called a medieval prophetic "deep structure" that lasted for centuries.[14]

That "deep structure," I believe, was lasting because it brought consolations. One was that the prophetic plan was written indelibly. The prophecies I have treated were not of the admonitory variety, issued to urge people to change their ways by revealing what would happen if they did not. On the contrary, they were meant to be statements of fixedly preordained events. At first it might seem as if admonitory prophecies might be more consoling than fixed ones, since they offer the hope that humans can alter their fates by their own actions. But most observers in the Middle Ages were too pessimistic to believe that the corruption of humanity would cease merely by exhortation. Fixed prophecies spoke well to them in eschewing contingencies.

Consolation was present all the more in promises of rewards. Of course the ultimate rewards were otherworldly, but it is a simplification to believe that high- and late-medieval readers of eschatological prophecies were consoled, like Molly Bloom's sour old lady, solely by

14. I study other examples of the medieval prophetic "deep structure" in my "Black Death and Western European Eschatological Mentalities," *American Historical Review*, 86 (1981), 533–552.

thinking that the just would soon see God while the sinful would roast in hell. Rather, they were consoled as well by the expectation of a penultimate time of betterment in the world. The prophecies they read strengthened their conviction that present evils were bound to get worse but also offered assurance of consequent good times on earth which some of them would live to experience. In the "Columbinus" version, the good earthly times would come after Antichrist and last for the gratifyingly long duration of two hundred twenty years. In the other prophecies, the good times were apparently shorter, although most of the texts are vague on this point. (Even the Tripoli prophecy's reference to fifteen years of peace and fruits does not present an unswervingly strict time limitation because the text leaves open the possibility that the time of the "glorification of Jerusalem" might be separate and longer.) But whatever the duration, the good times were always there.

In other words, the writers and believing readers of medieval eschatological prophecies were chiliasts. I have refrained from using the word chiliasm until now because it can easily convey false impressions. Most often chiliasts are conceived to be self-appointed messiahs, fanatical rabble-rousers, or "primitive rebels." Supposedly their hopes for the future are different from those of most of their contemporaries, grow out of or nourish social discontent, and foster insurrectionism. Certainly there are chiliasts like these, but chiliasm should be understood more generally as any hope for an impending, supernaturally inaugurated, marvelously better time on earth before the End.[15] In this sense, the author of the Tripoli prophecy was as much a chiliast as John of Leyden.

If this usage is accepted, then chiliastic beliefs in the Middle Ages were commonplace aids in coping with reality. The author of the Cistercian vision was not unusual in hoping for an imminent conversion of the world, and the author of the Tripoli prophecy was not eccentric but typical of prophets as a class in predicting the coming

15. On the consensus behind this definition, see my "Refreshment of the Saints," 98–99, n. 8. It is true that some modern writers tend to use the word *millenarianism* (or *millennialism*) in preference to *chiliasm*, but both come from the same origins (Latin and Greek for one thousand) and thus should be considered synonymous. I prefer chiliasm because it is less cumbersome.

of an imminent time of peace, abundance, and Christian triumph. Neither author was a wandering fanatic who aimed to whip up crowds of the discontented to frenzy. Almost certainly both were clerics; certainly clerics were the main readers of the various forms of the Cedar of Lebanon text in the first centuries of its circulation. As time went on more laymen joined the ranks of the readers and copyists of prophecies, but the identifiable laymen who copied the Tripoli prophecy—Pietro da Villola, Reginald Andrew, Johann Carion—were not underprivileged persons prone to riot. The view that medieval chiliasm was a monopoly of anomalous "revolutionary millenarians" must be put aside.[16]

Medieval chiliastic prophecies could, and usually did, have subversive implications, but such prophecies were rarely issued to encourage subversion.[17] Medieval eschatological prophets were usually displeased with the present, and they often castigated perceived

16. As against Norman Cohn, *The Pursuit of the Millennium*, 3rd ed. (New York, 1970). Cohn's work is open to criticism from several different points of view; for this line of criticism, see also my "Medieval Prophecy," esp. p. 19, and Hillel Schwartz, "The End of the Beginning: Millenarian Studies, 1969–1975," *Religious Studies Review*, 2, no. 3 (July, 1976), 1–15, who identifies a "second generation" of studies, as opposed to the first one represented by Cohn, which "describe millenarian beliefs and actions less often as the products of disease, more often as an arsenal of world-sustaining forces." (Richard Kieckhefer called my attention to the Schwartz piece.)

17. Even the chiliastic manifestoes of Fra Dolcino of 1300 and 1303 did not call for violence on the part of Dolcino's own followers, and whatever violence Dolcino may later have countenanced was defensive: see Töpfer, 302–303, 319–321. The only medieval chiliasts known to me who explicitly called for revolutionary violence from within their own camp were the Bohemian Taborites of 1419–1420: see Howard Kaminsky, *A History of the Hussite Revolution* (Berkeley, Calif., 1967), and German translations of the most important texts in Robert Kalivoda and A. Kolesnyk, *Das hussitische Denken im Lichte seiner Quellen* (Berlin, 1969), 296–327. *The Reformation of Kaiser Sigismund* and the *Book of One Hundred Chapters* also called for violence, but these were less prophecies than reform treatises with chiliastic content: on these two texts, see most recently, respectively, Tilman Struve, "Reform oder Revolution? Das Ringen um eine Neuordnung in Reich und Kirche im Lichte der 'Reformatio Sigismundi' und ihrer Ueberlieferung," *Zeitschrift für die Geschichte des Oberrheins*, 126 (1978), 73–129, and Klaus Arnold, " 'Oberrheinischer Revolutionär' oder 'Elsässischer Anonymus'? Zur Frage nach dem Verfasser einer Reformschrift vom Vorabend des deutschen Bauernkriegs," AfK, 58 (1976), 410–431. Several other prophetic texts do predict popular violence, but that is not the same as calling for it.

abuses vitriolically.[18] The Tripoli prophet was milder than most, but even he defamed the mendicants and foresaw their imminent annihilation. Yet medieval eschatological prophets hardly wrote as reformers or revolutionaries; their aim was to comprehend and make known God's plan without thinking that they or others could do anything to change it. Although they did not hesitate to express their prejudices and resentments, they did not mean to call for any human action other than "vigilance" and perseverance in Christian rectitude. Above all, consciously or unconsciously they meant to offer consolation to themselves and others in times of despair.

Most medieval people differed from most of us today in believing, or at least in being constantly exposed to the belief, that their world stood close to the edge of time. This, of course, does not mean that all medieval people always brooded about the End. Most men and women seem to have gone about their affairs under normal circumstances without eschatological preoccupations: wills and tombstone inscriptions usually took coming generations for granted. The clergy, however, was occupationally more inclined at all times to look for eschatological intimations, and some layfolk kept track of eschatological portents as well. Accordingly, eschatological prophecies were constantly copied, altered, and recopied; they were always on flyleaves and must often have been in the air to the extent that their readers talked or preached about them to others.[19]

18. For numerous examples, see my "Medieval Prophecy and Religious Dissent."

19. A thorough study of the treatment of eschatology and prophecy in late-medieval sermons is a desideratum that would call for much painstaking research since much of the evidence doubtless still lies buried in unpublished and unwieldy sermon collections. Those eschatological sermons I know run the gamut from (1) recitations of traditional Antichrist lore; to (2) careful reviews of different ways of computing the End, with the ultimate purpose of showing that the time of the End cannot be surely known; to (3) urgent adjurations that the End is near. In the third group I would place Pierre d'Ailly's little-known *Sermo tertius de adventu Domini* (=*Sermo de quadruplici adventu Domini*) of 1385, in, e.g., D'Ailly, *Tractatus et sermones* (Strasbourg, 1490), sig. t3^r–t6^r, which refers to prophecies of Pseudo-Methodius, Arnold of Villanova, Joachim, and Hildegard. See also the Paul's Cross sermon of 1388 of Thomas Wimbledon, in Nancy H. Owen, ed., "Thomas Wimbledon's Sermon: 'Redde Racionem villicacionis tue,'" *Mediaeval Studies*, 28 (1966), 176–197, which refers to Joachim, Hildegard, and a "doctor" who predicted the coming of the great Antichrist for 1400. In 1439

Given this pervasively eschatological and prophetic context, it was above all in times of perceived crises that people wrote or read prophecies which helped them make sense of perceived disasters and served to give them hope. The coming of the Mongols, the fall of the Holy Land, the onslaught of the Black Death, and later the appearance of Luther and the Turks before Vienna were major catalysts for the creation and intensified circulation of prophecy. In addition, less dramatic events that nonetheless disturbed given individuals provoked resort to prophecy as well. From the high Middle Ages until the medieval supernatural framework collapsed around 1700, details and interpretations of prophecies varied with circumstances, but the major outlines remained immobile. Writing around 1239, the author of the Cistercian vision predicted that there would be "mutations of faith," but in one sense he was surely mistaken, for there were no mutations of a basic prophetic faith from his own day until the dawn of the Enlightenment.

---

the doctor of theology Johannes Wünschelburg read the entire "Gamaleon" prophecy from the pulpit in the Bavarian town of Amberg; on this see, e.g., Friedrich Lauchert, "Materialien zur Geschichte der Kaiserprophetie im Mittelalter," *Historisches Jahrbuch*, 19 (1898), 844–872 (at 844–846), and further literature cited in my article, "Gamaleon," *Dictionnaire d'histoire et de géographie ecclésiastiques*, XIX, 957–958.

Appendix I

TEXTS OF THE
CISTERCIAN VISION

A. CONTINENTAL VERSIONS

The following is a composite edition of the three continental texts of
the Cistercian vision: UB Innsbruck 187, f. 2ʳ (prov. Ottobeuren)
(=I); Alberic of Trois-Fontaines's version as edited in MGH, *Scriptores*, 23, 949 (=A); and Vat. lat. 3822, f. 6ᵛ (=V). (The edition by
J. Bignami-Odier, "Notes sur deux manuscrits de la Bibliothèque du
Vatican," *Mélanges d'archéologie et d'histoire*, 54 [1937], 229, is defective.) The Innsbruck MS is used as the base text, except for two
instances in which it appears to be in error. In this and all following
editions, I adhere to the orthography of the base MS, except in writing *v* for consonantal *u*. I do not report minor orthographical variants
(e.g., *Libani* for *Lybani*). Punctuation and capitalization are modern-
ized. Uncertain readings are placed in pointed brackets ⟨ ⟩, and oblit-
erated or completely illegible passages are represented by a series of
dots within pointed brackets.

Anno[1] Domini M°CC°xl^mo apud Snusnyacum[2] monasterium Cysterciensis ordinis hec visio facta est cuidam monacho celebranti presentibus abbate et ministro. Apparuit quedam manus scribens in corporali verba hec. Cedrus alta Lybani succidetur. Prevalebit Mars Saturno et Iovi. Saturnus[3] in omnibus insidiabitur[4] Iovi. Infra xi annos erit[5] unus deus et una[6] monarchia. Secundus deus abiit. Filii Israel liberabuntur a captivitate. Quedam gens sine[7] capite dicta vel reputata vagans veniet. Ve[8] clero! Viget[9] ordo novus; si ceciderit, ve[10] ecclesie! Multa[11] prelia erunt in mundo. Fidei, legum, et regnorum mutaciones erunt. Terra Sarracenorum subvertetur.

B. ENGLISH VERSIONS

Since the English versions diverge greatly from each other, it seemed best not to present a composite edition of all four. Nonetheless it is certain that all four copies descended from a common ancestor because they all contain the following variants (or corruptions of such variants) not found in any of the surviving continental texts: *Mars prevalebit*; corruption of *et una monarchia*; omission of *dicta*; addition of *tota*. A second, later, common ancestor contains further variants (or corruptions of such) found in all the English copies except that of Matthew Paris: *ix annos*; *deus monarchie*; *obiit*; omission of *vagans*; *de clero*. As the following editions will show, none of the four surviving copies directly relied on any of the others.

---

1. *The preamble,* Anno ———— verba hec, *appears only in I. A has:* Ante aliquot annos contigit que secuntur. Cuidam Cisterciensis ordinis abbati et eius ministro apparuit manus scribens verba ista in corporali. *V lacks a preamble.*

2. *Could also be* Sunsnyacum, Sinisnyacum, Smisnyacum, *or* Simisnyacum.

3. Saturnus ———— Iovi *lacking A.*

4. insidiatur *I.*

5. *Followed by* post *V.*

6. monarcha *for* una monarchia *A.*

7. dicta sine capite *for* sine capite dicta *V.*

8. Vech, vech clero! *for* Ve clero! *V.*

9. *Lacking I.*

10. vech *V.*

11. Sic multa *for* Multa *V.*

1. Matthew Paris

I follow the edition of H. R. Luard, Matthew Paris, *Chronica majora* (RS 57; London, 1874–1884), III, 538.

> Eodem tempore [1239] cuidam monacho Cisterciensi apparuit manus candida scribens in corporali hec verba. Cedrus alta Libani succidetur. Mars prevalebit Saturno et Iovi. Saturnus vero in omnibus insidiabitur Iovi. Erit unus deus, id est monarcha. Secundus deus adiit. Filii Israel liberabuntur a captivitate infra undecim annos. Gens quedam sine capite reputata vagans veniet. Ve clero! Viget ordo novus; si ceciderit, ve ecclesie! Fidei, legum, et regnorum mutaciones erunt, et tota terra Sarracenorum subvertetur.

2. The Dunstable and Gilbertine Versions

The following is a composite edition of the versions found in the Annals of Dunstable, as edited by H. R. Luard, *Annales Monastici* (RS, 36; London, 1864–1869), III, 151 (=D), and in the Gilbertine copy in Cambridge, Saint John's College 239, rear flyleaf (=G). I use the Dunstable copy as the base text but accept variants from G when they appear clearly preferable.

> Eodem[1] anno [1239] cuidam monacho Cisterciensis ordinis, abbate et conventu presentibus, ministranti, apparuit manus scribens in corporali hec verba. Cedrus alta Libani succidetur. Mars prevalebit Saturno[2] et[3] Iovi. Saturnus in omnibus insidiabitur Iovi. Infra novem annos erit unus deus monarchie. Secundus[4] deus obiit. Filii Ysrael[5] liberabuntur a captivitate quadam. Gens sine capite, vel reputata,[6] veniet.[7] De clero viget

---

1. Anno Domini M°CC° quadrgesimo pervenit ad nos hec scriptura. Apparuit manus scribens hec verba *for* Eodem ——— hec verba G.

2. *Reading uncertain* G.

3. Et Iovi in omnibus insidiabitur *for* et Iovi ——— Iovi G.

4. Secundo *for* Secundus deus D.

5. *Lacking D.*

6. repudiata G.

7. *Reading uncertain but probably* veniet G.

ordo novus. Si[8] ceciderit, ve ecclesie! Multa prelia erunt in mundo. Fidei,[9] legum, et regnorum mutaciones[10] erunt.[11] Tota terra Saracenorum subvertetur.

3. The Walsingham Version

The following is taken from BL Royal 13 E IX, f. 27[v] (prov. Saint Albans).

Cedrus alta Libani succedetur. Tota terra Sarracenorum subvertetur. Maris prevalebit Saturno. Et Iovi Saturnus in omnibus insidiabitur. Infra ix annos erit unus deus tocius monarchie. Secundus obiit. Filii liberabuntur captivitati. Quedam gens sine velamine repudiata venit. De celo viget ordo novus. Et si ceciderit, ve ecclesie! Multa prelia erunt in mundo. Fidei, legum, et municiones erunt.

---

8. Cum G.

9. *This and the succeeding sentence are in reversed order in* G.

10. immutaciones D.

11. *Followed by* Paupertas est odibile bonum. ⟨Curarum remocio⟩. Possessio sine calumpnia. G.

Appendix II

WITNESSES OF
THE EARLIEST FORM OF
THE TRIPOLI PROPHECY

A. HYPOTHETICAL RECONSTRUCTION OF THE ORIGINAL PROPHECY OF CA. 1290

The earliest version of the Tripoli prophecy was unquestionably the one that alluded only to the fall of Tripoli (i.e., not Tripoli and Acre), that predicted the return of Frederick II, and that was fuller in several details toward the end than the more widely circulated revision done after the summer of 1291. I can identify four witnesses to this earliest form: the copy made by John of Paris in 1300, two fifteenth-century Italian copies—BN lat. 16021, f. 19^{r-v}, and Vat. lat. 793, f. 96^v—and the variant readings found in the Nicholas of Strassburg copy in Bodl., Bodley 140, f. 87^{r-v}. John's text is the most reliable single witness, but it can be corrected in numerous places where one or several of the three other witnesses correspond more closely either to the language of the Cistercian vision (the exemplar of ca. 1239) or to the language of the post-Acre revision.

> Anno Domini 1287 facta est quedam visio Tripolis cuidam
> monacho grisei ordinis celebranti missam coram abbate et alio

presente monacho. Infra oblacionem et communionem apparuit quedam manus scribens super corporale in quo dictus monachus consecrabat.

Cedrus alta Libani succidetur, et Tripolis in brevi destruetur. Mars Saturnum superabit. Et Saturnus insidiabitur Iovi. Vespertilio dominum apum subiugabit. Infra quindecim annos erit unus deus et una fides. Alter deus evanuit. Filii Israel a captivitate liberabuntur. Quedam gens que sine capite vocatur veniet. Ve tunc clero et tibi Christianitas! Navicula Petri iactabitur variis[1] fluctibus, sed evadet et dominabitur in fine dierum. In mundo erunt multa prelia, et multe strages, et fames valida, et hominum mortalitas per loca, et regnorum mutaciones. Terra barbarorum subvertetur. Ordines mendicancium et alie secte quamplures annichilabuntur. Tunc surget leo de cavernis moncium et montana transcendet, et alium leonem interficiet. Bestia occidentalis et leo orientalis totum mundum subiugabunt. Et tunc erit pax in toto orbe terrarum, et copia fructuum, et omnium rerum habundancia per quindecim annos. Tunc erit passagium commune ultra aquas congregatas ad terram sanctam. Et civitas Ierusalem gloriabitur, et omnes civitates Iudee reedificabuntur. Sepulchrum Domini ab omnibus honorabitur. Et in tanta tranquillitate audientur nova de Antichristo et cuncta mirabilia. Beatus qui tunc vicerit, quia non ledetur a morte perpetua.[2] Vigilate.

B. THE JOHN OF PARIS TEXT

Thomas Kaeppeli, *Scriptores Ordinis Praedicatorum Medii Aevi* (Rome, 1970–   ), II, 521, lists eight manuscript copies of John of Paris's *De adventu Antichristi et fine mundi* (*De Antichristo*). One of these, in BN lat. 3455, is mistakenly listed by Kaeppeli as belonging to the fifteenth century but is actually a sixteenth-century copy made from the printed edition of 1516 and accordingly may be excluded from consideration. Adding two copies unknown to Kaeppeli that I have located in manuscripts from Milan and Turin, a list of surviving manuscript witnesses to the text is as follows:

---

1. *Possibly* validis.

2. *Compare Rev. 2:11.*

Avignon, Bibliothèque Calvet 1087, fos. 206^r–219^r (ca. 1400) (=A)

Cues, Hospital 57, fos. 97^r–103^v (15th century) (=C)

Laon 275, fos. 1^r–11^r (14th century) (=L)

Milan, Ambrosiana I. 227 Inf., fos. 31^v–35^v (14th century) (=M)

Oxford, Bodl., Canon. Pat. lat. 19, fos. 14^r–35^v (14th century) (=O)

Paris, BN lat. 13781, fos. 81^r–95^v (14th century) (=P)

Turin, Biblioteca Nazionale Universitaria G. IV. 8, fos. 24^v–35^r (15th century) (=T)

Vat. Pal. lat. 924, fos. 226^v–238^v (15th century) (=Va)

Venice, San Marco III. 177 (2176), fos. 35^v–42^v (1469) (=Ve)

The printed edition—*Expositio . . . Joachim*, fos. 44^r–51^v—was made from the same exemplar once located in the Venetian monastery of San Giorgio Maggiore that was used by the scribe of Ve and thus has little value for reconstructing the text. The listed MSS break down into three families: (1) O; (2) PLCVa; (3) AMTVe. A comparison of the text of the Tripoli prophecy in each of the families with the original Cistercian vision, with independent early witnesses of the Tripoli prophecy, and with the post-Acre revision reveals that the first family, manuscript O (copied in the first half of the fourteenth century in northern Italy), is the best. Although P is indubitably a very early copy written near to the scene of John's activity (Saint-Germain-des-Prés, before ca. 1320, when it was used by Nicholas of Strassburg or an intervening copyist), it contains several serious corruptions. Manuscripts L, C, and Va descend from P. Those of the third family descend from an ancestor of O, but all have more corrupt readings than O and P, many of which arose from a contamination described in Chapter Four. The edition given below therefore follows O, except in a very few places where other witnesses show it to be clearly in error. Because a critical edition of John of Paris's entire treatise is being prepared as a Ph.D. dissertation by Mrs. Sara Clark of Cornell University, I refrain from providing an exhaustive list of variants. Instead I provide only the variants of P, since P was the basis of the Nicholas of Strassburg plagiarism; the variants of A that reveal contamination by a branch of the original version, a witness of which is found in Vat. lat. 793; and additional variants that show how later scribes endeavored to improve or alter the meaning of the text (i.e., changes in syntax—particularly frequent in M—or inadvertent omissions are excluded). Since A usually encompasses the same variants as M, T, and Ve, when A is given it may be assumed that M, T, and Ve (and also the printed edition) follow the noted variant unless otherwise indicated; when P is given it may be assumed that C, L, and Va follow it unless otherwise indicated.

> Anno[1] Domini millesimo ducentesimo 87[2] facta est quedam visio Tripolis[3] cuidam monacho grisei[4] ordinis celebranti missam coram[5] abbate et[6] alio presente monacho. Infra oblacionem[7] enim et communionem apparuit[8] quedam manus scribens[9] super corporale in quo dictus monachus consecrabat.[10]
>
> Cedrus alta Libani succidetur,[11] et Tripolis[12] in brevi destruetur. Mars Saturnum superabit. Et Saturnus insidiabitur Iovi. Vespertilio dominum apum superabit.[13] Infra tres annos

---

1. *Followed by* vero P.

2. *So in* O. 87 *appears to have been added by a later hand to the sufficient blank space left by the original scribe for completion of the date in Latin words.* 1287 *in Roman numerals or Latin words appears in all the other MSS except M, which gives* Mlxxv.

3. Tripoli *A;* in Tripolis *with changed syntax M.*

4. ordinis griseorum *for* grisei ordinis P.

5. eorum P.

6. *Followed by* eciam P.

7. enim oblacionem *for* oblacionem enim P.

8. Nam apparuit *for* apparuit A.

9. super corporale scribens *for* scribens super corporale P.

10. fuit [*added in margin in scribe's hand*] sic *for* consecrabat O; consecrabat P; corpus Domini consecravit *for* consecrabat A.

11. succeditur O.

12. in brevi Tripolis *for* Tripolis in brevi P; Tripolis *lacking* Va.

13. *Followed by* vel fugabit *in the margin of* P; *followed by* vel fugabit *in the text of* CL; fugabit *for* superabit Va.

unus deus[14] et una fides. Alter deus evanuit. Filii Israel a captivitate liberabuntur. Quedam gens que[15] sine capite vocatur
veniet. Ve tunc[16] clero et tibi[17] Christianitas! Navicula Petri
iactabitur variis[18] fluctibus, sed evadet et dominabitur in fine
dierum. Et in mundo erunt[19] multa prelia et multe strages, et
omnis terra turbabitur, et fames valida,[20] et hominum mortalitas[21] per loca, et regnorum mutaciones. Terra barbarorum
pervertetur. Ordines[22] mendicancium et[23] alie secte[24] quamplures adnichillabuntur. Tunc surget leo de cavernis moncium,
et montana transcendet, et alium leonem interficiet. Bestia occidentalis et leo orientalis totum mundum sibi[25] subiugabunt.
Et tunc erit pax in universo orbe, et copia fructuum, et omnium rerum habundancia per xv[26] annos. Tunc erit passagium
commune ad terram sanctam. Et civitas Ierusalem gloriabitur,[27] et omnes civitates Iudee rehedificabuntur.[28] Sepulchrum
Domini ab omnibus honorabitur. Et in tanta[29] tranquilitate
audientur nova de Antichristo. Cuncta[30] mirabillia. Beatus qui
tunc vicerit,[31] non ledetur a[32] morte perpetua.[33]

---

14. dominus *P*; *lacking A.*

15. sine capite veniet *for* que ———— veniet *P.*

16. autem *A*; *followed by* toti *CL.*

17. toti Christianitati *for* tibi Christianitas *P.*

18. magnis *A.*

19. *Followed by* tunc *O.*

20. *Followed by* erit *P.*

21. *Followed by* erit *O.*

22. Ordo *Va.*

23. ad *C.*

24. *Followed by* tam marium quam muliebrium *Ve.*

25. tibi *O.*

26. 25 *PL*; xxv *C*; xxvi *Va*; alias 30 *in the margin of O.*

27. *Lacking P.*

28. edificabuntur *P.*

29. finita *P*; illa *Va.*

30. *Lacking Va*; et cuncta *M.*

31. viserit *O.*

32. *Lacking O.*

33. secunda *A.*

C. THE NICHOLAS OF STRASSBURG TEXT

Adding three copies of Nicholas of Strassburg's *De Antichristo* that I have located in manuscripts from Basel, Frankfurt, and Naples to the hitherto fullest list provided by Thomas Kaeppeli, *Scriptores Ordinis Praedicatorum Medii Aevi* (Rome, 1970–   ), III, 144–145, a composite list is as follows:

Basel, UB A V 39, fos. 130^v–131^v (extracts) (14th century) (=B1)

Basel, UB A VI 6, fos. 303^r–314^v (15th century) (=B2)

Berlin, Staatsbibliothek Theol. lat. quart. 175, fos. 62^r–72^v (14th century) (=Be)

Erfurt, Amplon. quart. 154, fos. 1^r–76^r (14th century) (all three of Nicholas's treatises)

Frankfurt, UB Barth. 141, fos. 141^v–161^v (15th century) (=F)

Naples, VII. C. 20, fos. 106^v–114^r (15th century)

Oxford, Bodl., Bodley 140, fos. 60^r–96^r (14th century) (all three treatises) (=O)

Strasbourg, Bibliothèque Municipale C. 25, 4° (dedicated to John XXII; destroyed, 1870)

Trier, Historisches Archiv 551 (1296), fos. 40^r–78^r (15th century) (all three treatises: dedicated to John XXII)

Trier, Stadtbibliothek 651, fos. 93^r–155^r (1468) (all three treatises)

Utrecht, UB 386, fos. 190^r–199^v (15th century) (=U)

Warsaw, Codex Chart. Lat. Fol. I 109 (dedicated to John XXII; destroyed, 1944: photocopy reputedly owned by F. Stegmüller)

Since it is certain that Nicholas of Strassburg copied from John of Paris's *De Antichristo*, specifically from the MS tradition represented by P, and very likely from P itself, the Nicholas copies have no independent value for reconstructing the text. Accordingly, I have not gone to the trouble of gathering all ten surviving copies but have limited myself to collating six (those for which abbreviations are given above). Of these, the Berlin MS clearly gives the best text and therefore is used as the base. The Berlin MS contains all three treatises dedicated to Baldwin of Trier under the collective title *De adventu Christi*, with the *annus presens* of 1326. It was copied in the mid-fourteenth century in the Benedictine monastery of Saint Peter's, Erfurt. One can see at a glance that its readings are virtually identical with the P text of John of Paris.

The dating and provenance of the other five MSS can be specified with some exactitude. B1 is part of an eschatological miscellany from the Charterhouse of Basel, copied during the Great Schism around 1390; B2 is part of another eschatological miscellany, copied in or near Basel in the early fifteenth century; F is from the Bartholomaeus-stift of Frankfurt, copied around 1450; O is from an English Dominican house, probably Leicester, and was copied in the later fourteenth century; U is a fifteenth-century MS from the Augustinian canonry of Utrecht. The variant apparatus excludes orthographical and minor variants, such as *supra* for *super*, or omissions and additions of *et*, and also excludes numerous grammatical errors made by F. It shows clearly that the scribe of O presented a composite reading taken from Nicholas and an independent transmission of the earliest form of the prophecy. It also raises interesting questions about U that I find difficult to resolve.

> Anno vero[1] Domini M°CC°lxxxvii[2] facta est quedam visio Tripolis[3] cuidam monacho ordinis griseorum celebranti missam eorum[4] abbate et eciam alio monacho presente. Infra enim[5] oblacionem et communionem apparuit quedam manus super corporale scribens in quo dictus monachus consecrabat.
>
> Cedrus alta Libani succidetur et in brevi destruetur. Mars[6] Saturnum superabit.[7] Et Saturnus insidiabitur[8] Iovi. Vesper-

---

1. *Lacking B2*; videlicet O.
2. M°CC 77 F; M°CClxvi° U.
3. metropolis O.
4. coram *OU*.
5. *Lacking OU.*
6. Tripolis mare *for* Mars O.
7. *Followed by* vel fugabit *OU*.
8. insidialem B2.

tilio[9] dominum apum superabit vel fugabit.[10] Infra[11] tres annos unus dominus[12] et una fides. Alter deus evanuit.[13] Filii Israel a captivitate liberabuntur. Quedam[14] gens sine capite veniet.[15] Ve tunc clero et toti[16] Christianitati! Navicula Petri iactabitur variis[17] fluctibus, sed evadet et dominabitur in fine dierum. Et in mundo erunt multa prelia et multe strages, et[18] omnis terra turbabitur, et fames valida erit,[19] et hominum mortalitas per loca et regnorum mutaciones. Terra barbarorum pervertetur.[20] Ordines mendicancium et alie secte quamplures annichilabuntur. Tunc surget leo[21] de cavernis moncium, et montana transcendet, et alium leonem interficiet. Bestia occidentalis et leo orientalis[22] totum mundum sibi[23] subiugabunt. Et tunc erit pax in universo[24] orbe, et copia fructuum, et omnium rerum[25] habundancia per xxv[26] annos. Tunc erit[27] passagium commune ad terram sanctam.[28] Civitas[29] Ierusalem et omnes civitates

---

9. Vespertilio ――― fugabit *lacking OU.*

10. fulgabit *F.*

11. In fine MCCCxxxv erit *for* Infra tres annos *O.*

12. deus *supplied over erasure O.*

13. ⟨tumuit⟩ *F.*

14. Gens quedam que vocatur sine capite veniet *for* Quedam ――― veniet *O.*

15. venient *U.*

16. tote *B1F;* tibi *O.*

17. validis *O.*

18. et omnis terra turbabitur *lacking O.*

19. *Lacking O.*

20. subvertetur *O.*

21. *Lacking Be; present in all other copies.*

22. origentalis *B2.*

23. *Lacking F.*

24. toto orbe terrarum *for* universo orbe *O.*

25. *Lacking O.*

26. xv autem annos *for* xxv annos *O.*

27. passagium erit commune ultra aquas congregatas ad terram sanctam *for* erit ――― sanctam *O.*

28. *Lacking U.*

29. Et civitas Ierusalem gloriabitur *for* Civitas Ierusalem *O.*

Iudee[30] edificabuntur.[31] Sepulchrum[32] Domini ab omnibus honorabitur. Et finita[33] tranquillitate audientur[34] nova de Antichristo et [35] cuncta[36] miracula. Beatus qui tunc vicerit,[37] non[38] ledetur a morte perpetua.[39]

D. BN LAT. 16021, F. 19^r-v (CA. 1470; NORTHERN ITALY–PROBABLY MANTUA)

Prophetia[1] Abbatis Ioachim: Anno 1287 quidam monachus ordinis grisorum dixit missam coram abbate et alio monacho presente. In oblatione misse et comunione apparuit quedam manus super corporale in quo predictus monachus conferebat alta libamina, quod dixit fieri atripolis in brevi destruetur. Mars Saturnum superabit. Saturnus insidiabitur Iovi. Vespertilio dominum appium subiugabit. Infra quindecim annos erit unus deus et una fides. Et alter deus ⟨vero⟩ evanescet. Filii Ierusalem ab captivitate liberabuntur. Gens quedam que vocatur sine capite venient. Ve nunc clero et tibi Christianitas! Navicula Petri iactibitur vallidis fluctibus sed evadet et dominabitur in fine dierum. In mundo erunt prelia multa, et multe strages, et fames vallida. Ordines mendicantium et alie multe secte anichillabuntur. Bestia occidentalis et leo orientalis totum mundum subiugabunt. Et tunc pax erit in toto orbe, et copia frugum, et omnia habundantia. Et inter quindecim annos tunc passagium erit ecclesie ultra acquas congregatas ad terram sanctam. Et civitates Ierusalem honorabitur. Et omnes civitates nova audient et inde rehedificabuntur. Sepulcrum Christi ab universis

---

30. et in se *after* Iudee *erased* O.

31. reedificabuntur O.

32. Tunc sepulcrum honorabitur ab universis *for* Sepulchrum —— honorabitur O.

33. in tanta O.

34. nova audientur *for* audientur nova OU.

35. *Lacking Be; present in all other copies.*

36. mirabilia facta B1; miracula facta F; cuncta mirabilia O; ⟨conclusa⟩ miracula U; *all for* cuncta miracula.

37. vixerit O.

38. nam non *for* non B1B2FU; et *for* non O.

39. *Followed by* ergo vigilate fratres O.

1. *This scribe uses the spellings* prophetia *instead of* prophecia, *etc.*

honorabitur. Et in tanta tranquilitate nova audient de Antichristo et cuncta mirabilia. Beatus qui tunc nascerit, quia non ledetur a morte perpetua. Vigilate.

E. VAT. LAT. 793, F. 96ᵛ (CA. 1403; ITALY)

I reproduce the edition by August Pelzer, *Codices Vaticani Latini, II, 1: Codices 679–1134* (Vatican City, 1931), 122, altering the orthography of *prophecia* etc., as well as the punctuation and capitalization.

Visio seu prophecia facta Tripoli provincie Calabrie: Anno Domini MCCCC° facta est quedam visio Tripoli cuidam monaco ordinis Sancti Benedicti celebranti misam coram abbate et alio presente monaco infra comunionem et oblacionem. Nam aparuit quedam manus scribens super corporale in quo dictus monachus consecrabat corpus Domini. Cedrus alta Libani succeditur,[1] et Tripulis in brevi destruetur. Mars Saturnum[2] superabit. Et Saturnus[3] insidiabitur Iovi. Navicula Petri iactabitur magnis fluctibus. Ve autem clero et tibi Christianitati quia erunt in mundo multa prelia, multe strages, fames, mortalitates, ac regnorum mutaciones. Ordo Fratrum Minorum augmentabitur, et quamplures secte anichilabuntur. Deinde surget leo de cavernis moncium, et montanea transcendet, et serpens destruet eum. Bestia occidentalis quasi totum mundum subiugabit. Ferentes lilium sine aquila subpeditabuntur cum suis sequacibus. Hiis completis erit pax in universo orbe, copia fructuum, et omnium rerum abondancia per quindecim annos. Et fiet pasagium ad teram sanctam. Civitas[4] Yerusalem gloriabitur, et in die illo rehedificabitur. Sepulcrum Domini ab omnibus honorabitur. Beatus qui tunc vixerit, quia non ledetur a morte subitanea. Hec omnia prenominata debent adimpleri de anno currente MCCCC°iii[5] et MCCCCiiii°[6] ut determinatum est per astronomos.

1. *Corrected to* succidetur.
2. *Before correction,* Saturnium.
3. *Followed by* superabitur, *then erased.*
4. *Before correction,* Civitatis.
5. *Later altered to* MCCCC°lii.
6. *Later altered to* MCCCCliii°.

Appendix III

THE REVISED VERSIONS
OF THE TRIPOLI PROPHECY

A. HYPOTHETICAL RECONSTRUCTION OF THE
ORIGINAL POST-ACRE REVISION

The following is based on a comparison of the pre-Acre version with representatives of the best families of the post-Acre version. It is intended only to serve as a working model and point of reference.

> Anno Domini 1287 facta est quedam visio mirabilis in claustro grisei ordinis Tripolis. Quidam monachus dixit missam coram abbate suo et uno ministro presente. Infra ablucionem et communionem misse apparuit quedam manus scribens super corporale in quo dictus monachus corpus Domini confecerat.
>
> Cedrus alta Libani succidetur, et Tripolis in brevi destruetur, et Acharon capietur. Et Mars Saturnum superabit, et Saturnus insidiabitur Iovi. Et vespertilio subiugabit dominum apum. Infra quindecim annos erit unus deus et una fides. Et alter deus evanescet. Filii Israel a captivitate liberabuntur. Gens quedam veniet que vocatur sine capite. Ve tunc clero et tibi Christianitas! Navicula Petri iactabitur variis fluctibus, sed evadet et dominabitur in fine dierum. In mundo erunt multa prelia, et strages magna, et fames valida, et hominum

mortalitas per loca, et regnorum mutaciones. Terra barbarorum convertetur. Ordines mendicancium et alie secte quamplures annichilabuntur. Bestia occidentalis et leo orientalis universum mundum subiugabunt. Et tunc erit pax in toto orbe terrarum, et copia fructuum per quindecim annos. Tunc erit commune passagium ab omnibus fidelibus ultra aquas congregatas ad terram sanctam, et vincent. Et civitas Ierusalem gloriabitur, et sepulchrum Domini ab omnibus honorabitur. Et in tanta tranquillitate audientur nova de Antichristo et alia Dei mirabilia. Ergo vigilate.

B. THE BLOEMHOF AND LI MUISIS VERSIONS

The copy of the revised version of the Tripoli prophecy in the Bloemhof chronicle is probably the earliest surviving Latin one (although the single MS containing it is late). I follow MGH, *Scriptores*, 23, 567–568. To this I append the abbreviated version given by Gilles Li Muisis. This does not descend from the Bloemhof copy but appears to descend from a common source and is closer to the Bloemhof version than to any other. For Gilles's text I follow the edition of the single contemporary MS edited by J.-J. de Smet, *Corpus Chronicorum Flandriae* (Brussels, 1841), II, 151.

1. Bloemhof

Anno Domini 1287 facta est mirabilis in claustro grisei ordinis Tripolis. Monachus quidam qui dixit missam coram abbate suo, uno presente ministro. Intra ablucionem et communionem manus quedam missa aparuit scribens super corporale litteris aureis, in quo dictus monachus corpus Domini confecerat.

Cedrus alta Libani succidetur, et Tripolis in brevi capietur, destruetur, Acharon capietur. Et Mars Saturnum superabit, et Saturnus insidiabitur Iovi. Et vespertilio subiugabit dominum apum.[1] Infra quindecim annos erit unus deus et una fides. Et alter deus evanescet. Et filii Ierusalem a captivitate liberabuntur. Gens quedam veniet sine capite. Et tunc ve clero et

---

1. *MGH has* dominium apostolicum; *without having seen the MS I suspect that this is an overly learned reading of the abbreviation* d̄mn apm.

tibi Christianitas! Navicula Petri iactabitur variis fluctibus, sed evadet et dominabitur in fine. In mundo erunt multa prelia, strages magne, et fames valida, hominum mortalitas et regnorum mutaciones. Terra barbarorum convertetur. Ordines mendicorum et alie secte quamplurime annichelabuntur. Bestia occidentalis et leo orientalis universum mundum subiugabunt. Et tunc pax erit in toto orbe terrarum, et copia fructuum per quindecim annos erit. Et tunc erit commune passagium ab omnibus fidelibus ultra aquas congregatas ad terram sanctam, et vincunt. Et civitas Ierusalem gloriabitur, et sepulchrum Domini honorabitur. In tanta tranquillitate audientur de Antechristo et alia miracula. Ergo vigilate.

2. Li Muisis

Anno MCCLXXXVIII, unus monachus Cisterciensis dicens missam, vidit manum scribentem super corporale litteris aureis, et inter cetera scripsit quod in brevi Tripolis caperetur, et eciam post Acra caperetur.

C. THE GERMAN GROUP

Because of the survival of very pristine versions of the German group text in the Füssen (Oettingen-Wallerstein Bibliothek I, 2, 4°, 28) and Eberhard of Regensburg copies, it is possible to come close to reproducing the original progenitor of this family. I attempt to do this by following the Füssen MS in all but eight clearly mistaken readings in which it can be easily corrected by supplying the readings of Eberhard. The Weichard of Polhaim, version for 1396, and anonymous monk of Sankt Emmeram's texts all descend from Eberhard, as does most likely the copy in Donaueschingen 793. Thus the three main independent witnesses in the German group are the Füssen, Eberhard, and Breslau Dominican copies:

Version for 1396 copied by Andreas of Regensburg in Clm 903, f. 22ᵛ (ca. 1420) (=A)

Breslau Dominican in Breslau (Wrocław) UB IV F 6, f. 100ᵛ (ca. 1370) (=B) (This was edited by Joseph Klapper, *Exempla aus Handschriften des Mittelalters* [Heidelberg, 1911],

64: Klapper omits the words *et cetera Dei*, which should appear in his line 28, but otherwise presents a perfect edition.)

Anonymous compiler in Donaueschingen 793, fos. 62ᵛ–63ʳ (ca. 1460) (=D)

Eberhard of Regensburg (ca. 1305), as edited in MGH, *Scriptores*, 17, 605 (=E)

Version for 1396 in Eichstätt 698 (old 269), p. 380, (ca. 1400) (=Ei)

Copy located before 1500 in Sankt Mang's, Füssen, now Augsburg UB, Oettingen-Wallerstein'sche Bibliothek I, 2, 4°, 28, fos. 85ᵛ–86ʳ (ca. 1310) (=F)

Anonymous Monk of Sankt Emmeram's, Regensburg, in Clm 14594, f. 78ʳ (1380s) (=R)

Weichard of Polhaim (ca. 1307), as edited in MGH, *Scriptores*, 9, 811 (=W) (I follow the MGH's base MS for Weichard, excluding the variants from the other two, which are insignificant.)

Anno[1] Domini[2] MᵒCCᵒlxxxᵒviiᵃ [3] facta est quedam visio[4] mirabilis in claustro grisei ordinis[5] Tripolis. Quidam[6] monachus dixit missam coram suo abate et uno ministro presente. Infra[7] ablucionem[8] et communionem[9] misse[10] apparuit que-

---

1. *Rubrics*: Hec sunt determinaciones astrologorum de futuris provenientibus ab anno Domini MᵒCCCCᵒlxiᵒ usque ad annum lxxᵐ *D*; Prophecia mirabilis de cursibus mundi *AEi*.

2. Domini *lacking DR*.

3. MᵒCCᵒlxxvii *B*; MᵒCClxxxvi *DERW*; millesimo tricentesimo nonagesimo sexto *AEi*.

4. mirabilis visio *BF*.

5. monachi *D*.

6. Monachus quidam *W*.

7. Et infra *ABDEEiRW*.

8. oblivionem *D*.

9. communicacionem *AEi*.

10. *Lacking B*.

dam[11] manus scribens in[12] altari super corporale in quo predictus monachus corpus[13] Domini confecerat.[14]

Cedrus alta Libani succidetur, et Tripolis in brevi destruetur, et[15] Aharon[16] capietur. Et Mars Saturnum[17] superabit, et Saturnus insidiabitur Iovi. Et vespertilio fugabit dominum apum. Infra xv annos erit unus deus[18] et una fides. Et[19] alter deus evanescet. Filii[20] Israhel[21] a[22] captivitate liberabuntur. Gens quedam veniet que vocatur sine capite. Ve tunc clero et tibi Christianitas! Navicula Petri iactabitur in validis fluctibus, sed evadet et dominabitur in fine dierum. In mundo erunt multa prelia, et[23] strages magna, et fames valida, et hominum[24] mortalitas per loca, et[25] regnorum mutaciones. Terra barbarorum convertetur. Ordines mendicancium et alie secte quamplures[26] annichilabuntur.[27] Bestia occidentalis et leo orientalis universum mundum subiugabunt. Et tunc pax erit in toto orbe terrarum et copia fructuum per xv[28] annos. Tunc passagium[29]

---

11. manus quedam *F.*

12. super corporale in altari *for* in altari super corporale *ADEEiRW.*

13. dixit missam *for* corpus Domini confecerat *F.*

14. consecrat *for* confecerat *AEi.*

15. *Lacking R.*

16. Acharon *ADEEi*; Accaron *B*; Acaron *R*; Accharon *W.*

17. superabit Saturnum *for* Saturnum superabit *W.*

18. dominus *D.*

19. *Lacking F.*

20. Et filii *B.*

21. Irsahel *R.*

22. de *F.*

23. exstrages *for* et strages *F.*

24. huiusmodi *D.*

25. *Lacking B.*

26. ⟨quasi plures⟩ *Ei.*

27. destruentur *F.*

28. Christianos *for* xv annos *AEi.*

29. passaynum *F.*

commune[30] erit[31] ab omnibus fidelibus ultra[32] aquas congregatas[33] ad[34] terram sanctam, et[35] vincent. Et civitas Ierusalem gloriabitur,[36] et sepulcrum Domini ab universis honorabitur. Et in tanta tranquillitate nova audientur de Antichristo et cetera Dei mirabilia.[37] Ergo[38] vigilate.

D. THE FRENCH TRANSLATION OF CA. 1292

This early witness from the northeastern French linguistic area appears to have been made from a Latin cousin of the German family text. I reprint the edition made from the only known copy (prov. Saint Jacques, Liège; now MS Brussels II. 2212) by J. Van den Gheyn, "Note sur un manuscrit de l'*Excidium Aconis*, en 1291," *Revue de l'Orient Latin*, 6 (1898), 555–556. My only alterations are in punctuation.

> Lan de lincarnation nostre signour Ihesu Crist M.CC.IIII.
> XX et XI [1291] avint une mervelleuse vision en lenclostre
> de lordene de triple. Uns moines disoit messe par devant son
> abbeit, un sien menistre present. Avint ensi que entre le com-
> munion et le laver, une mains apparut seur l'autel, escrivans
> seur le corporel on queil li moines avoit sacreit le cors nostre
> saignour: Li haus cedeles de libes serat copeis. Tripes serat
> en brief tens destruit, et acre prise. Et markes seurmonterat
> saturne, et saturne materat iupiter. La chave soris en chacera
> le dieu de se oes. Dedens xxx ans, uns dies et une fois. Et li
> autre dieu seront evanuis. Et li fil dysrael seront delivre de
> chativisons. Une gens venront que on appellerat sens testes.

---

30. erit ab omnibus fidelibus commune *for* commune erit ab omnibus fidelibus *ADEEiRW*.

31. erit ita *B*.

32. ultra aquas *lacking AEi*.

33. congregati ibunt *for* congregatas *AEi*.

34. et *B*.

35. *Lacking B*.

36. glorificabitur *B*.

37. miracula *A*.

38. *Lacking D*; *followed by* etcetera *Ei*.

Adont avanrat mescheance a clergie en crestienteit. La nacelle saint piere sera getee en grans fluns, mais elle eschaperat, et arat saingnorie en la fin de iours. Moult de batailles seront au monde, et moult de grans rages, et de grans famines, mortaliteis seront en moult de lieus, mutations serat de regnes. La terre de sarrasins serat convertie. Les ordes mendians et moult dautres sectes iront a niant. Les bestes doccident et li lyons dorient metteront tout le monde en leur subiection. Adont serat pais par toutes terres, et grande habundance de fruis par xv ans. Adont serat communs passages outre mer de crestyens a la sainte terre, et venkeront. Et li citeis de iherusalem serat glorefye, et li sepucres nostre signor serat aoreis de ses homes. Et en teil tens orat on novelles datecrist.

E. THE PIETRO DA VILLOLA, DIETRICH ENGELHUS, AND PETER OF ARAGON VERSIONS

Like the French translation, these copies appear to descend from the German family. All are very corrupt and of interest primarily in revealing scribal confusion and liberties taken with the text. For Villola I reprint the edition made from MS Bologna, Biblioteca Universitaria 1456 by A. Sorbelli, *Corpus Chronicorum Bononiensium* (*Rerum Italicarum Scriptores*, XVIII, pt. 1; Città di Castello, 1905), 4–5; for Engelhus I follow G. W. Leibniz, *Scriptores rerum Brunsvicensium*, II (Hannover, 1710), 1121; and for Peter I reprint the edition made from Vat. Archivio Segreto, Arm. LIV, num. 17, fos. 129ʳ–130ʳ, by Alfonso Maria de Barcelona, *Estudios Franciscanos*, 15 (1915), 61–62.

1. Villola

Cedrus alta Libani succidetur. Tripolim in brevi destruetur. Acton capietur. Mars Saturnum superabit. Saturnus insidiabitur Iovi, et vespertilio fugabit dominum. Et infra apud xv annos erit unus deus et una fides. Alter deus evanescit. Filii Ysrael a captivitate liberabuntur. Gens quedam veniet que vocabitur sine capite. Tunc ve clero et tibi Christianitati! Navicula Petri iactabitur in vallidis fluctibus, sed evadet in fine dierum. In mundo erunt multa prelia, et strages magna, fames valide, et hominum mortalitates per loca, et regnorum mutaciones. Terre barbarorum convertentur. Ordo mendicancium et allie anulabuntur. Bestia orientalis et leo ocidentalis totum mundum subiugabunt. Et tunc pax erit in toto orbe terrarum. Copia fructuum per xv annos. Tunc passagium comune erit ab omnibus fidelibus ultra aquas et contratas ad terram sanctam, et vincet. Ierusalem glorificabitur, tunc sepulcrum Domini ab universis honorabitur. Et erit in magna tranquilitate et audietur nova de Antichristo.

2. Engelhus

Honorius quartus, Romanus, sedit annos [Leibniz: unnos] II [i.e., 1285–1287]. . . . Hoc tempore monachus quidam Tripolis, celebrans coram suo abbate, vidit manum scribentem in corporali hec verba: Cedrus alta Libani succidetur. Tripolis destruetur, Accaron capietur. Mars Saturnum superabit, Saturnus insidiabitur Iovi. Vespertilio fugabit deum apum. Ve tunc clero et terre Christianitatis. Ergo vigilate.

3. Peter

Anno Domini millesimo CC°xcvii facta est quedam visio mirabilis in claustro Cisterciensium. Quidam monachus dixit missam coram suo abbate et uno ministro presente. Et sit post ablucionem misse apparuit quedam manus in altari super corporali in quo predictum monachus corpus Domini confecerat. Et sequidur descripcio dicte manus.

Cedrus alta Libani succindetur, et Tripolis in brevi destruetur, et Acon capietur. Et Maris Saturnum superavit, et Saturnus insidiabitur Iovi. Et vespertilio fugavit eum. Et postea infra xv anno erit unus deus et una fides. Et alter deus evanescet. Filii Israel a captivitate liberabuntur. Et gens quedam que vocatur sine capite veniet. Ve tunc clero et tote xristianitate! Navicula Petri iactabitur in validimis fluctibus que evadet et durabit in fine dierum. In mundo erunt multa prelia, et strages magna, et fames valida, et hominum mortalitas, et plures regnorum mutaciones. Et terra barbarorum convertetur. Ordines mendicancium et alie secte quamplures anichilabuntur. Et bestia occidentalis et leo orientalis universum mundum subiugabunt. Et pax erit in toto orbe terrarum, et copia fructuum per xv annos. Tunc passagium ecclesie erit ab omnibus fidelibus ultra aquas congregatum ad terram sanctam, et vincent. Et civitas Iherusalem glorificabitur, et sepulcrum Domini ab omnibus honorabiliter. Et in magna tranquilitate nova audientur de Antichristo. Ergo dicit vigilate Ioachim venient dies in quibus Gallici Gallicos interficient.

F. THE REDATED VERSION FOR 1367

This version, the sole copy of which is in Paris, Sainte-Geneviève 792, f. 12ʳ (ca. 1379), is related to the German family. For its noteworthy variants see Chapter Six, n. 19. Unfortunately much of the writing toward the outer margin has become so faded as to be illegible.

Anno Domini MCCCᵒlxviiᵒ facta est quedam visio mirabilis in claustro Cisterciensis ordinis Tripolis. Qui⟨dam⟩ monachus ⟨dixit⟩ missam coram abbate et uno ministro. Et infra ablucionem et communionem misse apparuit quedam ⟨manus scribens in altari super⟩ corporale in quo predictus monachus corpus Domini confecerat.

Cedrus alta Libani sic sedetur, et Tripolis ⟨in⟩ brevi destruetur, et ⟨. . .⟩ capietur. Et Mars Saturnum superabit, et Saturnus insidiabitur Iovius. Et vespertilio fugabit deum apum. Infra ⟨. . . . . . .⟩ erit unus deus et una fides. Et alter deus evanescet. Filii Israel a captivitate liberabuntur. Gens quedam ve⟨niet que⟩ vocabitur sine capite. Ve tibi clero et tibi Christianitati! Navicula Petri iactabitur in validis fluctibus, sed ⟨. . . . .⟩ in fine dierum. In mundo erunt multa prelia, esuries magna, et fames valida, et hominum mortalitas per ⟨. . . . . .⟩ regnorum mutaciones. Et terra barbarorum convertetur. Et ordines mendicancium et alie secte quamplures ⟨. . . . .⟩ Bestia occidentalis et leo orientalis universum mundum ⟨subiugabunt⟩ et pax erit in toto orbe terrarum ⟨. . . . . . .⟩ fructuum per xii annos. Tunc passagium commune erit ab omnibus fidelibus ultra aquas congregatas ad terram ⟨sanctam et venirent⟩. Et civitas Jherusalem gloriabitur, et sepulcrum Domini ab omnibus honorabitur. Et in tanta tranquillitate ⟨nova⟩ audientur de Antichristo. Ergo vigilate.

G. THE ENGLISH COPIES

There is clearly no one English "family": many different copies must have arrived from the continent to influence diverging English traditions. Yet BL Royal 9 B IX, f. 2^r, from the Benedictine house of Bardney, Lincolnshire, copied shortly before 1300, is sufficiently related to the twins BL Harley 485, f. 98^v (=H) and Bodl., Bodley 158, f. 146^r (=B) (both copied in northern England in the middle or later fourteenth century) to allow the edition of the three as a group with the Bardney MS as the base. The copies made by the Welsh and Yorkist anthologists are sufficiently eccentric to necessitate separate presentation, as is the copy made by Henry of Kirkestede at Bury Saint Edmunds between ca. 1365 and ca. 1377. The latter shows traits from several different sources, indicating that contamination occurred somewhere in its transmission; otherwise its most noteworthy trait is that it is the only currently known copy, aside from some with the 1347 redating, that contains the final confirmation story. N.B.: After this book went to press, I learned that a close relative of the Yorkist anthology copy (without its sixteenth-century addition) exists in MS Cambridge, Gonville and Caius College 249, f. 183va. This copy was made under the direction of John Harryson, M.D., around 1464, probably in Ashwell (Hertfordshire), where Harryson was vicar. It lacks the Yorkist anthology's long rubric, supplying instead merely "Prognosticacio terre sancte," but otherwise displays only minor variants from its relative.

1. The Bardney and the Twin North-Country English Copies

Anno Domini M°CC°octuagesimo septimo facta est visio mirabilis in claustro[1] nigri ordinis in civitate Tripoli. Mona-chus[2] quidam dicit[3] missam coram[4] abbate suo et unico minis-tro presente. Infra[5] communionem et ⟨a⟩blucionem misse ap-

---

1. claustro nigri ordinis in *lacking HB.*

2. Quidam monachus *for* Monachus quidam *HB.*

3. dixerat *HB.*

4. ⟨scilicet⟩ [·s·] presente abbate et uno ministro m̄i [*corruption for* Domini?] *for* coram ——— presente *HB.*

5. Cum predictus monachus post communionem et manuum ablucionem ad

paruit quedam manus scribens super corporalia aureis litteris in quibus predictus monachus corpus Christi confecerat.

Cedrus alta Libani succedetur,[6] et[7] Tripolis[8] in brevi destruetur, et[9] Acon capietur. Et Mars Saturnum superabit, et Saturnus insidiabitur Iovi. Et verspertilio subiugabit[10] dominum apum. Infra xv annos erit unus deus et una fides. Et alter deus evanescet. Et filii[11] Ierusalem[12] a captivitate liberabuntur.[13] Gens quedam veniet que dicitur sine capite. Et tunc ve clero et tibi Christianitas![14] Navicula[15] Petri nutabit[16] in validis fluctibus, sed inde[17] evadet et dominabitur[18] in fine. Et in mundo erunt prelia, et strages magna, et fames valida, et mortalitas per loca, et[19] mutaciones regnorum. Et terra barbarorum convertetur. Et[20] ordines mendicorum[21] et alii quamplurimi adnichilabuntur. Bestia occidentalis et leo orientalis universum mundum subiugabunt. Et tunc erit pax in toto orbe terrarum, et copia fructuum per xv annos. Et tunc erit passagium[22] commune ab omnibus Christi fidelibus ultra aquas

---

altare verteretur aparuit quedam manus scribens super corporale in quo dictus monachus confecerat corpus Christi litteris aureis que sequntur *for* Infra ——— confecerat *HB.*

6. succidetur *HB.*

7. *Followed by* civitas *HB.*

8. *Followed by* propter peccata inhabitancium *HB.*

9. *Followed by* civitas *HB.*

10. superabit *HB.*

11. filius *HB.*

12. *Supplied by later hand over erasure in Bardney MS.*

13. liberabitur *HB.*

14. Christianitati *HB.*

15. *Followed by* beati HB.

16. iactabitur *HB.*

17. *Lacking HB.*

18. ditabitur *HB.*

19. regnorum et mutaciones *for* et mutaciones regnorum *HB.*

20. *Lacking HB.*

21. mendicancium *HB.*

22. commune passagium *for* passagium commune *HB.*

congregandis ad terram sanctam, et vincunt.[23] Et civitas Ierusalem gloriabitur et sepulcrum Christi[24] ab omnibus visitabitur.
Et in tanta tranquillitate nova[25] audientur de Antichristo et
alia mirabilia Dei.

2. The Welsh Copy, MS Aberystwyth Peniarth 50, pp. 245–246 (mid 15th century)

Anno Domini MᵒCClxxviiᵒ ffacta fuit hec mirabilis in
claustro griesei ordinis in civitate ⟨. .⟩ Tripolitana. Cuidam
monacho celebranti coram abbate et uno ministro ⟨tamen⟩
presente apparuit quedam manus scribens aureis litteris super
corporale quo corpus Christi conficeret.

Cedrus alta Libani succidetur. Tripolis et in brevi destruetur. Acon capietur. Mars Saturnum superabit, et Saturnus
insidiabitur Iovi. Et vespertilio subiugabit dominum apum. In
mundo erunt prelia multa, strages magna, et fames valida, et
per loca mortalitas, et regnorum mutaciones per xvi annos.
Unus deus erit et una fides, et dii gencium evanescent. Et
civitas Ierusalem gloriabitur. Terra barbarorum convertetur.
Gens quedam veniet que dicitur in capite. Et tunc ve clero et
Christianitati! Navicula Petri iactetur in validis fluctibus, sed
evadet et dominabitur in fine. Ordines mendicancium et alie
secte plurime adnichilabuntur. Leo orientalis et bestia occidentalis universum mundum subiugabunt. Et tunc erit pax
in toto orbe terrarum, et copia fructuum per xv annos. Et tunc
erit commune passagium ab omnibus Christi fidelibus ultra
aquas ad terram sanctam. Et sepulcrum Domini ab omnibus
visitab⟨itur⟩.

3. The Yorkist Anthology and its Seventeenth-century Completion: MS BL Cotton Vespasian E. VII, f. 90ʳ⁻ᵛ (ca. 1470)

a. *Rubric*: Anno Domini millesimo CC. octuagesimo septimo ffacta est visio mirabilis in claustro grisei ordinis in civi-

---

tate Tripolitana. Monachus quidam dixit missam coram abbate suo et uno ministro presente. Apparuit ei quedam manus scribens aureis litteris super corporale in quo corpus Christi conficeret. Pronosticacio terre sancte de eodem Sexto.

b. *Text*: Cedrus alta Libani succidetur. Tripolis in brevi destruetur. Acon⟨um⟩ capietur. Mars Saturnum superabit et Saturnus insidiabitur Iovi. Et vespertilio subiugabit dominum apum.[i] Sequitur: civitas Ierusalem glorificabitur et terra barbarorum convertetur. Idem: leo orientalis et bestia occidentalis universum mundum subiugabunt [*here in margin in same hand*: Animal occidentalis]. Et tunc erit pax in toto orbe terrarum et copia fructuum per xv annos. Et tunc erit commune passagium ab omnibus Christi fidelibus ultra aquas congregandas[ii] ad terram sanctam, et vincent. Et civitas Ierusalem glorificabitur. Et sepulcrum Domini ab omnibus visitabitur.[iii]

c. Seventeenth-century additions:

i. *An insertion after* dominum apum: infra 15 annos erit unus deus et una fides. Et alter deus evanescet. Et filii Hierusalem à captivitate liberabuntur. Gens quedam veniet, que dicitur sine capite. Et tunc ve clero et tibi Christianitas! Nam navicula Petri iactabitur in validis fluctibus, sed evadet et dominabitur in fine. In mundo erunt prelia, et strages magna, et fames valida, et mortalitas per loca, et regnorum mutaciones. Et terra barbarorum convertetur. Ordines mendicorum et alie secte quamplurime adnichilabuntur. Leo orientalis etc.

ii. *corrects* congregandas *to read* congregatas.

iii. *An insertion at the top of the page to be read after* visitabitur, *now largely cut off as a result of trimming*: ⟨in tanta tranquillitate nova audientur de Antichristo et alia mirabilia⟩.

4. Henry of Kirkestede: MS Cambridge, Corpus Christi College 404, f. 100[v]

Anno Domini MCClxxxviii⁰ facta est visio mirabilis in civitate Tripolis. Quidam ibi monachus Cisterciensis ordinis dixit missam coram abbate suo et uno ministro presente. Inter ablucionem et communionem misse apparuit quedam manus scribens super corporale aureis litteris in qua dictus monachus corpus Christi confecerat.

Cedrus alta Libani succidetur, et Tripolis in brevi destruetur, et Acon capietur. Et Mars Saturnum superabit, et Saturnus insidiabitur Iovi. Et vespertilio fugabit ducem apum. Infra xv annos erit unus deus et una fides. Et alter deus evanescet. Et filii Israel a captivitate liberabuntur. Gens quedam veniet que dicitur sine capite. Et tunc ve clero et tibi Christianitas! Navicula Petri iactabitur in validis fluctibus, sed evadet et dominabitur in fine dierum. In mundo erunt multa prelia, et strages magna, et fames valida, et hominum mortalitas per loca, et regnorum mutaciones. Et terra barbarorum convertetur. Ordines mendicancium et alie secte quamplures adnichilabuntur. Leo orientalis et bestia occidentalis universum mundum suo imperio subiugabunt. Et tunc pax erit in toto orbe terrarum, et copia fructuum per xv annos. Tunc erit commune passagium ab omnibus Christi fidelibus ultra aquas congregatas ad terram sanctam, et vincent. Et civitas Ierusalem glorificabitur, et sepulchrum Domini ab omnibus visitabitur. Et in tanta tranquillitate nova audientur de Antichristo et alia dici mirabilia. Vigilate ergo et orate.

Duo monachi missi ab abbate Cisterciensis civitat⟨e⟩ Tripolis retulerunt ista nova predicta coram summo pontifice in scriptis. Et summus pontifex fecit eos iurare super sacramentum suum si vera essent omnia que referebant.

H. THE REDATED VERSION FOR 1347

1. The Latin Original

The nearest post-Acre text to the 1347 version is the copy made by Henry of Kirkestede appearing directly above. From comparisons to this it can be seen that no single MS of the redating has consistently superior readings, but the best of the nine known Latin copies is Clm 28229, f. 21ʳ (Speyer, mid-14th century), which I use as a base despite its mistaken date of 1348 for the correct 1347. The eight other Latin copies are:

Bodl., Bodley 761, f. 184ᵛ (England, mid-14th century) (=B)

Bodl., Digby 218, f. 107ʳ (England, ca. 1400) (=D)

Bodl., Fairfax 27, f. 26ʳ (England, mid-14th century) (=F)

Bodl., Hatton 56, f. 32^v (England, ca. 1450) (=H)

Friar John of Kilkenny, *Annals of Ireland*, ed. R. Butler (Dublin, 1849), 36 (year 1349) (=K)

Lilienfeld 49, f. 357^r (Lilienfeld, mid-14th century) (=L)

BN franç. 902, f. 96^v (England, mid-14th century) (=P)

Yale University Marston 225, fos. 43^v–44^v (probably southern Germany, mid 14th century—edition by Leclercq, as cited in Chapter Six, n. 6, is faulty) (=Y)

Anno[1] Domini MCCC°xlviii°[2] facta[3] est quedam[4] visio[5] in claustro[6] Cisterciensis ordinis Tripoli.[7] Quidam monachus[8] celebrabat[9] missam[10] coram[11] abbate suo[12] et[13] uno ministro presente. Et[14] inter ablucionem[15] et communionem[16] misse[17]

---

1. Anno ——— MCCC°xlviii° *lacking F*; Anno ——— confecerat *lacking H*; *K begins*: De ista pestilencie facta est visio mirabilis, ut dicebatur, anno precedenti, scilicet 1347, in claustro Cisterciensium Tripolis sub hac forma. Quidam monachus. . . .

2. MCCC°xlvii *BDP*; millesimo CCC°xlvi° *Y*.

3. quedam visio facta est in claustro Cisterciensis ordinis Tripolym *for* facta ——— Tripoli *D*.

4. *Lacking F*; hec *L*.

5. visio quedam mirabilis *F*; mirabilis *added after* visio *in margin by correcting mid-14th century hand Y*.

6. claustro Cisterciensis ordinis *lacking L*.

7. Tripolis *P*; *lacking Y*.

8. monachus ordinis Cistersiensis *L*.

9. celebravit *BDFKP*.

10. *Lacking F*.

11. coram ——— presente *lacking Y*.

12. in uno mon ⟨. . . .⟩ *for* suo ——— presente *D*; ministro suo *for* suo ——— ministro *F*.

13. *Lacking BKP*.

14. *Lacking BDFP*.

15. absolucionem *FY*.

16. canonem *D*; conplendam *L*.

17. *Lacking DL*.

apparuit quedam manus scribens super corporali[18] in[19] quo[20] predictus[21] monachus confecerat.[22]

Cedrus alta Libani succidetur,[23] et[24] Tripolis[25] in brevi destruetur, et[26] Accaron[27] capietur.[28] Et[29] Mercurius[30] mundum superabit, et[31] Saturnus insidiabitur[32] Iovi.[33] Et[34] vespertilio fugabit[35] ducem Abim.[36] Infra xv annos erit[37] unus[38] deus et una[39] fides. Et[40] altera[41] evanescet.[42] Filius[43] Israel[44] a capti-

---

18. corporale *BDFKP*; corporalia *Y*.

19. *Lacking B*; in ———— confecerat *lacking FY*; scilicet *for* in ———— confecerat *P*.

20. que *B*.

21. dictus *D*; conficiebat hec verba *for* predictus ———— confecerat *L*.

22. *Lacking B*; confic⟨eret⟩ *D*.

23. succendetur *BDK*.

24. *Lacking DL*.

25. T⟨ri⟩polina *D*; ibidem Tripolis *for* Tripolis in brevi *K*.

26. *Lacking DHLY*.

27. Acon *BFKP*; Acone *D*; Acho ⟨. .⟩ *H*; Acharon *L*; Arcon *Y*.

28. *Lacking D*.

29. *Lacking DHL*.

30. marchiatus *BFHPY*; marchidat⟨it⟩ *D*; marchionatus *K*; falsitas *L*.

31. *Lacking DHL*.

32. mediabitur *B*; insidiatur *D*.

33. iam *B*.

34. *Lacking FHL*; Et ———— Abim *lacking P*.

35. superabit *D*.

36. ab huic *B*; adhuc *D*; ab insulis *F*; Albuch *H*; ab m̅. v̅ı. *K*; Ab̅mch̅ [Abimelech?] *Y*.

37. erit ———— fides *lacking FH*.

38. una fides et unus deus *for* unus deus et una fides *K*.

39. et *added after* una *above the line L*.

40. *Lacking F*.

41. altere *BDKY*; altero *FH*; alia *L*; cetere *P*.

42. avenissent *B*; evanescent *DFKPY*; evanes⟨cent⟩ *H*; simul evanescent *L*.

43. Filii *BDFHKPY*; Filius ———— liberabit *lacking L*.

44. Ierosolomitani *K*.

vitate liberabit.[45] Gens[46] quedam[47] veniet[48] que[49] nascetur[49a] sine capite. Ve tunc[50] clero et[51] sterilitate![52] Navicula Petri iactabitur in[53] validis fluctibus,[54] sed evadet[55] et[56] dominabitur[57] in fine[57a] dierum.[58] Et[59] in mundo erunt multa[60] prelia,[61] et[62] strages[63] magne,[64] et[65] fames valida,[66] hominum mortalitates[67] per loca, et[68] regnorum[69] mutaciones.[70] Et[71]

---

45. liberabuntur *BDFHKPY*.

46. Gens —— in *lacking H*.

47. *Lacking D*.

48. veniet que *lacking K*; venient *L*.

49. et *D*.

49a. nascentur *L*.

50. tunc erit *F*; in *K*; *lacking L*; tunc in *P*.

51. ve *L*; propter *P*.

52. sterilitati *BDFY*; sterilitati ve adusterio *L*; sterilitatem *P*.

53. *Lacking BDFKPY*.

54. fructibus *H*.

55. quedam *L*.

56. in f⟨ine⟩et dominabitur *for* et —— dierum *H*.

57. dominabitur usque *L*.

57a. finem *L*.

58. *Lacking F*.

59. *Lacking BDFHKPY*.

60. *Lacking F*; *added by correcting hand above the line Y*; prelia multa *for* multa prelia *D*.

61. pericula *F*.

62. *Lacking DL*.

63. stragens *L*.

64. *Lacking H*.

65. et —— valida *lacking FY*; et *lacking L*.

66. et valide *B*; validorum *D*; magna et *H*; valide *LP*.

67. mortalitastes *D*; mortalitas *HK*.

68. *Lacking BDFHKP*.

69. *Followed by* erunt inmutaciones cuius *D*.

70. co⟨. . .⟩caciones *L*.

71. in *F*; Et —— barbarorum *lacking H*; Et *lacking LP*.

terra barbarorum convertetur.[72] Ordines[73] mendicancium[74] ecclesie[75] al⟨ias⟩ certe quamplurimum adversabuntur. Bestia occidentalis[76] et leo orientalis[77] universum mundum[78] subiugabunt. Et[79] pax erit in toto orbe terrarum, et copia fructuum[80]
per xv[81] annos. Tunc[82] passagium[83] erit commune ab omnibus
fidelibus ultra[84] aquas congregatas[85] ad terram sanctam, et[86]
vincentur.[87] Et[88] civitas Ierusalem[89] glorificabitur, et sepulcrum Domini ab omnibus honorabitur. In[90] tanta tranquillitate
nova audientur[91] de Antichristo.[92] Ergo[93] vigilate.[94]

---

72. convertentur *F*; contingentur *H*.

73. Ordines ⟨. . .⟩ *H*.

74. certe mendicantes quamplures adverberantur *B*, mendicantes certe quamplures adversabuntur *K*, menducantes quamplures versabuntur *P*, *for* mendicancium ——— adversabuntur.

75. certe quamplures adversabuntur *DY*, terre quamplures adversabuntur *F*,
adversabuntur *L for* ecclesie ——— adversabuntur; ecclesie ——— adversabuntur *lacking H*.

76. orientalis *BDFHKPY*.

77. occidentalis *BDFHKPY*.

78. *Followed by* suo superio *B*; suorum imperio *D*; suo imperio *HP*; *followed
by* suo subiugabunt imperio *for* subiugabunt *K*.

79. Tunc *L*.

80. frugum post *for* fructuum per *L*.

81. xi *H*.

82. *Lacking L*.

83. erit passagium *for* passagium erit *DLY*.

84. ultra aquas *lacking BFP*; super *H*.

85. congregatis *BDFP*; *lacking H*; congregabit *L*.

86. *Lacking BDFHKLPY*.

87. *Lacking BDFHKLP*; vincant *Y*.

88. *Lacking DHY*.

89. Israel *B*.

90. Et in *H*.

91. de Antichristo audientur *for* audientur de Antichristo *L*.

92. *Text ends here DHF*.

93. Vigilate ergo *BPY*; *lacking K*; *texts ends with* ergo *Y*.

94. *Text ends here K*.

Ista[95] visio apparuit in Ierusalem seu Tripoli et fuit missa summo pontifici Avinionis.

2. The Catalan Translation: MS Carpentras 336, fos. 75ᵛ–76ᵛ (second half of the 15th century)

En l'any de nostre senyor Mccccxxxvii feyta fou aquesta visio en un loch qui s'apella Tripol. Car un monge de Sistell dehia missa, aparech una ma sobre lo corporal en que lo monge havia consegrada la ostia, la qual ma scrivia ço quis sequex:

Lo cedre molt alt del munt de Liban sera tallat, e Tripol en breu sera destroit. E Saturn ensemps sera pres, sera posat a guayt a Iupiter. E la rata pinyada en qual sera lo duch blanch. Entre xxv anys sera una fe. Vendra una gent sens cap, fort cars ses devendra[1] en los clergues. La naveta de Sant Pere sofferra gran tempestat, mas escapara e senyoreiara en la fi dels dies. Del mon seran batalles e morts sens fi, sera mortaldat en algun loch, seran mudaments de regnes. *Spanya,*[2] *nodrissa de la malvestat bravetat heretge de Mafumet, sera desconsolada. Perira dels uns als altres. E quant lo polli bestial haura complits iii septanaris d'anys crexera lo foch, cremant e destrohint, entro que lo rata pinyada destroira les mosques d'Espanya, e sotsmetra a si Affrica, e esclafara lo cap de la bistia, e pendra la senyoria general del mon, ço es L'imperi, e finalment humiliara los habitadors de Nil.* E la terra dels barbres sera convertida. E la bistia de occident e leo d'orient subiugara tot lo mon. E sera habundancia de fruytes. Lauors sera feyt comu passatge per tots los fels generalment a la terra santa. E a les aygues ainstades a la civtat de Jherusalem sera glorificada. E lo sepulcre de nostre senyor sera ahorat per tots. E dementre durara

---

95. *Alternate endings:* Duo monachi missi ab abbate Cisterciensis ordinis Tripolis ista predicta summo pontifici retulerunt. Et summus pontifex fecit eos iurare si vera referebant *BP*; Hec visio (missa) est Pape Clementi Avinionis de Ierusalem ⟨inde⟩ super ⟨esiatis⟩ quod talis pestilencia est in civitate Avinionis quod mille et septingenti domus sunt per ⟨minimis⟩ pestilenciam deserte et desolate *L*.

1. *This would mean "the clergy will be very dearly taxed"*; P. Bohigas (see *Chapter Six, n. 8), 30, provides* fort cas—*"the clergy will have a great fall"— which would be closer to the original, but the MS has* cars *and not* cas.

2. *The italicized passage is from the prophecy* Ve mundo in centum annos.

la tranquilitat de la pau seran hoydes de Antecrist novelles.
Donchs vellats.

I. THE FRENCH FAMILY

The missing progenitor of the French family must have ante-
dated 1320: see Chapter Six, n. 36. Of the three most complete surviving witnesses—Chartres 322, f. 1ᵛ (probably early 14th century)
(=C); Tours 520, fos. 103ᵛ–104ʳ (from a treatise of ca. 1350, copied
1422) (=T); Bodl., Lyell 35, fos. 16ᵛ–17ʳ (redating for 1487, copied
by Reginald Andrew late XV) (=O)—none is so clearly superior
that it can be used as a base. Accordingly, I present a hypothetical
reconstruction that draws from all three witnesses and comparison
to the original post-Acre revision. The variant apparatus ignores
minor discrepancies. I edit separately the relevant part of the early
sixteenth-century *Casleti paludum*: although this indubitably stems
from the French family, it has an entirely reconceived order of predictions. A final witness to the family is a scrap from Rupescissa that
appears in Chapter Seven, n. 4.

1. Hypothetical Reconstruction with Variants from the Major Three Witnesses

Anno[1] Domini MᵒCCᵒlxxxviiᵒ[2] quidam monachus grisei
ordinis in civitate Tripolis[3] dixit missam coram suo abbate et
uno ministro presente. Et apparuerunt articuli manus[4] scribentis super corporale inter ablucionem[5] et elevacionem hostie
salvatoris litteris aureis in hec verba.

Cedrus alta Libani succidetur. Tripolis[6] in[7] brevi capietur.[8]

---

1. Quasi anno priusquam civitas Tripolis destruetur *for* Anno ———— MᵒCCᵒlxxxviiᵒ *C.*

2. millesimo CCCClxxxviiᵒ *O.*

3. Neapoli *O.*

4. *Followed by* litteris aureis *with* litteris aureis *lacking at the end of the sentence* C.

5. elevacionem et oblacionem *C,* elevacionem et super ⟨. . . .⟩ *O, for* ablucionem,
et elevacionem.

6. ⟨Agindubium⟩ *for* Tripolis in brevi *O.*

7. in brevi *lacking* C.

8. destruetur C.

Acon[9] destruetur.[10] Mars Saturnum superabit. Saturnus[11] insidiabitur Iovi. Et infra xv annos surget gens que[12] vocatur[13]
sine[14] capite, et prevalebit. Tunc ve clero et[15] tibi[16] Christianitas! Navicula Petri iactabitur in validis fluctibus, sed evadet. Tunc erit unus[17] deus, et alius[18] deus[19] evanescet. Gens
barbarorum convertetur. Omnes ordines mendicantes adnichilabuntur. Vespertilio superabit dominum[20] apum. Bestia occidentalis[21] et leo orientalis subiugabunt[22] mundum universum.
Tunc erit commune passagium ultra[23] aquas ad terram sanctam.
Et filii[24] Israel[25] liberabuntur a captivitate sua.[26] Et civitas
Iherusalem gloriabitur,[27] et sepulcrum Domini[28] honorificabitur. Et erit summa pax per[29] xv annos. Et in tanta tranquillitate audientur nova de Antichristo. Ergo vigilate.[30]

---

9. in brevi Acris capietur *for* Acon destruetur *C*; Acon destruetur *lacking O*.

10. *Followed by* Et hec iam transierunt *T*.

11. *Followed by* inde *O*.

12. que vocatur *lacking O*.

13. vocabitur *T*.

14. ancefala *for* sine capite *C*.

15. Christianitatis *for* et tibi Christianitas *T*.

16. terror Christianis *for* tibi Christianitas *O*.

17. *Lacking T*.

18. alienus *O*.

19. *Lacking C*.

20. ducum *O*; deum *T*.

21. australis *C*.

22. superabunt *CO*.

23. ultra aquas *lacking OT*.

24. *Followed by* ac filie *O*.

25. Iherusalem *CO*.

26. *Followed by* civitate Ierusalem *O*.

27. glorificabitur *T*.

28. *Lacking C*.

29. xx^{ti} annis *for* per xv annos *O*.

30. *For final gloss in Tours MS, see Chapter Five, n. 49.*

2. *Casleti paludum* from Tours 522, f. i^v

Casleti paludum vermiculi leone captivat. [*Followed by four obscure emblematic lines.*] Navicula Petri iactabitur in validis fluctibus, sed evadet. Vespertilio superabit deum apum. Bestia occidentalis et leo orientalis superabit universum mundum. Rubea ⟨gente⟩ in albam cum accingentibus prius translata. Tunc erit unus deus, et alius deus evanescet.

Martinus comburetur. Sui contrarii pro parte ⟨in eveadem⟩ destruentur. Gloria ~~Lombardorum~~ [*sic*] barbarorum convertetur. Omnes ordines mendicancium adnichilabuntur. Beguine cum begardi prohibentur. Et Pauli lex augebitur. Presbiteris uxores dabuntur. Erit commune passagium ultra aquas ad terram sanctam. Filii Iherusalem a captivitate sua liberabuntur. Iherusalem glorificabitur. Legio lugebit et translabitur marchio cum gente sine capite. Plures destruet et suo ⟨d . . . . o⟩ subiugabit. Hildegaldis sine dente mordetur. Monoculus eciam victus exibit.

J. THE REDATED VERSION FOR 1387

This eccentric version is also not closely related to any of the others. I give a composite reading from the two surviving MSS— Schloss Pommersfelden 102, f. 67^v (Nürnberg, ca. 1460s) (=P) and Wolfenbüttel 366 Helmstedt, fos. 60^v–61^r (Regensburg, 1467)(=W) —with variants in the apparatus.

Anno Domini MCCClxxxvii facta est[1] visio valde mirabilis in quodam monasterio ordinis Cisterciensis. Quidam monachus[2] sanctissime vite dixit missam coram abbate suo et alio[3] ministro presente. Acciditque[4] infra sacram communionem corporis et sanguinis Domini nostri Ihesu Christi; et[5] apparuit quedam manus valde candida scribens in altari super corporale in quo predictus monachus Dominum tractavit.

---

1. fuit P.
2. monacho W.
3. quodam W.
4. Accidit W.
5. *Lacking* P.

Cedrus alta Libani succidetur. Ariopolim in brevi destruetur. Accaron[6] in brevi capietur. Mars Saturnum superabit.
Saturnus insidiabitur[7] Iovi. Vespertilio fugabit dominum apum.
Et infra sexaginta[8] sex annos erit unus deus,[9] una fides in terris.
Et alter deus evanescet. Filii Israel a captivitate liberantur.[10]
Genus quoddam sine capite veniet. Navicula periclitabitur
validis[11] fluctibus, sed evadet in fine dierum. In mundo erunt
prelia. Multa multorum regnorum mutaciones erunt. Ve tunc
clero et toti Christianitati! Terra barbarorum convertetur.
Et omnes ordines mendicancium et quamplures alie secte utriusque sexus annichilabuntur. Bestie orientales et leo occidentis
universum mundum subiugabunt.[12] Item[13] tunc pax erit in toto
orbe terrarum. Item copia frugum erit per xii annos. Tunc
passagium erit commune ab omnibus Christi fidelibus ultra
aquas ad[14] terram sanctam, vincent. Tunc civitas Ierusalem
glorificabitur, et sepulchrum Domini in pacis tranquillitate
honorificabitur. Et videbimus nova de Antichristo. Etc.[15]

K. THE MAGDEBURG PROPHECY OF 1531/32

For the report of the original Latin version in Luther's *Tischre-
den* see Chapter Eight, nn. 17 and 18. I give here the German version
from *Ettlich weissagung durch den hochgelarten Astronomum Jacob
Pflawmen zu Ulm zusamen getragen Anno M.CCCCC* (Wittenberg,
Nickel Schirlenz, 1532), f. 8ᵛ, with variants from Johann Carion,
Chronica (Augsburg, 1533), f. 144ᵛ.

---

6. Acaron *W*.

7. insidiatur *W*.

8. *Followed by* et *P*.

9. *Followed by* et *P*.

10. liberentur *P*.

11. variis *P*.

12. subiugabit *P*.

13. *Lacking W*.

14. et *PW*.

15. *Lacking W*.

Ein[1] Prophecy vor etlich hundert jaren warhafftig geschrieben zu Latein, gefunden zu Magdeburg.

Vom Stam[2] Keisers Caroli und der Könige aus Franckreich wird ein Keiser komen mit namen Carolus, der wird Herr sein[3] in gantzem Europa und wird reformiren die Christliche Kirchen[4] und das Reich.

Denn es wird ein volck komen das heisst das volck on ein heubt, und denn wee den Priestern. Das schiefflin Petri wird grosse not leiden. Aber es wird entlich wider zu rugen komen und den[5] sieg behalten. Es werden schreckliche verenderung aller Reich, und die Mönch werden unter gehen. Die bestia von Occident und der Leo von Orient werden herschen inn aller welt, und[6] denn wird friede sein inn gantzer welt, und werden die Christen frey zihen 15 jar lang inn Asien. Darnach wird man grewliche mehr vom Antichristo hören.

L. SPEYER GLOSSES, CA. 1527

I reproduce only the section of Clm 28229, f. 21[r], that is glossed: for the complete text, see section H.

Cedrus alta[a] Libani succidetur, et Tripolis[b] in brevi destruetur, et Accaron[c] capietur. Et Mercurius mundum superabit, et Saturnus[d] insidiabitur Iovi.[e] Et vespertilio[f] fugabit

---

1. Zů Magdeburg ist ein Chronica vor hundert jarn geschriben darinn dise wort Lateinisch am end stehen *for* Ein ——— Magdeburg.

2. stamm des

3. werden

4. kirch

5. *Lacking.*

6. und ——— welt *lacking.*

a. Turcus succumbet.

b. Ierusalem.

c. Soldanus.

d. Saturniani ⟨. . . . .⟩ et agrestes rustici.

e. omnibus literatis hominibus.

f. id est Machmetiste.

ducem[g] Abim. Infra xv annos erit unus deus et una fides. Et
altera[h] evanescet. Filius Israel a captivitate liberabit. Gens[i]
quedam veniet que nascetur sine capite.[j] Ve tunc[k] clero et
sterilitate! Navicula[l] Petri iactabitur in validis fluctibus, sed
evadet et dominabitur in fine dierum. Et in mundo erunt multa
prelia, et strages magne, et fames valida, hominum mortalitates
per loca, et regnorum mutaciones. Et terra barbarorum[m] convertetur. Ordines mendicancium ecclesie al⟨ias⟩ certe quamplurimum adversabuntur. Bestia occidentalis[n] et leo orientalis[o]
universum mundum subiugabunt, Et pax erit in toto orbe terrarum, et copia fructuum per xv annos. Tunc passagium erit
commune ab omnibus fidelibus ultra aquas congregatas ad
terram sanctam, et vincentur.[p]

---

g. regem Bohemie

h. scilicet Luteri.

i. Agareni; *then in margin*: ab Agar famula Abrahe nati Ismahelite.

j. rege.

k. iam tempus instaret.

l. id est omnes sacerdotes.

m. Saracenorum.

n. Rex Romanorum ex Hyspania in partibus inferioribus natus.

o. eius germanus.

p. Waradach.

INDEX OF
MANUSCRIPTS CITED

SUBJECT INDEX

Printed in the United States
217593BV00001B/6/P

To my F.R.I.E.N.D.S. Much of this book was written while waiting with you during our daughters' practices and competitions. Thank you for giving me much-needed brain breaks and motivating me to get the job done, and for being my friend and supporter.

To my children, Emma, Sophia, and Rémi. Thank you for allowing me the time to write this book. You understood right from the beginning that it was important for me to become a published author, and you gave me the time and freedom to make that happen. I am so thankful to have been able to share this experience with you and hope that you are all proud of what I have accomplished. Now that my goal has come to fruition, always remember that I will be behind you to support whatever dreams you may have, no matter how long it may take for you to attain them.

To my husband, Louis-Christian, thank you for supporting me through this process and for being my number one cheerleader. I am forever grateful that we have built a life together where we support one another unconditionally. Without your help, support, and encouragement, I would not have had the courage to attempt this endeavor. Thank you for giving me the little push to say yes and for following me all the way through to the end with it.

And finally, to all my past and present students. You are the reason this book is what it is. Without the experiences we have gone through together, my ideas that have become the basis of this book would not have developed, and I would not be the teacher that I am today. I learn as much from you as you do from me. Each one of you has left an imprint on my heart, and I carry that with me each and every day.

About the Author

Monica Dunbar is an enthusiastic educator with a passion for making connections with her students. Her love of education has led her to teaching in the Canadian Arctic, creating educational materials for educators around the world, and sharing her opinions, insights, and experiences on her blog at www.iheartgrade3.com.

When not in the classroom, Monica enjoys being at home with her husband, three children, and their lovable Samoyed, Nova. Most of her free time is spent at nearby arenas, with a cup of warm coffee in her hands, watching her children chase their dreams of Olympic gold medals and NHL stardom.